THE INSIGHT GUIDES SERIES RECEIVED SPECIAL AWARDS FOR EXCELLENCE FROM THE PACIFIC AREA TRAVEL ASSOCIATION.

JAMAICA

Fifth Edition (2nd Reprint)

APA PUBLICATIONS

Publisher: Hans Johannes Hoefer
General Manager: Henry Lee
Marketing Director: Aileen Lau
Editorial Director: Geoffrey Eu
Editorial Manager: Vivien Kim
Editorial Consultants: Adam Liptak (North America)
Brian Bell (Europe)
Heinz Vestner (German Editions)

Project Editors

Helen Abbott, Diana Ackland, Mohamed Amin, Ravindralal Anthonis, Roy Bailet, Louisa Cambell, Jon Carroll, Hillary Cunningham, John Eames, Janie Freeburg, Bikram Grewal, Virginia Hopkins, Samuel Israel, Jay Itzkowitz, Phil Jarratt, Tracy Johnson, Bèn Kalb, Wilhelm Klein, Saul Lockhart, Sylvia Mayuga, Gordon MaLauchlan, Kal Müller, Eric Oey, Daniel P. Reid, Kim Robinson, Ronn Ronck, Robert Seidenberg, Rolf Steinberg, Sriyani Tidball, Lisa Van Gruisen, Merin Wexler.

Contributing Writers

A.D. Aird, Ruth Armstrong, T. Terence Barrow, F. Lisa Beebe, Bruce Berger, Dor Bahadur Bista, Clinton V. Black, Star Black, Frena Bloomfield, John Borthwick, Roger Boschman, Tom Brosnahan, Jerry Carroll, Tom Chaffin, Nedra Chung, Tom Cole, Orman Day, Kunda Dixit, Richard Erdoes, Guillermo Gar-Oropeza, Ted Giannoulas, Barbara Gloudon, Harka Gurung, Sharifah Hamzah, Willard A. Hanna, Elizabeth Hawley, Sir Edmund Hillary, Tony Hillerman, Jerry Hopkins, Peter Hutton, Neil Jameson, Michael King, Michele Kort, Thomas Lucey, Leonard Lueras, Michael E. Macmillan, Derek Maitland, Buddy Mays, Craig McGregor, Reinhold Messner, Julie Michaels, M.R. Priya Rangsit, Al Read, Elizabeth V. Reyes, Victor Stafford Reid, Harry Rolnick, E.R. Sarachandra, Uli Schmetzer, Ilsa Sharp, Norman Sibley, Peter Spiro, Harold Stephens, Keith Stevens, Michael Stone, Desmond Tate, Colin Taylor, Deanna L. Thompson, Randy Udall, James Wade, Mallika Wanigasundara, William Warren, Cynthia Wee, Tony Wheeler, Linda White, H. Taft Wireback, Alfred A. Yuson, Paul Zach.

Contributing Photographers

Carole Allen, Ping Amarand, Tony Arruza, Marcello Bertinetti, Alberto Cassio, Pat Canova, Alain Compost, Ray Cranbourne, Alian Evrard, Ricardo Ferro, Lee Foster, Manfred Gottschalk, Werner Hahn, Dallas and John Heaton, Brent Hesselyn, Hans Hoefer, Luca Invernizzi, Ingo Jezierski, Wilhelm Klein, Dennis Lane, Max Lawrence, Lyle Lawson, Philip Little, Guy Marche, Antonio Martinelli, David Messent, Ben Nakayama, Vautier de Nanxe, Kal Müller, Günter Pfannmuller, Van Philips, Ronni Pinsler, Fitz Prenzel, G.P. Reichelt, Dan Rocovits, David Ryan, Frank Salmoiraghi, Thomas Schollhammer, Blair Seitz, David Stahl, Bill Wassman, Rendo Yap, Hisham Youssef.

While contributions to Insight Guides are very welcome, the publisher cannot assume responsibility for the care and return of unsolicited manuscripts or photographs. Return postage and/or a self-addressed envelope must accompany unsolicited material if it is to be returned. Please address all editorial contributions to Apa Photo Agency P.O. Box 219, Orchard Point Post Office, Singapore 9123.

Distributors:

Advertising and Special Sales Representatives

Advertising carried in Insight Guides gives readers direct access to quality merchandise and travel-related services. These advertisements are inserted in the Guide in Brief section of each book. Advertisers are requested to contact their nearest representatives, listed below.

Special sales, for promotion purposes within the international travel industry and for educational purposes, are also available. The advertising representatives listed here also handle special sales. Alternatively, interested parties can contact Apa Publications, P.O. Box 219, Orchard Point Post Office, Singapore 9123.

APA PHOTO AGENCY PTE. LTD.

Jamaica

Produced and Edited by Paul Zach
Directed and Designed by Hans Johannes Hoefer

APA PUBLICATIONS

Jamaica, the 16th volume in Apa Productions' award-winning *Insight Guides* series, is the result of a marriage of minds from three different worlds.

This long-dreamed-of book is primarily an outgrowth of the talents and energies of three people: Apa founder-publisher-photographer **Hans Johannes Hoefer**, a German who established this new-concept firm in Singapore in 1970; **Paul Zach**, an Ohio freelance journalist who shuttled from

Zach and Friends

Hoefer

Henry

Anderson

Stahl

Black

Reid

Tel Aviv to Tampa, Honolulu to Jakarta, before landing in the Caribbean; and publisher-politician **Mike Henry**, Jamaica's minister of state for information and the head of Kingston Publishers Ltd.

The seed that grew into this book was first planted way back in 1976 during a chance meeting of Hoefer and Henry at the "Olympic Games of book publishing," the Frankfurt Book Fair.

An immediate friendship blossomed between the flamboyant Henry and the tall, intense Hoefer. The Jamaican had been impressed by the *Insight Guides* series, already well established in the Southeast Asian region.

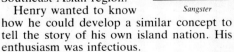
Sangster

Henry wanted to know how he could develop a similar concept to tell the story of his own island nation. His enthusiasm was infectious.

In fact, from the moment Hoefer launched the series with *Bali* in 1970, he had consciously been developing the books as

guides for the "second-generation" traveler. A "first-generation" traveler, Hoefer explained, was one who required a book to get him or her from airport to hotel to restaurant to tourist attraction, then back home again. And a "second-generation" traveler had transcended those needs, with the assistance of modern travel agencies and personal travel experience; but what he now needed was a book to explain the *why* of visiting a destination instead of the *how* of getting there.

Henry concurred. And when the Jamaican political atmosphere brightened in 1980 with the landslide victory of Henry's Labour Party over an incumbent, left-leaning socialist administration, he saw *Insight Guides* as a way to help boost his country back on the road to prosperity by contributing to the vital but sagging tourist industry.

Henry's personal fortunes in that political year helped even more. After winning election to Parliament from his native parish of Clarendon, he was tapped by the new prime minister, Edward Seaga, to serve as minister of state for information.

In 1981, Hoefer and Henry met again, and this time formally agreed to cooperate in the production of *Insight Guide: Jamaica*. To Hoefer, this was another milestone in the history of his growing company, the first step in a major new series of books canvassing the Caribbean as thoroughly as Apa had been doing in the Asia-Pacific region. To meet those ends, he is continuing to explore new avenues with publishers, businessmen and leaders in that part of the world.

Hoefer, a graduate of printing, book production, design and photography studies at

Krefeld and a disciple of Germany's famed Bauhaus tradition, had established a foothold on the North American continent with the release of *Florida* in early 1982. The so-called "pink book" had been well-received in the Sunshine State, so Hoefer again called upon Zach, who had edited and written much of *Florida*, to head for the Caribbean to coordinate work on *Jamaica*.

Maxwell

quickly developing an attachment to the Caribbean island. His "feel" for tropical islands developed during his years as a reporter for *The Honolulu Advertiser* and later as Gannett Fellow in Hawaii. He also had

Zach spent 2½ years covering Indonesia for the *Washington Post,* ABC News, McGraw-Hill World News and Reuters News Agency. Previously, in 1977 he had spent a year in Honolulu as a Gannett Fellow in Asian Studies at the University of Hawaii; worked for three years as a reporter for the *Evening Independent* in St. Petersburg, Florida; and dodged mortar shells and Katyusha rockets in Israel while an intern for the Associated Press during the Middle East war of 1973.

LaYacona

Hussey

Royes

worked as an editor for The *Seattle Post-Intelligencer* before joining Apa. Anderson edited Apa's guides to *Burma* and *Nepal* and was busy preparing the title on *Sri Lanka* when work on *Jamaica* took priority.

Zach arrived in Kingston in February 1982, immediately after the release of *Florida*, and set in motion the machinery necessary to produce an *Insight Guide*. With the assistance of Henry and his staff at Kingston Publishers, Zach pulled together the mounds of text, thousands of photographs, and piles of archival materials used in a book's preparation.

Moo Young

DaCosta

Stone

Carnegie

Back in Jamaica, Henry had opened the doors of the nation to Zach and Apa. He provided invaluable contacts with government officials, businessmen and other tourist industry leaders. He helped Apa photographers take their cameras to Pocomania rituals deep in the Jamaican bush and to tightly regulated government functions like the visit of U.S. President Ronald Reagan. He also contributed his own expertise in the field of Jamaican drink and cookery by writing "From Cho-cho to Kulu Kulu." Henry is the author of *Caribbean Cocktails*, published by his own company.

When his work in Jamaica was over, Zach flew to Apa headquarters in Singapore for final consultations and long sessions with another free-lance editor, **John Gottberg Anderson.** Together they shaped for the text into its final form, and with publisher Hoefer made final photo selections and design alterations.

Pressley

Anderson had never been closer to Jamaica than Florida, but he found himself

Apa's team of Jamaican writers was led by the Honorable **Victor Stafford Reid**, who has received the coveted Order of Jamaica for his work. Internationally known for his critically acclaimed novel, *The Leopard*, Reid has also authored such books as *New Day*, *Sixty Five*, *The Young Warriors*, *The*
(Continue on page 314)

TABLE OF CONTENTS

TABLE OF CONTENTS

Cover
    —by Paul Zach and David Stahl

Cartography
    —by Francis Tan

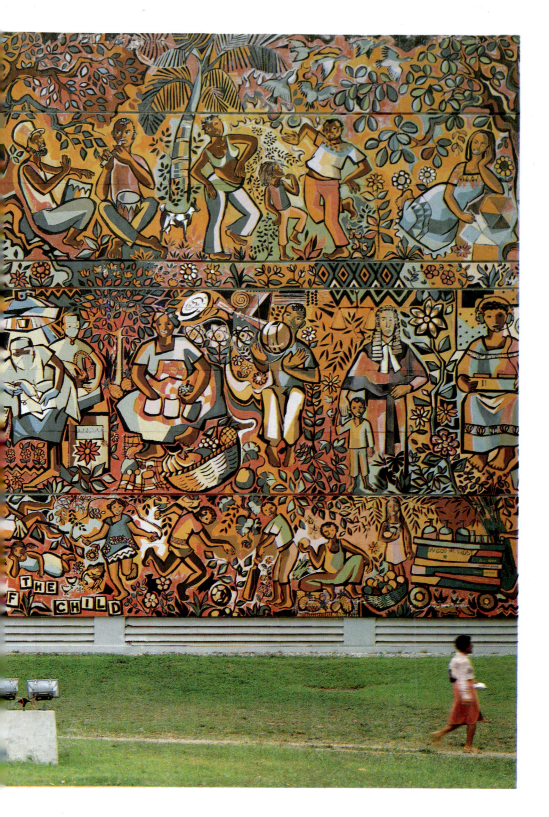

SEDUCTIVE SANDS, HYPNOTIC RHYTHMS

Never had I seen a land so beautiful.
Now I knew where the writers of the
Bible had got their description of Par-
adise. They had come here to
Jamaica.
— *Errol Flynn in* My Wicked, Wicked
Ways, *1959*

Errol Flynn, the swashbuckling movie idol
of the 1940s, literally washed up on the
shores of Jamaica in his yacht, *Zaca*, following a hurricane. Flynn, who had a reputation
for wooing and winning women, this time
was seduced by the siren of the Caribbean
Sea. He spent most of the last 13 years of his
life in Jamaica.

Jamaica has had the same persuasive
effect on mankind for centuries. There's
something sensuous in the undulating cut of
its contour, in the way the winds tease the
palm trees and the seas massage its sand.
There's a hypnotic quality to its people's
lilting patois and reggae rhythms, to the
deafening hush that hangs in the heights of
the Blue Mountains, to the hum and whistle
of its birds.

So "walk good," but be wary. Once it
grabs you, Jamaica might not let go.

Highlands and Cockpits

Few islands or countries of Jamaica's size
boast such a thrilling diversity of skin tones
and facial features, of landscapes and seascapes, of plant and animal life. With a total
land area of 4,244 square miles, Jamaica is
slightly smaller than the American state of
Connecticut but somewhat larger than the
Mideastern country of Lebanon. The island
stretches about 146 miles east to west from
Morant Point to Negril, and bulges to 51
miles at its greatest width. About 2.2 million
people live here, handsome blends of African, European, Arabic, Chinese and East
Indian stock who account for the National
Motto: "Out of Many, One People."

Jamaica floats in the Caribbean Sea at a
latitude 18 degrees north of the Equator. Its
reputation has grown around its fine
beaches, and most hotels and resorts crowd
powdery slivers of sand along the north
coast.

Preceding pages: Dunn's River Falls; Minard
Estate; Ocho Rios hat stand; and University of
West Indies mural. Left, schoolgirls at Minard.

Yet rugged highlands dominate the landscape. More than half of Jamaica hovers
1,000 feet above the Caribbean; 40 square
miles rise above the 5,000-foot level. The
highest point, Blue Mountain Peak, punc-
tures the clouds at 7,402 feet just 10 miles
from the coastal plain east of Kingston. In
the middle of the island sits cool Mandeville
on a plateau in the Don Figueroa Mountains, 2,000 feet above the checkered agricultural slopes of the countryside.

Jamaica's northwest is pockmarked by the
surrealistic karst landscapes of the Cockpit
Country—a "Me No Sen, You No Come"
land of the free-spirited Maroon peoples.
Sinkholes have settled in the brittle limestone surface, forming a pitted tundra that
resembles the inside of an enormous egg
carton.

Where the highlands plummet to the sea,
they have created spectacular cliffs like Lovers' Leap on the south coast, where the
duppies (ghosts) of forlorn sweethearts
mingle with the sea mists. Some 120 rivers
and streams gush from mountain ravines to
carve gashes in the coastal plains. Cloud-
bursts transform them into torrents that can
flood the lowlands; droughts make them into
parched ravines clogged with stones.

The Evolution of Paradise

Geologists believe Jamaica and its neighboring islands in the Caribbean evolved
from an arc of volcanos that bubbled up
from the seas billions of years ago. Lower
lands surrounding the peaks eased out of the
waters over 30 million years, the legacy
of minute skeletons of sea creatures and
marine organisms which accumulated on sea
beds elevated by volcanic activity. A cap of
white limestone, the residue of the
skeletons, still covers about two-thirds of the
island. This land-building process climaxed
about 20 million years ago when the island
emerged from the Caribbean.

The Cockpit Country and innumerable
cave systems betray the oceanic origins of the
country's surface. The limestone fractured
and cracked over the eons as rains rutted the
surface. Today, rivers like the Tangle River
near Maroon Town mysteriously disappear
underground, only to reappear in spring-
heads miles away. Cave systems include
Twin Sisters on the Hellshire Coast near
Kingston and a series of spectacular cham-

bers called Windsor Cave, nearly two miles long, in the Cockpit Country.

Primeval Jamaica was a rugged, rocky land. Eventually, climate and soil combined to spawn magnificent forests that covered every acre by the 15th Century. Its only native fruits at the time of Columbus' arrival were guava, pineapple, the sweetsop and possibly the star apple. Virtually everything that blooms today was imported either by the hands of humans or the droppings of birds. Europeans cleared timber from the plains, savannas and some mountain slopes for settlement and cultivation. Then they introduced sugar cane, bananas and citrus. Spanish traders brought coconuts from Malaya in the 17th Century. The ackee that is the staple of most Jamaican breakfasts came on slave ships from West Africa in 1778. Pimento is a native plant, as is the mahoe, Jamaica's national tree. Other natives include the Santa Maria, cedar, bulletwood, break axe, Spanish elm and ebony. The purple-blossomed lignum vitae is the national flower.

Nearly 3,000 varieties of flowering plants have been identified on the island, including 800 species found nowhere else in the world. Indigenous varieties include 200 species of wild orchids, 60 species of Bromeliads called "wild pine" by Jamaicans, and about 550 ferns.

This lush, perfumed Eden contains breathtaking hollows brimming with palm trees, mountains crowned by stunted elfin forests, and dusty plains full of dildo cacti and prickly pear. There are mistletoes called "scorn ground" and "God bush" and an aerial plant called "Old Man's Beard" that drips from telephone and power lines in most cities. Bamboo from China flourishes throughout the island. Tangles of vines contribute to the exotic scenery; they include a giant pea vine called "cacoon," with pods up to three feet in length that are stewed and eaten by Maroons.

Bountiful Birds

Jamaica's fauna pales in comparison with its visual feasts of flora. There are rats, of course, and mongooses introduced by 19th Century plantation owners to combat the rats. The native Jamaican coney closely resembles a large guinea pig, but is a relative of the rat. It lives in burrows in the ground but has become scarce and is rarely seen.

Bats are Jamaica's most numerous animals. About 25 varieties flitter through island belfries. The enormous gentle manatee that inspired tales of mermaids is another mammal, which still inhabits lonely waters along the south coast. Whales can sometimes be spotted off the coasts. Jamaica's rapidly dwindling numbers of crocodiles are called alligators. Frogs are called toads and moths are called bats. The ubiquitous gecko croaks and keeps the insect population in check. The comparatively large, ominous-looking ground lizard is common, but Jamaica has few snakes, all harmless.

Jamaica's bird population makes up in color and variety what its animals lack. Its national bird, the Doctor Bird, a streamer-tailed hummingbird found only in Jamaica, darts about the island's flower gardens. Bright yellow, orange and green parrots, parroquets and finches sing in the forests. On the ugly side, the John Crow turkey buzzards scavenge garbage and the entrails of dead animals. More than 200 species of birds have been spotted on the island, including 25 endemic species.

Breezes for the
Doctor and Undertaker

Jamaica's climate has always been its biggest attraction. The warmth that lured its earliest residents now brings hundreds of thousands of sun-worshipping visitors each year. Seasons are non-existent. Rains, averaging 77 inches annually, fall mainly in May and October although mountain trade winds pull down 200 inches a year in parts of the parishes of Portland and St. Thomas. Sunshine falls more often. It deposits annual average temperatures of 80 degrees Fahrenheit on the coast. But it can drop to the 60s and 70s in higher mountain elevations. Peaks in the Blue Mountains have been known to sustain "frigid" conditions below 50 degrees on rare occasions.

Mostly, the weather is perfect. Cooling trade winds that Jamaicans call the "Doctor Breeze" blow in from the seas to cool the daytime hours. Night brings the "Undertaker's Breeze" from the mountains. Jamaicans used to bundle up against it in fear of catching their deaths of cold. Now they revel in that wind. As artist-historian Howard-Pyle wrote in 1890:

The Air here, notwithstanding the heat, is very healthy. I have known blacks one hundred and twenty years of Age, and one hundred years old is very common amongst Temperate Livers.

At right, hot song stylist Burning Spear ignites the rhythms of reggae at Reggae Sunsplash, Montego Bay.

EXPLANATION

The Earliest Islanders

When Christopher Columbus "discovered" Jamaica on May 5, 1494, during his second voyage to the New World, he found a thriving colony of Arawak Indians such as he had met in the neighboring islands of Cuba and Haiti.

From an ancestral home in the Orinoco region of the Guianas and Venezuela, the Arawaks had long before sailed northward in their dugout canoes, settling in each of the islands of the Antilles from Trinidad to Cuba. They probably arrived in Jamaica in two waves—the first (the so-called "Red-

known and feared in Haiti and from time to time made murderous attacks even on Jamaica. But for the arrival of the Spaniards, the Caribs might have exterminated those first Jamaicans. As it happened, the newcomers from Europe were shortly to complete the work of destruction themselves.

The Arawak Civilization

An estimated 100,000 Arawaks at one time lived on the island. Aboriginal remains

ware People") around 650 A.D., the second between 850 and 900 A.D.

Some centuries later, the Arawaks' calm and peaceful lives were rudely disturbed by the arrival of another Indian tribe, the fierce man-eating Caribs (from whose name comes the word *cannibal*). Probably also originating in the Guiana region of South America, this warlike people began to spread through the islands in their war canoes, leaving death and destruction in their wake, slaughtering the men and abducting the women.

Farther and farther north they swarmed until by the time Columbus discovered the West Indies in 1492, they had taken the entire Lesser Antilles and were raiding the eastern end of Puerto Rico. They were

show that they lived in most parts of Jamaica, as far inland as Ewarton and Moneague and in such upland areas as the Long Mountain and Jack's Hill. The majority of their villages were close to the coast or near rivers, as the Arawaks were seagoing people and lived chiefly off seafood. (An interesting village site, and one of the most accessible, is that at White Marl, near Central Village, three miles from Spanish Town. On a hill adjacent to the site now stands the Arawak Indian Museum.)

Preceding pages: An early British rendering of the island. Above, Arawak drawings found in Mountain River Cave near Spanish Town and, right, Columbus meets an Arawak chief.

The Arawaks were a brown-skinned race, short and slightly built with straight, coarse black hair, broad faces and flat wide noses. Their only breadstuff, cassava, was doubtlessly introduced by them into the island in their migration from the South American mainland. In addition, they grew sweet potatoes, fruits, vegetables, cotton and tobacco. Jamaica was in fact well known for the cultivation of cotton. Much of the women's time was spent spinning and weaving it. Jamaica supplied hammocks (an Arawak invention) and cotton cloth to Cuba and

tobacco comes from the name of their pipe. They were a pleasure-loving people and enjoyed dancing, singing, and playing a ball game called *batos*.

As in Cuba, Jamaica's inhabitants divided their island into provinces, each ruled over by a *cacique* assisted by village headmen or sub-chiefs. *Caciques* were much respected; they alone enjoyed the privilege of polygamy, and they occupied the best and biggest houses, in which the family idols and images of spirit deities were kept. If a *cacique* were ill and dying he would be strangled

Haiti, and the Spaniards themselves had sailcloth made in Jamaica.

The Jamaican Arawaks were skilled artisans who left their paintings on the walls of many island caves. They were superb stoneworkers and their implements were particularly well shaped, smooth and beautifully finished. They fashioned their dugout canoes from the trunks of cedar and silk cotton trees, hollowing out the trunks first by charring, then by chipping with their stone axes and chisels. These canoes varied greatly in size: some held one person only, others 50 or more. Columbus saw one 96 feet long and eight feet wide!

Smoking was both a pastime and a religious ritual with the Arawaks, and the word

as a mark of special favor.

The Arawaks explained the mysteries of everyday life in their myths. Two supreme gods, Jocuahuma and his female counterpart, were associated with the sun and moon in a myth about the emergence of mankind from a cave. Souls of the departed were believed to go to *coyaba*, a place of ease and rest where there were no droughts, hurricanes or sickness, and where the time was spent in feasting and dancing.

The Arawaks often buried their dead in caves, placing the head and certain bones of the body in a pottery bowl. Some of the best preserved skulls and the finest examples of their pottery have been found in caves.

CHRISTOPHER COLUMBUS and his SONS DIEGO and FERDINAND.

Wilson sculp.t

From an ancient Spanish Picture in the possession of Edward Horne Esq.r
of Bevis Mount near Southampton.

P/21

28

SPANISH DISCOVERY AND COLONIZATION

Jamaica, like many another of the West India Islands, is like a woman with a history. She has had her experiences, and has lived her life rapidly. She has enjoyed a fever of prosperity founded upon those incalculable treasures poured into her lap by the old-time buccaneer pirates. She has suffered earthquake, famine, pestilence, fire, and death: and she has been the home of a cruel and merciless slavery, hardly second to that practised by the Spaniards themselves. Other countries have taken centuries to grow from their primitive life through the flower and fruit of prosperity into the seed-time of picturesque decrepitude. Jamaica has lived through it all in a few years.
    —*Howard Pyle, "Jamaica New and Old" in* Harper's New Monthly Magazine, *January 1890.*

As the 15th Century drew to a close, Jamaica was still primitive, its years of hardship and glory still ahead. In Europe, meanwhile, civilized man was entering the Renaissance. One of the most outstanding figures of the age was the Genoese seafarer Christopher Columbus, the man who was to discover the New World for the Old.

On Aug. 3, 1492, Columbus—in his flagship the *Santa Maria*, accompanied by two caravels, the *Niña* and *Pinta*, with a total crew of 90—sailed from Palos de la Frontera, Spain, on his first great voyage of discovery. On Oct. 12, he landed on one of the Bahamas, today's Watling Island. In gratitude to the Lord for bringing him safely to port, Columbus named it *San Salvador*, or "Holy Saviour." He later explored other islands in the Bahamas group and the north coasts of Cuba and Hispaniola.

It was on his second voyage, after revisiting Hispaniola and Cuba, that Columbus discovered Jamaica. He first heard of the island of *Xaymaca* (an indigenous name of disputed meaning) from the Cuban Indians who described it as "the land of the blessed gold." But Jamaica had no gold. This was a disappointment not only to Columbus but also to those who followed him.

The Christopher Columbus family contemplates their conquest of the West Indies in an 18th Century engraving.

On May 5, 1494, Columbus arrived at St. Ann's Bay, which he named *Santa Gloria*—"on account of the extreme beauty of its country," according to Columbus' biographer, Samuel Eliot Morison. He thought Jamaica itself "the fairest island that eyes have beheld . . . all full of valleys and fields and plains." Finding the Indians hostile, however, he anchored off the port for the night and sailed down the coast the following day to a harbor "shaped like a horse-shoe."

Here also the Indians were unfriendly, but Columbus was determined to land: he needed wood and water and a chance to repair his vessels The Indians scattered before the advance of a fierce dog and Spanish crossbow men, leaving some of their number killed and wounded on the beach. Columbus claimed Jamaica in the name of his patron sovereigns, Ferdinand and Isabella of Spain. He called it "St. Jago" or "Santiago" after his country's patron saint. The following day, six Indians brought peace offerings of cassava, fruit and fish. For the rest of the admiral's stay, the Indians supplied him and his men regularly with provisions in exchange for trinkets and other trade goods.

'El Golfo de Buen Tiempo'

On May 9, the fleet sailed westward to Montego Bay—*El Golfo de Buen Tiempo*, as Columbus called it, "Fair Weather Gulf." He then continued his cruise along the Cuban coast before crossing over again to Jamaica to complete the exploration of this island.

Nine years later, on his fourth voyage, Columbus visited Jamaica again—this time in sad and tragic circumstances. After leaving the American mainland, it had become clear that his two battered, worm-eaten caravels were not fit for the Atlantic crossing. He tried to make for Hispaniola but got no farther than St. Ann's Bay before the ships were stranded side by side, a bow's shot from the shore. With heavy hearts, the Admiral and his company—including his young son Ferdinand and his brother Bartholomew—watched the vessels fill with water and settle for good in the soft sand of the bay.

Here he was to spend 12 months, beset by hardships, hunger, doubts and sickness, abandoned by the Indians and deserted by many of his followers—some of whom even staged an abortive mutiny.

Eventually, two of his company—Diego Méndez and Bartolomé Fieschi—made the arduous sea journey to Hispaniola, where they managed to charter a small caravel from a Spanish colony. Towards the end of June 1504, the little vessel arrived at St. Ann's Bay and the desperate year-long wait was at an end. On the 29th, she left for Hispaniola with Columbus and the survivors of his crew, about 100 in all. In September, Columbus sailed for Spain. He was never to see the New World again.

'Sevilla la Nueva' And 'Villa de la Vega'

It was not until 1510 that colonists arrived in Jamaica, under the island's first Spanish governor, Juan de Esquivel. *Sevilla la Nueva*, or "New Seville," as they called their settlement on St. Ann's Bay, was conceived on a large and not unimpressive scale. It included among the principal buildings a fort, a castle and a church. But the location, close to swamps, proved unhealthy; it was soon abandoned in favor of a new site on the south side of what is now Spanish Town.

Little survives today of New Seville. Finely carved stone panels, semi-columns, door jambs, friezes and other artifacts found on the site are now in the possession of the Institute of Jamaica.

Spanish Town (the *Villa de la Vega* of the Spaniards) quickly became a center of activity. It is sometimes said that Columbus himself laid the foundations, but he had died some years before the royal decree for the establishment of the town was issued. Besides its convenient and healthful situation, with an ample water supply and fertile surroundings, Spanish Town enjoyed protection from direct sea attack while being sufficiently near to two good harbors.

A number of interesting accounts of the town were written during the Spanish period. A Carmelite missionary, Antonio Vázquez de Espinosa, writing around 1628, says the site was "marvellously attractive . . . very well built and laid out." An unwelcome English visitor, Captain William Jackson, who plundered Spanish Town 15 years later, thought it a fair town, consisting of 400 or 500 houses, five or six stately churches and chapels, and one monastery of Franciscan friars. Unfortunately, no Spanish buildings still exist, having in time deteriorated beyond repair.

The Spaniards enslaved the native Arawaks and so overworked and ill-treated them that in a short time they had all died out. The process was doubtlessly aided by the introduction of European diseases to which they would have had little or no immunity.

Today our only reminders of these first Jamaicans are their artifacts, found chiefly on their village sites; a small group of words, like *barbecue, hurricane, hammock, tobacco* and *canoe*; and a few place names, including *Jamaica* itself.

Upon the demise of the Arawaks, the Spaniards began importing black slaves from Africa. The first of them arrived in 1517, the earliest Jamaican ancestors of today's majority race.

Jamaica as a Spanish colony was largely a failure. Its main use to Spain was that of a supply base. In the early days of colonization, men, horses, arms and food from here helped in the conquest of Cuba and much of the American mainland; but after that, the island's importance waned until it sank to the position of an unimportant, badly governed and largely neglected outpost.

Almost nothing was done to develop the natural resources. The chief trade was the supply of fresh provisions to passing ships and the export of hides and lard to Havana and the Main. In exchange, the ships that touched here brought supplies of clothing, oil, wine, wheaten flour and a few luxury items.

The colonists devoted themselves chiefly to pastoral and agricultural pursuits. From Spain they brought all the familiar varieties of citrus (except grapefruit). They carried the banana and plantain to Jamaica from the Canary Islands via Hispaniola. They also introduced cattle, horses and swine, which they kept in *hatos*, or ranches, on the open savanna. Chief among the *hatos* were Morante (the name lingers in Morant Bay), Liguanea (in lower St. Andrew) and Guanaboa (in St. Catherine).

Roads in Spanish times were mostly bridle paths. Settlements, with the exception of the capital, were scarcely better than townships. These included Caguaya (Passage Fort), Oristan (Bluefields), Las Chorreras (near Ocho Rios), Savanna-la-Mar and Puerto Anton.

Although strictly speaking the island was under the control of Spain, it was to some extent self-governing. The Spanish governor ruled with the aid of a *cabildo*, a council of nominated members. A strong governor ruled largely by himself; a weak one was controlled by the *cabildo*. A tactless governor quickly ran into trouble with church authorities.

The church played an important part in

the life of the times. There is still a Red Church Street and a White Church Street in Spanish Town, both named for Spanish chapels, as well as a Monk Street—a reminder of the dark-robed, sandaled, figures who were once a familiar feature of the old town.

The End of Spanish Control

By the last years of the Spanish occupation, internal strife had weakened the colony. The governors were not properly supported from home, and quarrels with the church authorities undermined their control. In the 12 years before the English conquest, three governors rapidly met their demise. Francisco Ladrón de Zegama died a prisoner

challenge the justice of this division. "I should like to see the clause of Adam's will that excludes me from a share of the world," declared Francis I, King of France.

So national rivalries in Europe spread to distant lands, and from the mid 1500s to the end of the 18th Century, the rich countries of the Caribbean were the scene of international and commercial competition. As early as 1506, French ships appeared in the Caribbean, attacking small Spanish settlements and capturing vessels. In 1555, the Jamaican colonists chased two French ships away. But other Frenchmen followed, as did Dutch, Italian, Portuguese and English, all bent on trade and plunder. In 1596, the Elizabethan adventurer Sir Anthony Shirley raided the island. Other raids by English forces took

in his own house; Caballero died violently; and Sedeño was deprived of office after a riot and sent away to prison.

Frequent attacks by pirates were another corrupting influence in the colony. These were not limited to Jamaica, but formed part of a general effort on the part of certain European nations to loosen Spain's grip on the region. When Columbus discovered the New World, the Pope had issued proclamations neatly dividing the Indies between Spain and Portugal; but it was not long before other European nations began to

Virtually the only evidence of the Spanish occupation of Jamaica are place names. Above, King's House in Spanish Town.

place in 1603, 1640 and 1643.

These incursions had a demoralizing effect on the colonists. They also opened the eyes of more and more people to the attractions and strategic value of the island. During the English raid of 1643, a number of men deserted and had to be left behind. The question was: how long would it be before some foreign power attempted to take and hold Jamaica?

The answer came on May 10, 1655, when a large English expeditionary force sailed into Kingston Harbour (as it is now called). Once again the people of Spanish Town prepared for a marauding raid. But this time the fleet's arrival spelled the end of Spanish rule in Jamaica.

THE BRITISH TAKEOVER

The expeditionary force which captured Jamaica had been sent out by the Lord Protector, Oliver Cromwell, as part of a plan known as "The Western Design," aimed against the Spanish power and trade monopoly. The "Design," if successful, would have been a serious blow to Spain. Cromwell hastily gathered a fleet under Admiral William Penn and General Robert Venables. He also appointed a council of three commissioners to accompany the important expedition.

But the omens for success were not favorable. "No worse prepared and equipped expedition ever left the English shores," wrote Sir Charles Firth, the Cromwellian scholar, "and the consequences of these initial mistakes and negligences were all aggravated by the mistakes and quarrels of those charged with its command." Ruffians and thieves made up the majority of the troops, with a sprinkling of good soldiers, seasoned and better principled. In short, the crew was a mixture, as one of the captains described it, "of little wine with much water, the one losing its proper strength and vigour, and the other thereby little bettered."

Sailing from Portsmouth at the end of December 1654, the expedition stopped first at Barbados to raise levies from the plantations and take on provisions. In the Leeward Islands, additional recruits were also signed on. Then they sailed for Hispaniola on their great mission to attack the capital city of Santo Domingo.

But there they met disaster. The expedition was roundly defeated, the complete massacre of the forces being averted only by the landing of a party of sailors to cover their flight back to the ships. As it was, a third of their number was left behind as dead or missing.

Fearful of Cromwell's rage at the failure at Santo Domingo, it was decided to attack some other Spanish settlement. Jamaica, known to be thinly populated and weakly defended, was eventually chosen as the target of invasion.

On May 10, 1655, the fleet of 38 ships and about 8,000 men anchored off Caguaya, the landing place for Spanish Town, later to be

A portrait of Oliver Cromwell painted while he was engineering Great Britain's takeover of Jamaica (left). Right, an ancient British cannon that still guards the gates of Spanish Town.

known as Passage Fort. A few shots fired into the little fort dispersed the defenders. Soon the English flag waved above the walls of the fortification. The commanders of the expedition may have hoped to have been able to attack some stronger place from here later; but as it happened, Jamaica was to prove the end of Cromwell's ambitious "Western Design."

An early opportunity of occupying the capital, Spanish Town itself, was missed. Combined with a further delay by the Spaniards on the plea of considering surrender

terms, this gave most of the inhabitants an opportunity to escape with their valuables to the north side of Jamaica and on to Cuba. When the English troops finally marched into the town, they found it empty and bare of booty. In anger and disappointment, they destroyed much of the place, burning the churches and even melting the bells down for shot.

Confident that they would in time recover the island, the fleeing Spaniards had freed and armed their slaves and left them behind in the trackless interior. According to plan, these freedmen would harry the invaders with guerrilla warfare until an army for the Spanish reconquest could be collected. Instead, these people and their descendants were later to win fame as the redoubtable Maroons. A century and a half of constant battle with the British settlers eventually earned them a remarkable measure of self-government.

Although disappointed over the Santo Domingo fiasco, Cromwell decided nevertheless to make the most of the new colony, offering very attractive terms in the way of land grants and other perquisites to "such as shall transplant themselves to Jamaica."

Cromwell decided to import immigrants to help solve the problem of colonization. He gave orders for 1,000 Irish girls, and a large number of boys, to be rounded up and transported to Jamaica. The former were to become wives of the soldiers, the latter servants of the officers. There is some doubt

D'Oyley, proved equal to the challenge. As soon as news of the landing reached him, he called out 750 of his best officers and men. They sailed around the island to the attack. D'Oyley offered Ysassi honorable surrender terms, but received in reply a jar of sweetmeats and a courteous refusal.

The battle that took place on June 27 made amends for the failure at Santo Domingo. More than 300 Spaniards were killed and valuable supplies of food and arms captured, together with the Spanish royal standard and 10 colors. It was the most important battle ever fought in Jamaica and put an end to Spanish hopes of reconquest, although the war was to drag on for two more years. Ysassi held out in the mountains to which he had escaped, always

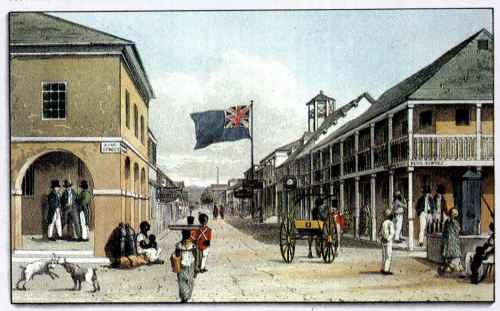

whether this order was ever carried out. In any case, Irish Town was not named for these early arrivals.

Colonel D'Oyley And
The Battle of Jamaica

Meanwhile, under the courageous and determined Governor Christobal Arnaldo de Ysassi, stout but unsuccessful efforts were made by the displaced Spanish to recapture the island. The decisive battle was fought in June 1658. A large force consisting mainly of Mexican contingents landed at Rio Nuevo and dug in behind a strong fort, armed with cannon, on a cliff near the river's west bank.

The British commander, Colonel Edward

hoping for the relieving force which never arrived. With his eventual escape by canoe to Cuba, all Spanish influence in Jamaica ended, and the island was officially ceded to the British Crown under the Treaty of Madrid in 1670.

Like the Arawak, the Spaniard has vanished from the Jamaican scene. Apart from the Seville carvings, already mentioned, there are almost no visible traces of Spanish occupation. Only place names, especially river names, survive to remind of

The Union Jack flies over Kingston's King Street during Jamaica's years as a British colony (above). The good life of expatriates as depicted in 18th Century cartoon (right).

past links with Spain.

The defeat of the Spaniards removed the danger of foreign invasion. But in August 1660 the threat of internal rebellion arose. It took the form of a mutiny of troops led by colonels Raymond and Tyson, the latter having command of one of the regiments quartered at Guanaboa Vale, nine miles from Spanish Town.

The reasons for the mutiny are not clear. Dislike of Colonel D'Oyley and his iron-handed methods played a part, as did rivalry between those who favored the Monarchy and those who preferred the Commonwealth. But the root cause may have been impatience with the continuation of military rule and a longing to settle down as colonists. After all, provisions were now plentiful,

in England arrived soon after. Within a year, D'Oyley was appointed governor—the first of more than 60 administrators who were to guide the destiny of the island.

It is ironic that D'Oyley's instructions conferred, in effect, the very privileges for which the rebellious colonels had grasped too soon. Among other things, D'Oyley was ordered to release the army and encourage planters, merchants and traders. Civil government was established and law courts set up. This was the groundwork that in time would lead Jamaica to become one of the most valuable possessions in the New World.

Under D'Oyley and his successors, despite war conditions in the Caribbean and serious internal difficulties, Jamaica gradual-

trade was increasing, and the general health of the community was improving.

Court-Martial

D'Oyley acted with characteristic promptness to meet this new danger. He tried fair words at first; but when these failed, he brought reinforcements into the town and persuaded the troops to hand over their leaders and disperse in exchange for a complete pardon. A court-martial was quickly convened and the colonels were adjudged to be deserving of death. Without delay, they were executed in sight of both the government and their troops.

News of the Restoration of the Monarchy

ly elevated itself to relative prosperity by the early 18th Century. Island-born proprietors rose in power and wealth. Politics and island economy were put on a sound footing as sugar production increased rapidly and cattle breeding, logging and coffee cultivation proved more and more profitable.

The British abandoned Spanish Town and gradually shifted their colonial government operations to the Liguanea Plain with its excellent access to the sea. It was here that the British molded Kingston Town into a proper English port city. Kingston Town, meanwhile, saw a spectacular rise in size and importance with good entertainment enabling a lavish lifestyle for the privileged rich and by 1872 became the capital of Jamaica.

The Spanish Armada def

ed by Captaine Morgan

Sʳ HEN: MORGAN

Part. 2. Chap. 4.

Yo Ho Ho! And a Bottle of Rum

Although the war with Spain, sparked by Cromwell's "Design," ended with the restoration of King Charles II to the British throne, the fighting never really ceased in the West Indies. Jamaica, as it turned out, was even better situated than Hispaniola for harassing the Spaniards. Early on, official British encouragement was given to the bucaneers—a rough, wild and ruthless collection of sea-rovers—to continue hostilities against Spain's West Indian possessions. They played a role of the first importance in the history of Jamaica and of the Caribbean as a whole.

They were an odd lot, these early rebels. They included runaway bondsmen, castaways, escaped criminals, political and religious refugees, who had gravitated in time towards the small, rocky island of Tortuga off the northern coast of Hispaniola, where they set up a sort of international port. Their early activities were limited to hunting the wild pigs and cattle which roamed the forests of western Hispaniola, to provide meat, hides and tallow. These they bartered to passing ships for ammunition and rough stores. They usually worked in pairs, to each man a partner with whom everything was shared. Armed with knives and long barreled muskets, they tracked their quarry with the help of dogs. From their method of curing the meat on a wooden frame called a *boucan* (the French adaptation of a Carib Indian word), they earned the name *buccaneer*.

Bucc-ing the System

Spain, of course, resented their presence on Spanish soil and hunted them relentlessly from the Hispaniolan forests. Driven to desperation and the realization that survival lay in unity, this scattered, ragged bunch of men banded together as the *Confederacy of the Brethren of the Coast* and took to the sea. At first they used whatever craft were available—chiefly canoes. But as they captured Spanish ships by surprise attacks, their fleet soon swelled in size. With captured guns and arms they fortified Tortuga. Each success brought new recruits, and the stronger and bolder they grew, the farther they raided, anywhere "against the Spaniard with his hoards of plate and gold."

How many of the big names in buccaneer history started as cow-killers remains uncertain. How many buccaneers deserved the name of "pirate" is another matter. Going to sea meant giving up buccaneering and become a freebooter. Later, when England and France began to issue them with regular commissions called *letters of marque*, their activities became technically legal and their status that of privateers. But there were

Preceding pages: Captain Henry Morgan blasts a Spanish armada. At left, the vaunted governor/buccaneer himself. Above, the execution of Three-Fingered Jack.

many cases where it was difficult to draw too fine a line between name and status.

These buccaneers were a hardy breed. Immune or seasoned to the climate and its ills, they were ruthless, fearless and—except in their communal dealings—lawless. As Brethren, they were welded together by a stern code of discipline which accounted for much of their success. They usually sailed under strict articles, the first of which was: "No prey, no pay." All plunder went into a common pool to be divided according to the share-out scales and disability pensions laid down in the articles. The loss of a finger, for example, rated 100 pieces-of-eight or one slave, while compensation for the loss of both eyes was 1,000 pieces-of-eight or 10 slaves.

Sir Thomas Modyford began his term as governor of Jamaica in June 1664 by suppressing buccaneering. But the outbreak of the Second Dutch War in March of the following year caused an about-face in policy. The hard-pressed Admiralty could not spare a fleet for the West Indies, the defense of which was placed in the hands of the wild Brethren. Edward Long was later to write in his *History* of the island: "It is to the Bucaniers that we owe the possession of Jamaica at this hour."

In Port Royal, the buccaneers found what they needed most: a ready market for their Spanish loot, facilities for the repair and equipping of their vessels, and ample opportunities for amusing themselves in the ways

Sir Henry Morgan, Buccaneer

It was about this time that a new buccaneer-captain appeared on the scene and instantly claimed the limelight. Under the leadership of Henry Morgan, a tough, thickset young Welshman, the buccaneers and Port Royal were to reach the pinnacle of their gilded if sodden glory.

Morgan—whose later career was climaxed with a knighthood, the governorship of Jamaica, and other official appointments—started humbly enough. Born about 1635, as the son of a Welsh land-owning farmer, he went to Barbados, possibly as an indentured servant, then made his way to Tortuga where he joined the Brethren and became Governor Modyford's strongest

they liked. They flocked to the Port in ever-growing numbers. "Such of these Pirates," wrote the buccaneer-historian John Esquemeling, "are found who will spend two or three thousand pieces-of-eight in one night...I saw one of them give unto a common strumpet five hundred pieces-of-eight only that he might see her naked."

And so Port Royal, until that time regarded as of no consequence except as a careening place for vessels, soon became home base for the buccaneers. Nourished by the almost fabulous wealth these corsairs brought in, the town grew and prospered at such a rate that within a decade and a half it had earned the title of the richest—and wickedest—city in the world.

ally. The ruthless, resourceful buccaneer leader was the one man who could hold the wild Brethren together and direct their main efforts towards the defense of the island.

The sacking of Puerto Principe (near Camagüey, Cuba), Porto Bello (Panama) and Maracaibo (Venezuela) stand out as incredible milestones in Morgan's equally incredible career. That he was a hater of Spaniards, not averse to extremes of violence and debauchery, is clear in this description by Esquemeling of the sacking of

Calico Jack's "Pirate Princesses," Anne Bonney and Mary Read, take a break from the drudgery of pillaging (above). Kingston in the 19th Century (right).

Porto Bello:

Having shut up all the Souldiers and Officers, as prisoners, into one room, they instantly set fire unto the powder (whereof they found great quantity) and blew up the whole Castle into the air, with all the Spaniards that were within. This being done, they pursued the course of their victory, falling upon the City . . . They fell to eating and drinking, after their usual manner; that is to say, committing in both these things all manner of debauchery and excess. These two vices were immediately followed by many insolent actions of Rape and Adultery committed upon many very honest women, as well married as virgins; Who being threatened with the Sword, were con-

own right, Port Royal remained Morgan's spiritual home and favorite stomping ground. His ponderous body was entombed here in 1688, and his death presaged the end for Port Royal as a buccaneering port. On June 7, 1692, a violent earthquake broke with a terrible roar under the town, plunging the better part of it beneath the sea, together with the burial ground in which stood Morgan's grave.

Already the Jamaican government had been cracking down on buccaneering, which had achieved its end and was now going out of fashion. A decision was made to abandon the stricken port and found a new settlement, soon to be known as Kingston, across the harbor. But in spite of the earthquake and later disastrous fires and hurricanes,

strained to submit their bodies to the violence of these lewd and wicked men. . . .

Morgan's crowning achievement was the destruction of Spain's supreme New World city of Panama. Peace had previously been sealed between Spain and England by the Treaty of Madrid, and Morgan's exploits—which shattered the treaty—earned both himself and Modyford the deep displeasure of their monarch in England. Eventually, however, the two daring and far-sighted friends were cleared of all disgrace and reunited in Jamaica, Morgan as governor and Modyford as chief justice.

Although he was a rich landowner in his

Port Royal survived to become an important naval station in the following century.

The French Invasion

As a prelude to 100 years of wars and alarms, the 17th Century closed with the only real invasion attempt Jamaica was to know. Taking advantage of the damage and confusion caused by the Port Royal earthquake, a large French force under Admiral Jean du Casse descended on the eastern part of the island and ravaged the countryside in true and terrible buccaneer fashion. But at Carlisle Bay, Clarendon, where the next landing was made, Jamaica's scanty but gallant forces engaged the invaders, 700 of whom were killed before the rest retired to the safety of their ships.

Although the island was saved it had suffered severely from the attack. About 100 settlers had been killed or wounded, scores of plantations burnt, 50 sugar works destroyed and some 1,300 slaves as well as enormous loot carted away.

The war dragged to a close in September 1697 with the Treaty of Ryswick. Spain recognized the French claim to the western part of Hispaniola, which they called St. Domingue. The Spanish called their part Santo Domingo. Today the island is still shared by two independent states, French-speaking Haiti and the Spanish-speaking Dominican Republic.

The ensuing peace was short-lived. The 18th Century was only two years old when the War of the Spanish Succession broke out in Europe. England and the Netherlands ranged against France and Spain. Although Europe was the main theater of war, the Caribbean saw a modicum of naval activity, including Admiral John Benbow's memorable engagement of a French fleet under the redoubtable Admiral du Casse.

On Aug. 19, Benbow in the 90-gun *Breda* sighted du Casse's squadron off Santa Marta, Colombia. The ensuing six-day battle, though indecisive, was notable for Benbow's obstinate courage in carrying on the running fight in spite of the desertion of four of his captains. At one point, the gallant admiral engaged the entire French squadron single-handed and succeeded in recapturing a British galley previously taken by the French! But at length, with the *Breda* badly damaged, his own right leg shattered by chainshot, and his captains staunchly refusing to engage the enemy, Benbow was forced reluctantly to break off the action and return to Port Royal. On arrival he immediately court-martialed the defecting captains, two of whom were sentenced to be shot. He himself died of his wounds at the old port and was buried in the Kingston Parish Church, where his tomb may still be seen.

Slaves and Pirates

The war was brought to an end in 1713 by the Treaty of Utrecht. Britain was awarded France's *Asiento*, or contract, for the supply of slaves to Spanish New World settlements. Jamaica quickly became the entrepôt for the trade, the majority of the slaves being shipped from here to Spanish ports in vessels locally owned and manned.

But all was not well with the island. Pursuing its aggressive policy, the House of Assembly was constantly at loggerheads with the governors representing the Crown, especially over money matters. Epidemics raged, violent hurricanes caused grievous loss of life and property, and troubles with the Maroons added to the general confusion.

So did attacks by pirates now plaguing the Caribbean in growing numbers. Coastal vessels were constantly molested by them and isolated plantations plundered. On one occasion Nicholas Brown, the "Grand Pirate," and his companion Christopher Winter burnt down a house near the coast in St. Ann with 16 people locked in it! A reward of £500 for his capture was earned by one John Drudge, who captured Brown after a fight on one of the South Cays of Cuba. Brown died of his wounds on the way to Jamaica

but Drudge, not to be cheated of the rewards, cut off the pirate's head, pickled it in a keg of rum, and later produced it in Jamaica in support of his claim.

Among the pirates who flourished at this time was Edward Teach, better known as "Blackbeard," believed by some to have been born in Jamaica. A powerful giant of a man, Teach is said to have struck terror into the hearts of his enemies by going into action with flaming matches plaited into his flowing black beard and hair. He was eventually

Edward Teach (above), fearfully known as "Blackbeard", started his pirate career in Jamaica. Sir George Rodney bombards the French fleet on April 12, 1782 (right).

killed in a sea fight off North Carolina.

Captain Charles Vane, another notorious pirate of this period, was captured after a successful career of robbery and murder and brought to Port Royal, where he was hanged on Gallows Point. But perhaps the most romantic of the lot was Captain Jack Rackham, called "Calico Jack" because of his penchant for calico underclothes. He started his career as a member of Vane's crew, rising in time to be its leader.

After terrorizing the Caribbean for more than two years, he made the mistake of lingering longer than a man of his business ought on Jamaica's north coast during November 1720. News of his presence at Ocho Rios was carried to Governor Sir Nicholas Lawes, who immediately dispatch-

Rackham's Cay, as a grim warning to other pirates.

The War of Jenkins' Ear

But the pirates, of course, were not the only people raising their pistols on the bounding main. Old rivalries between Britain, Spain and France resulted in almost continuous conflict in the Caribbean.

One of the more notable tiffs of the time was the so-called War of Jenkins' Ear, which broke out in 1739 over the old bugaboo of illegal trade. The stopping of British ships and ill-treatment of their crews by Spanish *guarda costas*, patrol vessels whose captains claimed the right of search, led to reprisals by the Englishmen.

ed a Captain Barnet and a swift sloop in pursuit. Barnet found Rackham anchored in Negril Bay, enjoying a rum punch party. After a short running fight, he captured the pirate and his crew.

At the trial at the Court of Vice-Admiralty in Spanish Town, the startling discovery was made that two of Rackham's toughest crew members were women! Both Anne Bonney and Mary Read were condemned to death, but Bonney managed to escape punishment and Read died of fever, in prison, before sentence could be carried out. "Calico Jack" was executed. His body was squeezed into an iron frame and hung off Port Royal, on a sandy islet still called

A seaman named Robert Jenkins added fuel to the fire. He had been captured by a *guarda costa* whose captain, he said, had slashed off one of his ears and told him to take it to England as a warning of the fate awaiting others who broke Spain's trade laws. Jenkins appeared before a committee of the House of Commons in London and waved a shriveled leathery object he claimed to be his ear. Those in the Caribbean who knew Jenkins as a scalawag insisted he had both his ears safely under his wig—but the clamor he created in Parliament was enough to incite a declaration of war against Spain.

The war itself was not a happy one for the British. Admiral "Old Grog" Vernon, so named because he ordered the sailors' rum diluted in an effort to reduce drunkenness among the crew, mounted one disastrous campaign after another from Jamaica, costing the lives of some 20,000 men.

The peace which followed the Treaty of Aix-la-Chapelle in 1748 was a fragile one. By 1756, the old rivals found themselves embroiled in the Seven Years War. In the West Indies, almost every French island fell to the British by the time the war ended in 1763 with the Treaty of Paris.

The Exploits Of
Admiral George Rodney

Tensions were high in Jamaica in the late 18th Century. The famous bandit Three-Fingered Jack caused alarm everywhere.

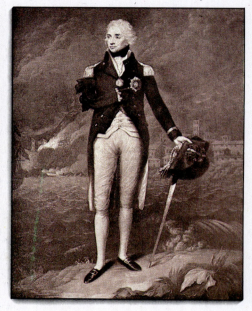

Fires and hurricanes ravaged the island, taking a heavy toll of life and property. A storm in October 1780 completely destroyed the town of Savanna-la-Mar, capital of Westmoreland parish. Fortunately, Admiral George Rodney—who now commanded the British fleet in these waters—had sailed for North America at the onset of the hurricane season and so saved his ships from one of the most destructive of all West Indian storms.

Of more long-term effect was the American War of Independence, which started in April 1775 with the historic skirmish at Lexington Green near Boston. Britain's West Indies colonies had little or no sympathy with the motherland over this war. In fact, the Jamaica House of Assembly made

its sentiments clear in a petition to the King, justifying the actions of the American colonists. France and Spain, meanwhile, were anxious to avenge their past losses in the Caribbean while England was preoccupied elsewhere.

In 1781, British forces surrendered to American General George Washington at Yorktown. By the following year, their status in the Caribbean was exceedingly dim. Only Jamaica, Barbados and Antigua remained in British hands, and they did not appear likely to stay that way.

The Count de Grasse, Admiral of France, joined forces with the Spanish and launched an invasion of Jamaica in April 1782. But they were intercepted by Rodney on April 9 off the island of Dominica. In a three-day running engagement, Rodney masterfully maneuvered his 36-ship fleet to break the enemy lines near the tiny Iles des Saintes between Dominica and Guadeloupe. To this day, the conflict is remembered as "The Battle of the Saints."

When the victorious British admiral sailed into Kingston Harbour with his prizes of war in tow, the island went wild with jubilation. The splendid French flagship *Ville de Paris*, with the count himself aboard as prisoner, was in English hands. Rodney was honored by the British Crown with a barony and a pension of £2,000 a year. Today a monumental statue of Rodney, sculpted by John Bacon, dominates the Square in Jamaica's Spanish Town. The statue is flanked by two of De Grasse's cannons.

Toward the end of the 18th Century, the youthful Horatio Nelson visited Jamaica. While awaiting the arrival of his ship, the *Hinchinbrooke*, he was put in command of the batteries at Port Royal's Fort Charles in preparation for a threatened French invasion which never materialized. Later he led an expedition from Jamaica to Nicaragua; it failed when yellow fever wiped out two-thirds of his forces. But Nelson went on to fame as one of the greatest of all British naval commanders, and his residence in Jamaica is commemorated by a marble tablet fixed to the wall of Fort Charles. It reads:

IN THIS PLACE DWELT HORATIO
NELSON
You who tread his footprints
Remember his glory.

British Commander Lord Horatio Nelson (above). France's Admiral Count de Grasse surrenders to British Admiral George Rodney (left) in an 18th Century engraving.

Hamilton delin.

Thornton sculp.

The French Admiral COUNT De GRASSE, Delivering his Sword to ADMIRAL (now LORD) RODNEY, (Being a more Exact Representation of that Memorable Event than is given in any other Work of this kind.) On Board the Ville de Paris, after being Defeated by that Gallant Commander on the Glorious 12th of April 1782 — in the West Indies —

London Published by Wm Holland No 11 Cockspur Street Oct. 1. 1800

Johnny comes.

Johnny perseveres and takes his Leave of Townend

Desires all Mosquitoes, and calls for Sangaree.

Feels his Pulse and trembles.

Johnny glooms the Thunder Storm wakes as Comes

Johnny Triptoes and Puffs Sidney's away.

John gets into a Rage the Devil with Doughto

Johnny ravies again and domesticates.

The Barons Island. New comes.

Johnny lies awake for the Jews.

The Salt & Body of John are consigned to earth. The Soul & Body of John are consigned to earth.

John writes by the tuck a state of his case.

JOHNNY NEWCOME IN LOVE IN THE WEST INDIES.

Smitten with the charms of Mimbo Wampo, a sable Venus, daughter of Wampo Wampo; King of the Silver Sand Hills in Congo.

Consulting Old Mimbo Jumbo the Oby Man, how to get Possession of the charming Mimbo Wampo.

"Lib me alone for dat Massa."

A few of the hopeful young Newcomes

1. 2. 3.
4. 5. 6.
7. 8. 9.

Delicately declaring his Love to the amiable Mimbo Wampo, while she is picking his Oagoes

"You lub me Massa" ch. 1 ch. 9.

Mr Newcome taking leave of his Ladies & Kickamorees, previous to his departure from Prying Pan Island, to graze a little in his Native Land.

Lucretia Diana Newcome, a delicate Girl very much like her Mother; only that she has a great antipathy to a Pipe, and cannot bear the smell of Rum.

Mr Newcome happy. — Mimbo made Queen of the Harem.

Published April 1st 1815, by William Holland, Oxford Street, London.

1. Lucretia Diana Newcome. 2. Penelope Mimbo Newcome. 3. Quam Dash Newcome prodigiously like his father. — 4. Curly Cato Newcome. 5. Cæsar Quffee Newcome. 6. Helena Quawichah Newcome. 7. Aricida Juba Newcome. 8. Hector Sammy Newcome. 9. Hanibal Pompo Wampo Newcome. a child of great spirit, who already Dreams of Liberty and Equality and promises fair to be the Toussaint of his Country.

TO BE SOLD & LET

BY PUBLIC AUCTION,

On MONDAY the 18th of MAY, 1829,

UNDER THE TREES.

FOR SALE,

THE THREE FOLLOWING

SLAVES,

viz.

HANNIBAL, about 30 Years old, an excellent House Servant, of Good Character.
WILLIAM, about 35 Years old, a Labourer.
NANCY, an excellent House Servant and Nurse.

The MEN Belonging to "LEECH'S" Estate, and the WOMAN to Mrs. D. SMIT

TO BE LET,

On the usual conditions of the Hirer finding them in Food, Clot in and Medical ance,

THE FOLLOWING

MALE and FEMALE

SLAVES,

OF GOOD CHARACTERS.

ROBERT BAGLEY, about 20 Years old, a good House Servant.
WILLIAM BAGLEY, about 18 Years old, a Labourer.
JOHN ARMS, about 18 Years old.
JACK ANTONIA, about 40 Years old, a Labourer.
PHILIP, an Excellent Fisherman.
HARRY, about 27 Years old, a good House Servant.
LUCY, a Young Woman of good Character, used to House Work and the Nursery.
ELIZA, an Excellent Washerwoman.
CLARA, an Excellent Washerwoman.
FANNY, about 14 Years old, House Servant.
SARAH, about 14 Years old, House Servant.

Also for Sale, at Eleven o'Clock,

Fine Rice, Gram, Paddy, Books, Muslins, Needles, Pins, Ribbons, &c. &c.

AT ONE O'CLOCK, THAT CELEBRATED ENGLISH HORSE

BLUCHER,

CKDAW NO. 12 THE SLAVE TRADE AND ITS ABOLITION   ADDISON PRINTER GOVERNMENT OFFICE.   PRINTED IN GREAT BRITAIN

SUGAR, SLAVES AND MAROONS

Within a year of the English takeover of Jamaica in 1658, one of the commissioners—Major-General Robert Sedgwick—predicted that the Maroons would become "a thorn in the sides of the English." His words proved truer than perhaps even he himself expected.

These former slaves who had escaped to the wild mountain country and earned the name *cimarrón*, Spanish for "wild" or "untamed," entrenched themselves for centuries, even developing a culture of their own.

As the island became more settled and English plantations spread farther inland, the Maroons found it easier to swoop from the hills at night, set fire to the fields, and steal cattle and other stock. Runaway slaves from the new plantations swelled their numbers and gave them greater confidence. In 1663, they ignored an offer of land and full freedom to every Maroon who surrendered to authorities; and for the next 76 years, irregular warfare resulted in a government expenditure of nearly £250,000 and the passing of some 44 Acts of the Assembly.

In time, the original Maroons settled chiefly in the eastern and northern parts of the island. In 1690, however, the Clarendon slaves—consisting mainly of Coromantees, an extremely brave and warlike people from Africa's Gold Coast—rebelled and escaped into the woods. Led by a general named Cudjoe, they joined forces with the Maroons and launched a campaign known to history as the First Maroon War. Cudjoe's brothers, Accompong and Johnny, carried the war in the west, and sub-chiefs Quao and Cuffee controlled affairs in the east.

The First Maroon War

Concentrated on the northern slopes of the Blue Mountains and in the forested interior, including the weird and trackless Cockpit Country, the Maroons developed a baffling method of warfare. Skilled in woodcraft and familiar with the untracked forests, they avoided open fights. Instead, disguised from head to foot with leaves and tree boughs, they preferred ambush. What's more, it was almost impossible to surprise

Preceding pages: William Holland's biting Johnny Newcome cartoons of 1800. At left, a sign typical of pre-emancipation Jamaica. Above, Maroon Chief Cudjoe makes peace.

them in their settlements. Keen-eyed lookouts spotted approaching forces hours before their arrival, and spread the warning by means of an *abeng*, a cow's-horn bugle.

British troops, unaccustomed to the country and climate as well as the guerrilla warfare, suffered heavily in their early clashes with the Maroons. But as more and more troops were thrown into the campaign, including Mosquito Coast Indians, tracker dogs, and companies of mulattoes and free negroes, the tide began to turn. The pivotal point may have come with the successful

storming of Nanny Town, the stronghold of Queen Nanny and her Windward Maroons high in the vast wilderness of the Blue Mountains. The town was destroyed and never rebuilt, and to this day the site is believed to be haunted by the ghosts of those who died in the bloody engagement.

Pressured on all sides and faced with starvation, as most of their provision grounds had been systematically destroyed, the Maroons agreed to listen to surrender terms. The English commissioned a Colonel Guthrie to seek out the great old warrior Cudjoe in his Cockpit Country hideout and conclude a treaty of peace. Formalities were carried out on March 1, 1739, under a large cotton tree amidst a cluster of Maroon huts at the entrance of the passage to Petty River Bottom Cockpit.

The new amity was confirmed by a symbolic exchange of hats between Cudjoe and Guthrie. Under the terms of the treaty, the Maroons were guaranteed full freedom and liberty, and were allotted 1,500 acres of land between Trelawny Town and the Cockpits. Cudjoe was appointed chief commander in Trelawny Town, and his successors were named in order, beginning with his two brothers, Accompong and Johnny. The chief was empowered to impose any punishment he regarded as fitting for crimes committed by his own people, except those requiring the death sentence; these cases had to be referred to a government judge. Two white men, named by the governor, were to live

which could easily be sold in Europe or North America. Tobacco, indigo and cocoa all achieved modest success, but sugar turned out to be the most profitable of all.

A large labor force was required for sugar production, and it was from this need that the African slave trade to the West Indies grew. At the same time, the small cultivator disappeared from the fabric of the islands' social structure, phased out as ever-larger areas of land came into the hands of a few powerful sugar planters with their armies of slaves.

The English first started the systematic cultivation of sugar cane in Barbados in 1640. So profitable was the crop that within 10 years, the wealth of the planters had multiplied 20-fold and the slave population

permanently with the Maroons to maintain friendly contact between them and the colonists.

The Maroons, on their part, were to cease all hostilities against the British. They were to reject asylum pleas from runaway slaves, helping instead to recapture them in exchange for a reward. And they were to assist the government as necessary in suppressing local uprisings or foreign invasions.

The following year, a similar treaty was concluded with Quao, chief of the Maroons left in the Blue Mountains. The First Maroon War was ended, and more than 50 years of peace were to follow.

The First settlers in the West Indies had concerned themselves with tropical crops

had risen from a few hundred to more than 20,000.

The capture of Jamaica opened up a piece of land more than 26 times that of Barbados. Governor Modyford, upon his appointment in 1664, promptly set about establishing a sound footing for Jamaica's sugar industry. It grew prodigiously. By 1673, there were 57 estates, and another 66 years later, 430 sugar estates dotted the island. Jamaica was on its way to becoming the single largest producer of sugar on earth.

Maroons demonstrate guerrilla tactics as they prepare for an ambush on the Dromilly estate in Trelawny in 1796 (above). Slaves toiling on a West Indies sugar plantation (right).

During their 18th Century heyday, the West Indies "sugar colonies" were the most valuable possessions in any empire. They were fiercely fought over in every war and fiercely bargained for at every peace conference. Their importance was out of all proportion to their size; indeed, the British West Indies had more political influence with the Crown than did all 13 of the American mainland colonies!

The large Jamaican sugar estates were villages in themselves. They consisted of the overseer's house and offices; the sugar works and mill; the boiling house, curing houses and still house; the stables which housed the grinding cattle; lodging for the white book-keepers; workshops for the blacksmiths, carpenters and coopers; and streets of

and the expression "as rich as a West Indian planter" became the accepted description of any very wealthy person.

A Specter of Fear

Despite this ostentation, a specter of fear walked the sugar estates day and night. Eighteenth Century plantation life was founded on force, and despite the tyranny which held him in bondage, the slave did not accept his lot without a struggle. Whenever he saw a way, the slave rebelled, killing his white masters and destroying their hated plantations. Many African blacks did not even wait until they had arrived in the new land to start their resistance: slave-trading voyages often ended in failure because of an

houses for the black slaves. On rising ground—usually some distance from the sugar works themselves—the planters built their great houses. Constructed of finely cut stone blocks and seasoned timber, with handsome carved woodwork and highly polished floors, they set the elegant style of the day.

The ambition of most planters was to live in Europe as absentee proprietors, luxuriating off their estate profits and leaving the cares and troubles of management to paid attorneys and overseers. Generous, hospitable and hearty, the planters liked to make a great show of their riches, especially in Europe. Such displays strengthened the belief in the great wealth of the sugar colonies,

uprising among the slaves.

In the early days of the slave trade, Africans shipped to the West Indies were mainly prisoners of war or criminals, bought from local chiefs in exchange for European goods. But as the slave traffic increased, other means had to be found to maintain the supply. African tribal wars were stirred up, for no other reason than to replenish the supply of prisoners who could later be sold as slaves. Stragglers were captured from neighboring villages for the same purpose, and regular man-hunting raids were organized by tribes with the help of white hunters. Slaves so taken were usually chained to one another and brutally driven to the coast, where they were stored in "factories"—large fortified castles built especially for the purpose—until the slave ships arrived for the dreaded "middle passage" to the West Indies.

Lasting from six to 12 weeks, the middle passage was perhaps the most dreadful of all experiences a slave endured. On arrival, he was put ashore, exhibited and auctioned to planters and local dealers. The price range normally varied from £25 to £75. Of the tens of thousands of black Africans imported into Jamaica during the 18th Century, about 5,000 were retained each year as slaves. The rest were re-exported.

Those days of yore are still very much a part of the Jamaican consciousness. Reggae superstar Bob Marley spoke of it in "Redemption Song," the last track on the final album

Punishment was a regular part of estate life. A planter could do pretty much as he liked with his slaves. In time, a revision of slave laws brought the master under stricter control, but the early slave code was very brutal. One reason for its severity was a belief that only by terrorism and tight discipline could slaves be prevented from rising and killing their masters, whom they greatly outnumbered.

The slaves were given provision grounds on which to grow their own yams, potatoes, plantains and other foodstuffs. They worked their grounds in the few free hours allowed them daily, producing almost all the food they needed to subsist. They sold their surplus produce in Sunday markets, thereby earning a little extra money which they

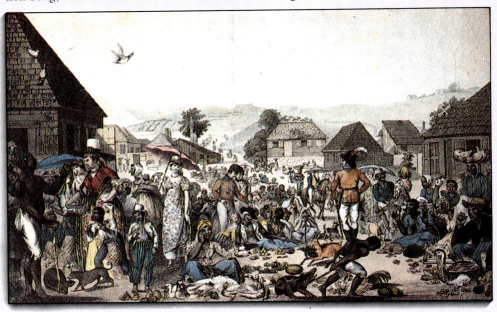

(*Uprising*) released before his death:
Old pirates, yes they rob I
Sold I to the merchants ships
Minutes after they took I from the
bottomless pit . . .

Life on the Plantation

The majority of plantation slaves were *predial*, or field, workers. Many more did domestic duties in the great house and overseer's residence as cooks, maids, butlers and grooms. Domestic service was generally much lighter than field labor under the driver's lash, and domestic slaves dreaded being transferred to the fields more than anything else.

hoped in time might be sufficient to buy their freedom. If a slave's owner wished, he could set his subject free, either in his own lifetime or by his will.

The lot of a slave, dependent as it was on the whims and fancies of others, could be terrible indeed. But he wasn't always alone in his struggle for rights. Among his friends were the early church missionaries—first the Moravians and later the Wesleyan Methodists and the Baptists. They taught the slave Christianity, did what they could to protect

A typical "Negro Market in the West Indies" in 1806 (above). A British emancipation society revealed this view of slaves being tortured in "A Jamaica House of Correction" (right).

52

him from cruelty, and later took part in the struggle for the abolition of slavery itself.

Slaves had few opportunities for recreation, but they learned to make the most of them. During the Christmas and New Year holidays, colorful gay John Canoe bands roamed the streets, and teams of pretty Set Girls dressed in the rich clothes and jewelry of their mistresses to compete with one another in the lavishness of their costumes. And once a week, there was the noise and merriment of the Sunday Market. A carnival atmosphere prevailed as thousands of people came to sell or trade pigs, goats and fowls; yams and other vegetables; small homemade articles like mats, baskets, bark ropes and jars; and delicacies like grapes, melons and strawberries from the high, cool

began in the parish of St. Mary but spread throughout most of the country. Tacky, its leader, was a Coromantee slave who had been a chief in Africa. He gathered a small party of trusted followers, mostly Coromantees like himself from the Frontier and Trinity plantations, and laid his plans in secrecy and with great care.

Before daybreak on Easter Monday, Tacky and his band stole down to Port Maria, murdered the fort's drowsy storekeeper, and made off with a supply of muskets, powder and shot. By dawn, hundreds of slaves had joined Tacky. They moved inland according to plan, overrunning the estates and killing the surprised or sleeping white settlers.

Meanwhile, a slave from the overrun

St. Andrew mountains.

Apart from these moments of pleasure, there were nightly gatherings outside the huts when the day's work was over. Then there was singing, dancing, and the telling of stories—stories of Anansi, the cunning spider man, of gods and animals, of Africa and its many wonders; stories of longing and despair, and stories of hope.

Rebellion!

In 1760, the most serious slave revolt in the island's history broke out. The government called upon the Maroons' assistance, as provided for in their 1739 treaty.

Known as Tacky's Rebellion, the revolt

Esher plantation slipped away and spread the alarm. A troop of mounted militia galloped off toward the trouble area. The governor in Spanish Town, as soon as he received the news by overland express, promptly dispatched two companies of regular troops and called out the Maroons from their Scott's Hall settlement.

The engagements that followed were fought with great skill and daring by the slaves. But as the conflict wore on, the prospects of success grew dim, and a number of slaves lost heart and returned to their plantations. Not so Tacky: he and a band of about 25 men held out until overwhelmed by greater numbers, whereupon they fought free and took to the woods. They were pursued by the Maroons, one of whom—a sharpshooter named Davy—caught up with Tacky. Both were running at full speed when Davy raised his rifle and shot the rebel leader dead. The rest of Tacky's band were later found in a cave. They had committed suicide rather than be captured.

By this time, slave revolts were breaking out in parishes throughout the island. An uprising of Coromantees in Westmoreland proved almost as serious as Tacky's Rebellion, and again Maroons were called upon to help suppress it. Other conspiracies, a number of which were discovered and quelled before real trouble started, flared up in St. Thomas-in-the-East, St. John (now a part of St. Catherine), St. James and Kingston. Months passed before peace returned to the

everywhere. From the time it began in 1789, there was fear in Jamaica that the spirit of subversion might spread to the slaves. There was no hiding the news. European refugees poured into the islands, bringing faithful slaves who carried the news of what was taking place on Hispaniola, only 100 miles away. This flow of refugees, and later of French prisoners of war, was itself a danger to Jamaica's security: it gave spies and agents of the revolution an opportunity to enter unnoticed and stir up disorder.

The events also caused alarm to the Spanish government in Santo Domingo, which shared a common border with St. Domingue. In 1793, when Spain and England both went to war with revolutionary France, they sent separate expeditions to invade St.

island. By that time, 60 whites and between 300 and 400 black slaves had been killed. Two of the revolts' ringleaders had been executed by burning alive, and two others were hung in iron cages on the Kingston Parade and left to starve to death.

Inspiration From Abroad

In the late 18th Century, two events of worldwide importance began to be felt in Jamaica: the French Revolution and the anti-slavery movement in England.

The revolution in France, and the ensuing conflict which gave rise to the black republic of Haiti out of the colony of St. Domingue, provided inspiration for the disaffected

Domingue. The British succeeded in capturing Port-au-Prince in March 1794. They hung onto the city for four years, but the invasion eventually collapsed, decimated by yellow fever and by the superior numbers and military skill of Toussaint l'Ouverture, the first of a remarkable series of black Haitian leaders.

The Jamaican government was unable to send assistance to the British troops in Haiti. There were problems enough at home. In 1795, the Second Maroon War broke out,

Cartoons like the one above published in London in 1838 played a role in freeing the slaves in Jamaica and other British colonies. Abolitionist William Wilberforce (right).

encouraged by the example of the French islands and—said some—by actual French agents.

The immediate cause of the Maroon War is said to have been the flogging in Montego Bay of two Trelawnys for pig-stealing. But it was well known that trouble had been brewing among the Trelawny Town Maroons for some time. The flogging, carried out under sentence of court, was not objected to; in fact, the men would have been far more severely dealt with by their own people for such an offense. The real rub was that the work-house driver who wielded the whip, and most of the prisoners who were allowed to look on and mock, were runaway slaves whom the Maroons themselves had previously captured and handed over to the

authorities for punishment.

This was a harsh blow to Maroon pride. When word of the incident reached Trelawny Town, there was an instant uproar, and wild threats of vengeance were voiced against the people of Montego Bay. Alarmed by this reaction, magistrates asked for troops to reinforce the local militia—and thus were the first tragic steps taken.

The Earl of Balcarres, who had recently arrived as Jamaican governor, treated the matter most seriously. A veteran of the American War of Independence, he believed in strong measures. The earl declared martial law, took command of all forces, and set up headquarters at Montego Bay.

One of his first moves was to send a detachment of men inland to destroy the Trelawny Town provision grounds. But when the detachment reached its destination, it found the grounds already razed. And the Maroons had vanished! But not for long—for on the return march to Montego Bay, the detachment was caught in a devastating Maroon ambush. The colonel and a number of officers and other men were killed or wounded, and the survivors fled in disorder.

With this skirmish, the Second Maroon War began in earnest. For the next five months, a mere 300 or so hardy, determined mountain men held out against 1,500 chosen European troops and more than twice that number of local militia.

As the war dragged on, the whole life of the island was disrupted. Jamaica, in the words of a writer of the time, seemed "more like a garrison ... than a country of commerce and agriculture."

It became increasingly clear to the Earl of Balcarres that no one could search out a Maroon but another Maroon. So the governor and his council decided on the use of dogs. A shipload of 100 of these terrifying beasts was imported from Cuba, where they were in common use for hunting runaway slaves and robbers, together with 40 handlers called *chasseurs*, strong and vigorous men accustomed to great exertion and hardship.

The news of the dogs' arrival caused a panic among the Maroons. In the wild and uncharted Cockpit Country, the Maroons had shown that they could elude almost any number of troops sent against them; but there was no escape from savage bloodhounds that tracked by scent. Before the dogs could be released against them, the Trelawnys sued for peace.

One of the terms of surrender was that the Maroons would not be transported from the island. But using a slim technical pretext as a loophole, the determined Balcarres secured the transportation of some 600 Trelawnys to Nova Scotia, from where they were later removed to Sierra Leone. Trelawny Town was turned over to a detachment of British troops, for whom a barrack was built on the site. The Maroon menace had been laid aside forever.

An End to Slavery

Developments which took place as the 18th Century drew to a close helped to bring the system of plantation slavery crashing down. In Great Britain, changes in the industrial and commerical life were causing doubts about the soundness of supporting the West Indies' slave-based economy. More important, a wave of humanitarian reform was sweeping Britain, part of a new demand for liberty being voiced throughout Europe.

A movement led by William Wilberforce succeeded in securing the abolition of the slave trade in 1807, and complete emancipation from slavery itself in 1838. In Jamaica, abolitionists found valuable allies in the missionaries of non-conformist churches, by now well-established and making heartening Christian progress among the black population. It was another matter, however, with the planter-dominated House of Assembly and with the majority of slave owners. They fiercely opposed the measures for as long as they could, seeing in them nought but disas-

ter and ruin.

In the end, the planters defeated themselves by exhausting the patience of the British Parliament. It only required one more slave uprising to hurry the day of freedom.

As it turned out, that final uprising was the most serious in the island's history. It broke out during the 1831 Christmas holidays, and its influence was felt far and wide. Disorder was centered in St. James. "Daddy" Sam Sharpe, a Baptist leader who sparked the revolt, is now regarded as National Hero. He was hanged in the Montego Bay square that today bears his name.

And so slavery came to an end in Jamaica. The freed slaves widely believed that their

emancipation was the personal act of Queen Victoria, who came to be known as "Missus Queen." Songs of their freedom are still heard today:

Jubilee, Jubilee
This is the year of Jubilee
Queen Victoria set we free
This is the year of Jubilee

With emancipation, sugar production fell sharply. The old plantation economy slowly died and estates were sold for whatever they would fetch. An attempt was made in the 1840s to provide alternative labor with indentured workers from East India, but the result was neglible.

Although the original white planter class had gradually given way to a new class of owners—chiefly mixed-bloods and Jews—the old oligarchic system of government remained unchanged. The island legislature was still elected by a handful of voters who met qualifications of property and income. The magistrates did the will of those in power, and the black peasantry was left to manage as best it might. To add to the distress of the latter, the American Civil War had cut off supplies of their staple foods, while severe droughts at home ruined their own crops. In addition, Edward John Eyre, who became governor in 1862, had little sympathy with the poorer classes and did almost nothing to assist them.

Matters came to a head in October 1865 with an uprising in St. Thomas-in-the-East. Known as the Morant Bay Rebellion and led by Paul Bogle, it resulted in the killing of a number of whites. The uprising was put down by Governor Eyre with great severity. More than 430 persons were executed or shot, hundreds more were flogged, and 1,000 dwellings were destroyed. Bogle, as well as George William Gordon, a prominent mulatto legislator of the day, was hanged. Gordon was blamed by Eyre for the trouble; in retrospect, he appears to have been a scapegoat. A century later, both Bogle and Gordon were declared National Heroes. A statue of Bogle by sculptress Edna Manley now dominates the courthouse square where the rebellion started.

Eyre's scandalous handling of the uprising caused an outcry in Britain and led to his eventual recall. But before leaving Jamaica, he induced the frightened members of the Assembly to surrender their ancient constitution in exchange for the Crown Colony form of government.

Paul Bogle (above) still stands undefeated and defiant in Morant Bay's town square in a sculpture (right) by Edna Manley.

THE TRANSITION TO INDEPENDENCE

Throughout the last decades of the 19th Century and the first decades of the 20th Century, Jamaica's governors wielded wide powers under the Crown Colony system. Sir John Peter Grant in the 1870s was particularly successful in pushing through reforms and improvements of far-reaching importance, and island leaders who followed Grant continued his brisk pace.

Local government was reorganized. The judicial system was completely overhauled and an up-to-date police system was formed. Education, health and social services saw

end, and by the 1930s, the island was moving toward another crisis. There were many contributing factors. Discontent at the slow pace of political advance was coupled with fallout from the worldwide Great Depression, which resulted in falling sugar prices and other economic problems. Growing unemployment was aggravated by the curtailment of emigration opportunities. Meanwhile, Panama disease ruined the banana industry, and the population growth rate was steeply rising. Dissatisfaction came to a head in 1938 with widespread violence and riot-

major progress. Among the government agencies created was one for the protection of East Indian immigrant laborers. An island-wide savings-bank system was organized. A public-works department was established and roads, bridges and railways were built. Cable communication with Europe was established. The banana trade, of great benefit to the island economy throughout the 20th Century, got its start.

The capital was transferred from Spanish Town to Kingston in 1872. The city weathered several major fires and a violent earthquake in January 1907, but was rebuilt on each occasion.

The outbreak of the First World War brought this era of Jamaica's history to an

ing, especially at Frome in Westmoreland.

Out of these disorders came the island's first lasting labor unions and the formation of associated political parties. The first two of these were Alexander Bustamante's Industrial Trade Union, later to be associated with the Labour Party formed by him; and the socialist People's National Party founded by Norman Manley, the island's foremost barrister, later to be closely linked with the Trade Union Congress and the National Worker's Union.

Preceding: Jamaicans spill into the streets of Kingston during pre-independence celebrations. Coke Chapel crumbles during the 1907 earthquake (above); King Street 1920 (right).

The rise of labor to political power was a new and dramatic development. Its leaders pressed not only for increased wages and working conditions, but for political reform as well. One result of this was the new Constitution of 1944, based on full adult suffrage. This brought the Crown Colony period to an end and placed the island securely on the road to self-government.

Further constitutional advances followed in 1953 and 1957, the latter providing for Cabinet government and virtual internal self-rule. By 1959, the island was self-governing with only defense and international relations referred to the Crown.

The years that brought these rapid constitutional advances to Jamaica also saw the development of natural resources, notably in

By February 1962, agreement had been reached. A new Constitution had been approved, and Jamaica's Independence Day was set for Aug. 6, 1962. General elections held on April 10 resulted in a victory for Bustamante's Jamaican Labour Party. Two weeks of celebration and rejoicing, such as Jamaica had never seen before, preceded the first session of the new Parliament on Aug. 7. Princess Margaret, standing in for her sister, Queen Elizabeth II, presented the Prime Minister with the constitutional instruments of independence.

Jamaica moved smoothly and without fanfare into its new sovereignty. Institutions vital to independence were operating efficiently—the administration of justice,

the field of bauxite mining; industrialization; the expansion of the tourist trade; and the growth of nationalism.

An experiment in closer association with other units of the British Caribbean led to establishment of the West Indies Federation in 1958. But the Federation was beset by problems from the start. Its collapse commenced in May 1960 when Bustamante declared his party's opposition to Jamaica's membership. Manley, whose party was then in power, put the issue to the Jamaican people for a referendum vote that resulted in secession. The British government offered no objection, and discussions began almost immediately on the question of Jamaica's separate statehood.

the civil service establishment, development corporations and the central bank. In short, the tried and tested machinery was there, backed by a well-developed political maturity.

Veteran and self-assured politician that he was, Bustamante stepped easily into the role of director of the island's political affairs. There were new initiatives in a number of areas, including agriculture, and by July 1963 a Five-Year Development Plan went to Parliament. It was prepared by 32-year-old Edward Seaga, a Harvard-trained social scientist, then Minister of Development of Welfare. Seaga proved even more successful as Minister of Finance and Planning in the JLP's second five-year term, and he succeeded to the prime ministership himself in 1980.

Jamaica became the 109th member of the United Nations, sought membership in its specialized agencies, and established a permanent mission at the world body's headquarters. The government's ideological stand was enunciated by Bustamante in his declaration: "I am for the West. I am against Communism."

Bustamante retired shortly before the JLP's next general election victory in 1967. He was succeeded by Donald Sangster, whose sudden death brought Hugh Shearer, a prominent trade unionist, into power as prime minister.

The expansion of industry, bauxite, oil-refining, cement-making and clothing manu-

"time for a change" theme and promised social and economic reform.

The social change proved to be a move to the left. Manley described it as "democratic socialism." This movement gained momentum after the party was returned to power in 1976. But it couldn't solve the nation's economic difficulties. Aggravated by the drastic increase in world oil prices, hardship and consternation dominated the economy. Growing unemployment, severe shortages of even basic necessities, dwindling foreign exchange reserves, and successive years of negative growth bred a sense of despair in many quarters. This led to the flight of much-needed capital and the migration of many skilled and professional Jamaicans to the comparative security of the United

facture all contributed to the island's growth. But there were serious impediments to the spread of prosperity, notably a rapidly increasing population. For a time, emigration to Britain helped relieve the pressure; but as the decade of the 1970s dawned, the island was still grappling with unemployment and the problem of balancing its books.

In the meantime, the People's National Party—under the persuasive leadership of Michael Manley, son of Norman, an economist and seasoned trade unionist—had swept to victory in the general elections of 1972, winning 37 seats to the JLP's 16. With its youthful image, the PNP had stressed a

States and Canada.

As the 1980s began, the JLP, reorganized, refreshed and led now by Edward Seaga, laid down its challenge for leadership. Its main political theme was "deliverance"—especially from economic mismanagement and the threat of an alien political system. Seaga placed greater emphasis on private enterprise and promised closer links with the U.S.A. His policies led to an overwhelming victory for the Jamaica Labour Party in the elections of October 1980.

Jamaica Labour Party leader Alexandra Bustamante rides into Kingston during political activities of the 1950s (above). Kingston's Daily Gleaner newspaper (right).

INSTITUTE OF JAMAICA
WEST INDIA REFERENCE LIBRARY

The Daily Gleaner

LARGEST CIRCULATION   ESTABLISHED 1834   Price: THREEPENCE

KINGSTON, JAMAICA, W.I., WEDNESDAY, AUGUST 8, 1962   THIRTY-TWO PAGES

JAMAICA CELEBRATES INDEPENDENCE
Princess opens first Parliament

MER ROYAL HIGHNESS the Princess Margaret at Gordon House, reads the Queen's Speech which opened the first Parliament of independent Jamaica. Seated on the dais with her are His Excellency the Governor-

General, Sir Kenneth Blackburne; the Earl of Snowdon (the Princess' husband) and Lady Blackburne, the members of the Royal party among those standing behind (to front of the dais on left) are the Principal Speaker of the House of Representatives, the Hon. Tacius Lindo, and the President of the Senate, the Hon. Senator G. C. Campbell. In front is (front are clerks at the Legislature and at right members of the Parliamentary Opposition.

'…News received with satisfaction…'
Khrush's telegram to Busta

Her Royal Highness in Throne speech:
UK and Jamaica wish to maintain bonds of friendship

THE FIRST PARLIAMENT of the independent Jamaica, summoned to a joint sitting by proclamation of Her Majesty the Queen, was opened in state at Gordon House yesterday morning by the Queen's sister, Her Royal Highness the Princess Margaret.

Multi-co-oured

From China

Queen's message:
I warmly welcome Jamaica to Commonwealth

Plea for UN membership

Busta on taxes:
Those who can pay will have to pay more

That taxation is likely to be increased among people in the higher income brackets, was indicated at the Prime Minister's first Press conference yesterday afternoon at Vinton Hall, University of the West Indies.

Ashenheim Ambassador to Washington

Mr. Ashenheim was a former member of the Legislative Council from 1960 and became Minister without Portfolio and Leader of Government Business following the April 10 general election.

Midnight…then bonfires, fireworks…
Down the Union Jack, up the Black, Gold and Green

With pomp and ceremony, and in an atmosphere of general rejoicing all over the country, Jamaica became an independent nation at midnight Sunday.

More than 20,000 people crowded the National Stadium Sunday night to see the Union Jack hauled down and the Jamaica National Flag hoisted in its place to the joy of the flag-off while eager spectators sang the Jamaica National Anthem.

From Macmillan —
Jamaica equal partner with UK

The Rt. Hon. Harold Macmillan, Prime Minister of the United Kingdom.

'Out of many …'

MARILYN MONROE FOUND DEAD
Sleeping pills nearby

HOLLYWOOD, August 7 (AP) Blonde and beautiful Marilyn Monroe, a glamorous symbol of the gay, carefree life of Hollywood, died tragically Sunday.

Prime Minister's message:
I know you will respond to the challenge

Sir Alexander Bustamante Prime Minister of Jamaica, in a special message to the people of Jamaica on the occasion of the country's attainment of Independence, said yesterday, that he spoke with pride and courage whether the deliberately lauded her life—that a special "natural" note before it makes a final report on her death.

FOLLOW ME TO 59 HWT. RD.

THE POLITICAL CANVAS: A PAINTING OF HOPE

JLP Zone: PNP enter at own risk!
  —Graffiti on a west Kingston wall
PNP Zone: JLP enter at own risk!
  —Graffiti on an east Kingston wall

To many visitors, Jamaica is a place awash in political slogans. Unseen poets and propagandists, armed with spray paint or brush, conduct word duels on the sides of buildings, on walls fronting villas and factories, even on the streets of the island. The literary devastation wanes and vanishes under fresh coats of post-election paint, only to reappear when another campaign begins. The practice is frowned upon by tourism officials and government agencies involved in beautification efforts. But in Jamaica the politics of spray-paint poetry is a paean to a democracy that is alive and working.

By the standards of many Third World governments, Jamaica's political system is an anomaly. Here, the two parties that have alternated in office since 1944 espouse platforms so different, they make the extreme wings of the U.S. Democratic and Republican parties look like limbs of the same bird. Members of the House and Senate engage in spirited debates, vigorously pounding their tabletops in support of their colleagues' positions, jeering and wise-cracking statements made by opponents. Their constituents eagerly exercise their rights of free speech in the editorial and letter columns of a press that is as free from government control as that of any major Western democracy. Sharp criticism of the ruling party by the Opposition occasionally earns front-page headlines. National issues are also intensively debated on popular public affairs "phone-in" radio programs.

The most dramatic demonstrations of Jamaica's healthy democratic spirit are the open-air mass meetings that characterize election campaigns. More than 100,000 people may travel for miles to hear and cheer their favorite candidates. A correspondent for Jamaica's *Daily Gleaner* described the phenomenon:

> Jamaicans dearly love speeches. They will listen obediently even to the monotonous. But it isn't the "sounds" that make political meetings exciting.

It is the sum of the "sounds"—the spectacle, the music, the illusion of togetherness, of high drama, of hope, the diversity of the people and their reactions. In short, the crowd: the long-suffering, over-optimistic, volatile, pragmatic, bawdy, exuberant Jamaican, multiplied by thousands. It is the crowd's almost tangible need to be led, to be shepherded, that makes political meetings frightening and moving.

All in the Family

Unfortunately, the passions stirred by intense politicking erupted into violence during the 1976 and 1980 parliamentary election campaigns. At the core of the warring were zealous supporters of the two powers in Jamican politics, the People's National Party (PNP) and the Jamaica Labour Party (JLP). Both parties evolved in turbulent times in the late 1930s and early 1940s when Jamaica was struggling to find its own political identity after nearly 400 years of British colonial rule.

The political parties provide the major means of integrating the society. They cut across racial and class lines, bringing together coalitions of interest groups that share a common concern in the political fortunes of the parties. More importantly, the parties represent the centerpiece of the political power structure in the country and have replaced the traditional domain of private power controlled by planters and merchants in the 1930s and 1940s.

A nationalist lawyer named Norman Washington Manley helped found the PNP in 1938 in hopes that it would lead his people to independent rule over a society free of class and economic distinctions. The JLP evolved soon afterward from a trade union established by a tall, charismatic leader named Sir William Alexander Bustamante.

From those early beginnings, the parties and their leaders were at odds with each other. Manley respected the British and their traditions but wished to see an early end to colonial rule and some basic changes in the society. He and his party spearheaded the movement for self-government. Bustamante, by contrast, was not as anxious to see these colonial ties severed. He felt that Jamaica had more to gain from British paternalism and economic aid than from a sudden plunge toward independence. Only reluctantly did he change his mind and support Manley in the 1950s in the cause of self-rule.

The divergent political philosophies of these two national heroes was demonstrated in Jamaica's choice of design for a national flag. Bustamante told newspaper editor T.E. Sealy: "Give me any flag, but put a little Union Jack in it." Manley told Sealy: "Our flag must represent all our races." The final result incorporates a piece of the personality of both leaders. It has the black color of Jamaica's majority race, as well as green and yellow, and a diagonal cross reminiscent of the British banner.

An ironic footnote to this tale: Bustamante and Manley were cousins. In fact,

ment in 1944.

In the ensuing years, the popularity of the party of "Busta," as Jamaicans fondly called the man with his lion's mane of white hair, slowly eroded. Manley's PNP took its turn at leadership beginning in 1955. The PNP flirted with the development of a West Indies Federation, a kind of United States of the Caribbean. Manley also engineered a revised constitution that paved the way for full independence from the British.

Differences with Trinidad led Jamaica to secede from the Federation in 1961 and the JLP rode that issue back into power the following year. Princess Margaret, filling in for her sister, Queen Elizabeth II, formally declared Jamaica an independent nation on August 6, 1962. What seemed like the is-

three of Jamaica's first five prime ministers—Bustamante, Michael Manley (Norman's son) and Hugh Shearer—hailed from the same family.

Taking Turns at the Top

Manley and Bustamante share the mantle as fathers of modern Jamaica, just as their remains now share the hallowed grounds of the National Heroes Park in the governmental district of Kingston. It was Bustamante who first captured the fancy of the population. His party rolled to victory when Jamaica elected its first parliament by universal adult suffrage, under a new constitution that introduced representative govern-

land's entire population poured into the streets to celebrate. Bustamante earned his victorious party's blessing to become Jamaica's first prime minister. Norman Manley died before he could take his turn as PM.

The political machinery tooled by the parties of Manley and Bustamante still looks somewhat British. One has only to attend a session of Parliament at Gordon House and watch as the meeting is called to order by a Speaker whose black face is incongruously framed in a white wig of flowing wool. He

Bustamante flashes his pleasure at another victory for the Jamaica Labour Party (above), and a somber Norman Manley, People's National Party founder (right).

sits above a desk containing a silver tea service and a table containing books of constitutional law and a gold sceptre.

This bicameral Parliament consists of a 60-member House of Representatives freely elected by a plurality of voters from the country's 13 parishes and the corporate areas of Kingston and St. Andrew. All parishes, including Kingston and St. Andrew, are run by parish councils elected by voters. Every Jamaican citizen aged 18 or over is eligible to vote.

Technically, Jamaica is still a member of the British Commonwealth and a constitutional monarchy; thus, the Queen of England is the titular head of state. Another ceremonial throwback to British rule, as a result, is the Queen's appointment of a

governor general as her local representative. But the "G.G.," as Jamaicans call him, is a Jamaican recommended by the prime minister. The real power remains vested in the leader of the ruling party who is appointed prime minister after Jamaicans vote his party into power.

The prime minister surrounds himself with a variable number of cabinet ministers. He also recommends the appointment of 13 members of the 21-seat Senate. The governor general appoints the balance upon the advice of the leader of the Opposition.

The Senate was originally supposed to function like the British House of Lords, as a chamber in which distinguished citizens, businessmen and outstanding professionals who were not caught up in the hurly-burly of party politics could be appointed to bring expertise and objectivity to governmental deliberations. This has not happened. The Senate has instead become a chamber dominated by retired and aspiring politicians who provide a mere echo of the partisan debates in the lower house.

Representatives are elected to the 60 single-member constituencies of Parliament. The constitution makes the House dominant, giving it control over finances and the power to override the Senate. However, its actions are subject to considerable influence from the executive branch, which controls voting through strong party loyalties and discipline, and by determination of the House's agenda of activities.

Joshua and the Syrian

Voter preferences continued to seesaw during the '60s. At least two-thirds of the population eligible to vote lined up behind either the PNP or the JLP, while a handful of minor parties failed to muster much support.

In spite of a decade of slow progress under the JLP following independence, support for the PNP pushed Michael Manley, the handsome son of Norman, into Jamaica House in 1972. Under Prime Minister Michael Manley, Jamaica's political culture became even more issue-oriented and ideologically polarized than it had been in the days of Norman Manley and cousin "Busta." However, the highly personalized and leader-centered tradition of party politics continued.

A graduate of London University, Manley entered politics after a stint as a labor union negotiator. His movie-star looks and commanding presence endeared him to women and awed men. People traveled hundreds of miles along treacherous mountain roads just to hear him speak. Manley even visited Ethiopia and had an audience with former Emperor Haile Selassie, winning him points among the traditionally apolitical Rastafarian subculture. Manley received a staff from Selassie, a "rod of correction" which he said he would wave to right wrongs and transform the country's deteriorating social fabric. The PNP then promoted Manley as a modern-day "Joshua" who would lead the people to the Promised Land.

Notwithstanding his penchant for showmanship, Manley initiated important changes in a social structure sharply divided between rich and poor. He passed minimum wage laws and introduced new labor legislation recognizing workers' rights. He also attempted land reform and increased the construction of low-income housing. Manley imposed a levy on multinational bauxite companies that gave Jamaica a bigger, more deserved chunk of the earnings from its most important natural resource. He expanded the program of electrifying rural areas. Poor farmers also received a fairer share of fertile lands that had been concentrated in the hands of a few wealthy property barons. Manley called his program Democratic Socialism.

Unfortunately, many of Manley's policies were instituted with little regard for their economic consequences. For example, major utilities were nationalized, but the government's lack of foreign exchange for the

purchase of new machinery, parts and replacements, led to the deterioration of electric plants and water purification and pumping stations. The sharp swing toward socialism also alienated many middle-class and big businessmen. Some left for greener pastures in the United States and Canada, taking their expertise and foreign exchange with them. Manley's foreign interests leaned increasingly toward Cuba and the Soviet Union, and he became a popular spokesman for Third World "have-not" countries. Consequently, the U.S. aid upon which Jamaica had been dependent began dwindling.

At the same time that Manley found his government's financial problems mounting, an economics wizard named Edward P. Sea-

ga was rising through the ranks of the Opposition to become leader of the JLP. Although Seaga's business background and Lebanese (in Jamaica, "Syrian") ancestry were decided disadvantages, he'd shown an uncanny ability to consistently win elections in the constituency of West Kingston, Jamaica's poorest, most troubled area of enclaves like Trench Town and Rema. The Harvard-educated sociologist delivered on political promises, transforming a grim ghetto called Back O' Wall into a model inner-city community called Tivoli Gardens.

In contrast to Manley, Seaga believed a return to free enterprise and friendship with the United States was the way to lead Jamaica to prosperity. He stood staunchly against Cuba and communism. Those stark differences between two ambitious men led to Jamaica's most explosive election campaigns in 1976 and 1980.

The Politics of Polarization

The political traditions of Jamaica differ markedly from those found in the liberal democracies in Europe and North America. Party feelings are more intense and militant. JLP and PNP supporters tend to be hostile toward each other. Over the years, they have developed negative stereotypes about the attributes of persons who support the opposing party. These inter-party hostilities reach critical temperatures during the heat of election campaigns and often boil over into personal abuse, attacks on political meetings, even murder. But, as the Jamaica Tourist Board understandably insists on pointing out, visitors have remained virtually immune to the violence, and trouble has rarely spilled out of certain constituencies in urban Kingston. Still, the political problems made headlines in countries where many of Jamaica's annual visitors live.

In other developing countries, the military often plays a major role in running political parties if not the government itself. However, the Jamaica Defence Forces (JDF) have generally maintained their independence from the party that is in—or out—of power. The highly trained group of about 2,000 men and women is not large by Caribbean standards. It is an offshoot of the crack West India Regiment that distinguished itself in Great Britain's campaigns in Egypt, Europe and Africa. The intimidating symbol of a crocodile identifies JDF trucks, jeeps and uniforms. Although the army has tried to avoid party politics, troops have joined with the policemen during the past decade to help put down political flare-ups.

The police force in its red and blue-striped uniforms outnumbers the military and thus maintains a higher profile. They are not averse to flagging down visitors during security checks on various parts of the island, to inspect cars for illegal drugs or weapons, and passengers for proper car ownership or rental papers, drivers licenses and valid visas or visiting permits. They also brave busy intersections to direct or untangle traffic with white-gloved hands; graciously provide directions to lost travelers; and constantly risk their lives apprehending armed criminals, collectively called "gunmen" in island vernacular.

Possibly as an alternative to controlling the military, Jamaica's political parties enlisted their own gun-toting gangs to try to shooting matches. Small factions within the PNP and JLP turned the harmless threats of the political graffiti into action.

Even beloved reggae superstar Bob Marley became a target. A gang of gunmen burst into his "Island House" home, now the Tuff Gong studio on Hope Road, and machine-gunned Marley, his road manager and others—two days before a scheduled free "Smile Jamaica" concert at National Heroes Park which Marley hoped would help cool the overheated political climate. Marley later wrote about the attack in his song "Ambush in the Night":

Ambush in the night—four guns aiming at me. They open fire on me.... See them fighting for power, but they know not the hour. So they bribe us,

scare voters to their sides during the '70s. The JLP charged Cuba and its sympathizers with smuggling American-made M-16 rifles to PNP henchmen. The PNP countered with claims that the weapons must be coming from the United States itself in a CIA (Central Intelligence Agency) plot to overthrow Manley's government.

The party violence became serious as voters prepared to go to the polls in December 1976. The natural tendency of Jamaicans to engage in shouting matches escalated into

PNP leader Michael Manley makes a campaign speech (left). Manley, Reggae star Bob Marley and JLP leader Edward Seaga join hands at the 1978 "One Love" concert (above).

with their guns and spare parts and money, trying to belittle out integrity.

Marley bandaged his wounds and bravely went through with his "Smile Jamaica" concert, albeit somewhat reluctantly. Prime Minister Manley mounted the stage to personally congratulate the singer for his courage at the close of the show. And Manley later met Seaga to sign a "Pledge of Peace" drawn up by a local church.

The truce proved temporary. The stakes were much too high. High levels of unemployment and the existence of significant urban and rural poverty made party patrons dependent upon the favors granted by their respective parties. Election contests, therefore, become even more intense because of material rewards like jobs, contracts, concessions, housing, government land, and a range of other benefits.

The parties tend to have a strong sense of territoriality at the local community level. Efforts are made to keep members of the opposing party out of local strongholds. So some violence results from efforts to preserve local "territorial hegemony." Consequently, there have been skirmishes between adjacent communities that support opposing parties.

In an attempt to restore order, Manley declared a state of emergency to increase his police powers under the constitution. The police and military began rounding up people suspected of instigating the pre-election trouble. JLP members immediately charged the PNP with singling out JLP candidates and supporters, and warned voters that Manley had misused the constitution merely to jail his critics and make himself more powerful.

Earlier, Manley had toughened criminal laws under a new Ministry of National Security act. That spawned the sinister, barbed-wire Gun Court on Up Park Camp Road. The court attempted to curb crimes committed with guns by speeding up trials, eliminating bail, and dealing out severe life-sentence penalties.

Otherwise, Jamaica's judiciary, like the legislative branch of government, has remained strongly rooted in British traditions. An 18-member Supreme Court, in full regalia of red robes and white wigs, acts as the venue of final appeal in reality. In theory, the Privy Council of England still has the last word in criminal cases. That may change, however, as progressive chief justices and attorneys work to streamline and improve Jamaica's jury system.

Manley's state-of-emergency declaration and the creation of the Gun Court initially produced some concern that he had tampered with matters that were the traditional jurisdiction of the judiciary. Among the most important provisions of Jamaica's constitution are the protection of fundamental human rights and freedoms of the individual, including protection from arbitrary arrest or detention and against discriminatory treatment, the protection of freedom of movement, and freedom of expression.

Exodus

Despite objections to the PNP action, the new measures strengthened the hands of the military, the police and courts. A lull in violence and terrorism resulted, however, temporary. And the people of Jamaica apparently saw nothing wrong in the actions of the Manley government. Manley won the 1976 election—in a landslide.

The euphoria of the huge election mandate soon gave way to harsh reality. One month after the vote, Manley announced that Jamaica had entered a state of economic crisis. The International Monetary Fund (IMF) agreed to bail out the country with a loan, but Manley balked at the strings that were attached. The IMF wanted a 40 percent devaluation of the Jamaican dollar and a boost in tax benefits that appeared weighted in favor of the rich. Manley finally accepted those distasteful terms and the loan when he found his country teetering on the brink of bankruptcy.

The prime minister's flirtation with left-leaning countries of the Third World, however, led to a continuing erosion of confidence among Jamaica's traditional Western allies. Manley became a spokesman for the Non-aligned Movement. He paid visits to Cuba and Moscow. As a result, foreign investment and other aid from the West dried up. Cuba stepped in and built the Jose Marti School on the outskirts of Kingston, but its government had its own financial problems to cope with and could do little more for its Jamaican friends.

Meanwhile, the exodus of middle and upper-class mainstays of the Jamaican economy turned into a flood. Even leaders in education and technology began leaving their country. Manley angrily told them if they did not like his policies they should leave. Consequently, businesses shut down and the lack of skilled workers led to a deterioration in maintenance of public utilities like the water and electric departments. One striking example of the exodus was the mass departure of the influential Chinese Jamaicans. Here in Jamaica, as in other countries, they had used their vaunted business acumen to work themselves out of indentured servitude in the 19th Century into lucrative enterprises in the 20th Century. The number of Chinese dwindled from a peak of about 40,000 in the 1960s to just 4,000 by the end of the 1970s.

The IMF loan proved to be only a stop-gap measure. Jamaica found itself in the humiliating position of accepting loans from Caribbean neighbors like Trinidad and tiny Barbados. Still, foreign debts mounted to more than 1 billion dollars, the cost of living soared, and unemployment rose to 30 percent. Foreign exchange reserves vanished. Potholes appeared in city streets. Interruptions in electric service became more frequent. Basic necessities like cooking oil and soap dwindled and brought exorbitant prices on the black market. In an article for *Geo* magazine, part-Jamaican Clifford Mason reported a poignant conversation he had with an old woman in Mandeville: "Imagine. I haf fe work all day long in a sun hot and when I come home fe cook dinner fe mi man, I cahn't even get likkle soap fe wash de sweat offa me," the woman said.

By 1979, Manley's government found itself $150 million in debt. Seaga and the JLP started their next campaign early.

Silencing the Guns

By 1978, clashes between supporters of the PNP and JLP were again on the increase.

prompted Manley to call for new parliamentary elections in October 1980.

The election announcement appeared to heighten the urgency of both parties' campaigns. That election year saw an unprecedented political bloodbath that made international headlines. More than 514 people died in violence blamed on the bitter campaign. Frightened tourists stayed away.

As usual, however, urban Kingston suffered the worst of it. Olympic Gardens, Jones Town, Trench Town, Hannah Town and neighboring areas, already miserable pools of poverty, became battlegrounds. Huge ads appeared in the daily newspapers demanding an end to the insanity. Some offered rewards of up to $10,000 for information leading to the conviction of gun

Marley, now an international musical superstar, again tried to intervene. He staged a "One Love" concert in April to commemorate the 12th anniversary of the 1966 visit to Jamaica by Haile Selassie, the messiah of his Rastafarian creed. More than 25,000 Jamaicans watched Marley call JLP leader Seaga and Prime Minister Manley to the stage, lock hands with both in a raised pyramid, and sing:

> One Love, One heart
> Let's get together and
> feel all right.

Again, the Marley magic silenced the guns. Again, the truce proved temporary. Increasingly bloody clashes between the JLP and PNP forces and the crumbling economy

smugglers. Both Manley and Seaga had bullets fired at them. Great Britain's *The Guardian* summed up the ugly air that hung over this beautiful island as election day 1980 neared:

> As the elections approach in October, violence and terror have become the permanent preoccupation of the 700,000 citizens of this hot unruly city. Soldiers and police point their guns at crowded pavement from their Toyota land cruisers; helicopters rattle over-

Prime Minister Edward Seaga, flanked by members of his party and cabinet, addresses Jamaicans from the tomb of Alexander Bustamante in National Heroes Park (above).

head at nights shining searchlights in dark side streets, gunfire wakes you in the small hours. Night life has dwindled with two cinemas closing this week for lack of business. Tourists, thinking mistakenly that the whole island is ablaze, have reduced bookings. . .

Oblivious to all this, people swarmed to JLP rallies to join cries of "Go deh, Eddie. We ready." Turnouts at the PNP meetings diminished noticeably from earlier years.

On October 30, 1980, more than 85 percent of Jamaica's registered electorate bravely left their locked-and-barred domiciles to exercise their right to vote. Seaga's rejuvenated JLP won 51 of Parliament's 60 seats, the biggest margin of victory since 1944. Michael Manley conceded defeat before all the votes had been cast.

A Minister's Prayer, A New Start

The resounding victory of the JLP in 1980 triggered tidal waves of optimism in Jamaica that still appear to be rattling the island's foundations. Seaga's first act as prime minister-elect was to call his parish minister to pray with him and his family. He then set about trying to mend the rifts in Jamaican society that had been ripped open by the parties and their candidates during the campaign. But he did not stray from his platform. One of his first official acts as prime minister was to clearly signal his foreign policy preference. Seaga became the first head of state to pay a visit to the newly inaugurated U.S. President, Ronald Reagan, who had been elected only a few days after his own victory. Reagan later repaid the visit with an overnight stop in Jamaica in April 1982, becoming the first reigning American president to set foot on the island. The Cuban Embassy on Trafalgar Road in Kingston, meanwhile, was closed and its officials expelled from Jamaica.

These newsmaking foreign-policy shifts played an important part in Seaga's main priority—rebuilding Jamaica's shattered economy. Western investors interpreted the moves as an invitation to begin returning. Western governments earmarked aid increases for Jamaica. Within six months of the election, the new government concluded agreements with the IMF for loans of nearly $700 million over three years. Seaga also set about returning hotels and other government-absorbed enterprises to private hands.

The policies had an immediate impact on the economy. In little more than a year, Seaga halted the negative slide of the na-

tion's economic indicators and boosted them back into the plus column. Jamaica registered a modest two percent increase in its rate of economic growth in 1981, better than many developed countries. Inflation declined dramatically from 29 percent in 1980 to just six percent in 1981. Soaring unemployment leveled off and even decreased slightly from 27 percent in November 1980 to 26 percent a year later. The government also recorded its first balance of payments surplus in seven years.

After this promising beginning, the economic and political fortunes of Seaga's government have tumbled. Decline in hard currency earnings combined with increased imports encouraged by government policies triggered a deterioration of the country's balance of payments problems. This escalated to crisis proportions due to adverse world market conditions for bauxite and alumina. As a consequence, tight austerity measures have had to be adopted. These have visited hardships on the population in terms of lay-offs, severe cost of living increases, and declining consumption and purchasing power. As a result, a welfare Food Stamps program has been developed to supplement the diet and nutritional levels of the poorest in the country. It is intended to benefit indigents, schoolchildren and expectant mothers in particular.

Tight monetary policies and a big devaluation of the Jamaican dollar designed to ease pressure on the balance of payments problem have had some adverse effects. Cut-backs in public spending have affected educational and health services as well as the maintenance of the infrastructure, such as roads.

These austerity measures combined with large increases in taxes designed to reduce the big budget deficit have weakened the popularity of the government. After winning an election held in 1983 in which the opposition party, the PNP, refused to take part, the popularity of Seaga's JLP fell considerably.

All of this has triggered demands from the PNP new elections. After four years of political quiescence, the political temperature has again been raised as the country's economic conditions have declined.

In spite of all these difficulties, Prime Minister Seaga remains optimistic that his policies will produce positive gains and results. He looks beyond the austerity measures and their inevitable negative impact to hopes for success base on tourism expansion and export-led growth.

The influence of British protocol is evident as Jamaica's Speaker of the House presides over a session of Parliament (right).

THE JAMAICANS

The Jamaica consciousness is just burning out of sight. Its history is African. Its culture is European. Its politics are Third World. We're producing a totally new breed of human being.
—*Perry Henzell, director of* The Harder They Come

One unfailing factor has knitted the Jamaican people closely throughout their island's turbulent history: the enthusiastic affection of one for another. Centuries of sharing a beautiful land of astonishing fertility have created a people as warm as noontime in a canefield; as good-natured as a market lady busing home into the hills on a Saturday night, full of tales of the city to tell an attentive and reciprocal audience.

This enthusiasm for one another, has enriched the "pure" Jamaican with the racial genes of Africa, Asia and Europe. It has proven to be immeasurably difficult—indeed, impossible—for serious rifts to occur when all know they share a common stock. Some say it is the rule, rather than the exception, that skin tones in most Jamaican families range from Nordic to Nubian. Sly wit greets any *moko*-head who pretends it to be otherwise. And those who would take issue with this for the sake of pretentiousness, whether they are black or of the somewhat pejorative "Jamaica-white," are sent into the wings to chew their genealogies.

Issues involving jobs or social acceptance rate other responses. Here, tempers can rush like rum from a demijohn, explosively directed at locals who would hire foreign whites for reasons of prestige. The wake of the conquerors is still visible in the Caribbean. On the other hand, there is now a rush of foreign whites for work permits; their line has begun to look more like the local queues seeking visas to America.

Finally, the fun-Jamaica has been zested by the labor of the other two great races, the Indians and Chinese; and of the trading "Syrians" (actually Lebanese) who have given up many man-hours of hard business to the great Jamaican game of "him-gawn-a-bed."

In another 50 years, this lively old colony

Preceding pages: A Jamaican bride and her bridesmaids at Devon House. At left, J. Mullings, justice of the peace and proprieter of DeMontevin's Lodge.

will be well on its way to having tripled its population. It is as comfortably nestled in the higher percentages of world population density as it is up there in ethnic mix. And its young enlightened government has not hesitated to assist. Recent legislation provides that all babies are legitimate, whether born in or out of wedlock. Naturally, that action spawned new reggaes, including the very popular, "No more bastard no-deh!"

Early Arrivals

The story of Jamaica's unique ethnic evolution began when Mongoloid peoples crossed the Siberian land-bridge into Alaska many millennia ago. They worked their way down the frost-free McKenzie Valley into the warm south, crossed the Central American isthmus into South America, and subsequently voyaged into the Caribbean, pausing to drop off several cultures, including the Aztec and Mayan civilizations. As they continued south and east, some members of the march broke off the long hike, took to the sea and became Canoe People.

The Canoe People evolved into distinct groups—Ciboneys, Arawaks and Caribs—and sailed into the Caribbean on a deadly chevy chase: the Ciboneys fleeing the Arawaks, the Arawaks fleeing the Caribs. The Caribs, who brought up the rear, were fierce unneighborly man-eaters. The Ciboneys, along with a few stray Arawaks, found shelter on the island of Cuba. The balance of the Arawaks settled in Jamaica. Christopher Columbus ran into them when he was searching for a new route to India, so he assumed they were all Indians.

The Emerging 'Ethnic Mix'

In the meantime, the 4,411 square miles of tall mountains, deep valleys and spectacular beaches had called up other Old World folk from the Arab nations, China, and real Indians from India. Jews came early with the Spaniards; some even hold that Columbus was a Jew, Christopher Colon, turned Christian.

Of the first Indians, the Arawaks, only traces remained by the time of the 17th Century English conquest. All had been killed off by enslavement, murder and disease during the Spanish years. But great endeavor was made to see that all died Christians.

The Spaniards, with regard for their conquistador image, had been horseback colonists who needed foot servants for gold digging, wild-pig hunting, and breaking wild horses for sale to passing expeditions. The gentle Arawaks had been unable to cope with the rough adventurers after a life of ease in a cornucopia of manioc and pork, fruit, fowl and fish, and above all, the two blessings of *cohiba* (tobacco) and *coyaba* (heaven). The Canoe People had met the Spanish Boat People, to the Indians' lament.

The demise of the Indians meant that new attendants were urgently needed by the dons who prized their siestas. So the Spanish brought in a second group of Boat People. Unlike the first, the Africans came not by choice or chance but by chain. A minority of

miles from Kingston, the Blue Mountains tower to more than 7,000 feet. Half of the island hovers upwards of 1,000 feet above the azure seas, and these uplands enjoy a dry, ideal average of 60 to 70 degrees Fahrenheit. The spectacular scenery owes much of its beauty to the thick foliage cover—just the kind ideal for harboring guerrilla fighters.

So when the black slaves struck their blows for freedom, they naturally took to the mountains. Their African forebears had been good fighting people: Akim, Ashanti, Fanti, Mandigo and Angola. Some went off to the mountains on their own; others didn't bother to return when sent out by their masters to hunt wild pigs, cattle, the succulent coney, and horses for the plantations.

British whites were later brought in as "almost slaves" or indentured workers, and some Africans joined the rush as voluntary immigrants. The indentured whites were treated worse than the black slaves, since they were only on lease and if worked to death could be replaced free-of-charge.

Black slavery under the Spaniards in Jamaica was not the squalid, somber savagery that slavery usually is. The blacks saw to that. Soon after their arrival, they discovered the mountains.

Half the area of New Hampshire U.S.A (and more than twice its population), Jamaica has a great backbone of mountains which runs the length of the island. The highlands descend only at the coasts. Just 10

The Spaniards made a few attempts to find them, then gave up. In any case, it was a fairly easy relationship until the English conquest. Then the remaining blacks were set free as the Spanish fled. They moved to the mountains and entered island annals as the Maroons.

Maroons of the Cockpit Country

Up in Maroon country it gets dark early in the winter months, and the evening turns

A resident of Jamaica's German community in Seaford Town holds up portraits of her children (above). Colonel C.L.G. Harris, leader of the Windward Maroons (right).

cool and fragrant with pimento and jasmine and the night-blooming cereus. There is a grand throating of frogs, the nighthawk's *gi'e-me-me-bit*, whistling toads, and the eerie "Creech Owl." But on the eve of Cudjoe Day, there is little dark in Accompong, one of the ancient fortress towns of the Maroon people. The great chief, Cudjoe, harried the English army from here and other strongholds for 50 years after the day in 1690 he walked away from a slave plantation at a place called Suttons.

Every year on Jan. 6, Accompong Maroons gather to celebrate The Day. They come from home or abroad, wherever they have followed the Money Fly. Maroons will tell you that the Money Fly is a shiny, bluish insect that is seldom seen unless it's on its

his guerrilla campaign, working his variants of ambush and attrition, taking the Redcoats at a gulp or wearing down the columns as they struggled with the precipitous slopes, the nervous English soldiers named the district "The Land of Look Behind."

At daybreak on Cudjoe Day, the drums commence. The drumming is complex, the rhythms twisting and changing as intricately as the carvings on the instruments. The singing is a series of surging harmonies fitted for the stomping march. In probably the most important event of the day, the Maroons make a pilgrimage to Old Town, Accompong's burial place, and to the Treaty Place. Here, under a silk cotton tree, on March 1, 1739, after the English had sued for peace, the First Maroon War ended. The

way out of the window. But if it lands on your hand, *wayah-O*! That is bankable! Jamaicans have followed the Money Fly to Panama to build the Panama canal; to New York to help settle Harlem before the 1920s; to Cuba to ensure the phenomenon of sugar in the early 20th Century; to Britain to run the buses and hospitals and even to soldier in its wars, from the guns of Morro Castle to the guns of August, from the War of 1812 (where old Stonewall Jackson personally commended their battle quality) to the Second World War.

Accompong and Cudjoe Town are close to each other, located in the wildest heights of the island in an area today known as the Cockpit Country. But when Cudjoe was into

Second Maroon War came some 50 years later. Many fire fights kept the mountains alight for one and a half centuries.

After the pilgrimage come the ceremonies of unveiling the monument to Cudjoe and the ancient Maroon fighters, put up by the National Trust. The Trust, which is state-funded, has established a series of monuments around the country to mark the sites of "folk" struggles ignored in the older history books written by English scholars.

The Windward Maroons

One hundred miles to the east, in the Blue Mountains, the Windward Maroons—descendants of the Nanny Town fighters—also

have their government monument. It honors the legendary Nanny of the Maroons, a warrior priestess who, like Cudjoe, waged her own great war against the English. She is now a National Hero with the rather sweet title, "The Right Excellent Nanny."

The Windward Maroons set up strongholds in 1658 during the English conquest, before any of the other Maroon companies. As Spanish blacks under their elected leader, Juan de Serras, they went into the Blue Mountains, the *Sierras de Bastidas,* to establish a base from which to attack the English. For the next 100 years they did so. Then they too, like the Accompongs in the west, were petitioned by the British government to make peace. The Maroons became virtually an independent nation within a nation. They remain so today with their own governmental subdivisions that are headed by colonels.

The fantastic exploits of the Maroon men and women, who by skill and courage kept the British empire builders at bay, rank in quality if not in scope with the next-century activities of those other colonials up Boston way. The Maroons clashed with Cromwell and every English monarch from Charles II in 1658 through to George III in 1795.

Using the mountains and forests as allies, the Maroons were feared for their "bush ambush." Wearing branches cut from the trees, and standing as immobile as actual foliage, they would lay a trail that led the Redcoats into their "funny glade." Then, with their ubiquitous *combola* (machetes), they hacked inward from the flanks. Although the Maroons were outnumbered and outgunned by their foes, the British arms were of little use in the deadly game of "Birnamwood to Dunsinane," as near-contemporary Will Shakespeare might have described the skirmishes.

Not all Maroons were of Afro-Spanish origin. In time, their numbers were considerably strengthened by Breakaways, slaves who escaped from the English plantations into the mountains. In fact, Cudjoe himself was a Breakaway. So was Quao, the almost equally famous war chief who served under Queen Mother Nanny.

The Maroons still live in their towns today. No longer the "untamed ones"—the name derived from the Spanish *cimarrón*— they retain traditions as proud as the mountain peaks around them. But isolation has fled before the advent of television and motor roads.

Imbued with the warrior quality, many of these early Afro-Jamaicans left their modest-sized island and traveled overseas to war. Breakaways tended to swim out to join private ventures, making their mark aboard pirate ships where their services were appreciatively engaged. The prize money for returning these "we-backs" was nothing compared to what could be stolen from white cutthroats. Many Breakaways canoed off to Cuba in great unsinkable crafts gouged from massive silk cotton trees and capable of accommodating 50 or more.

Many Jamaican Maroons went to war for the same British forces they were harassing at home. Among their legitimate battle honors were expeditions in the Napoleonic Wars, the capture of Cuba and Haiti, and sackings of Campeche, Porto Bello, Panama, Santo Domingo, Cartagena and Nicaragua. They had a "no-go" from Britain when they volunteered for service in the Boer War against white South Africans rebelling against English rule. But they were welcomed by Britain in the other African wars waged against black Ashantis fighting colonization.

Late in the 18th Century, the Jamaican fighters were drawn into a regular army and named the West India Regiment. Their forces were beefed up with black and white American Loyalists of the Carolina Regiment. The West India Regiment persisted for 150 years before it was deactivated. The regiment's famous band has become the Jamaica Military Band and still parades at state functions in Zouave uniforms.

The Fighting Spirit

On the plantations, the blacks were swinging blows for freedom with gusto and frequency. But it was the wrong terrain for a fire fight against trained, mounted troops, modernly armed. The plantation blacks lost. They did not have the advantages of the Maroons, who lived in freedom so close to the mountains.

Inside the forests and caves, the Maroons had learned to use the mountains to blunt the edge of the British weaponry—by the "bush ambush;" by sharpshooting from sniper posts in the high rocks; by vanishing like a slate wiped clean, slipping into caves behind the several waterfalls. Yet the captives on the flatlands continued to rebel, straight into the last years before emancipation. The final flareup was the Sam Sharpe Christmas Rebellion of 1831-32. The slave system was abandoned in 1834 when a four-

A warm smile from Cornelia Roxanne Parchment, Miss Jamaica World 1982. Her heritage is German and African—"pure" Jamaican.

year "apprenticeship"—a blandly titled law that allowed for one last hurrah of unbridled cruelties in hurriedly constructed slave prisons—led to full emancipation in 1838.

Until then, Africa and England had been the two ancestral lands of nearly all Jamaicans, except for a sprinkling of Spanish and Portuguese Jews. But white landowners, correctly fearing that after emancipation the blacks would desert the plantations for the free hills, began importing hundreds of white laborers from Germany, Scotland and Ireland. Surprisingly, thousands of blacks immigrated from Africa about the same time.

The Germans of Westmoreland

The white migration never amounted to much, but it left a few pockets of rural "poor-whites" with English and German names. The most noted, Seaford Town in the parish of Westmoreland, still exists— although migration to Canada in recent years has depleted its population.

With skins and features as Caucasian as Germans living in Europe, it is surprising to find this group of people in the middle of Jamaica, living and talking like poor blacks around them. Nearly a century of inbreeding has sadly had a degenerate effect on the population of 200 or so residents, nearly all of whom have one of four family names: Somers, Eldermeyer, Wedermeyer or Kameka. Their ancestors emigrated to Jamaica at the beckoning of a Prussian doctor, William Lemonius, settling on land provided by Lord Seaford. Those Germans who began intermarrying with Jamaican blacks in the 1930s contributed to a dilution of the number of whites living in the area.

Other evidence of the German influence are contemporary Jamaican place names like Hanover, Blenheim, Berlin, Potsdam, Saxony and Bohemia. Along the south coast in the parish of St. Elizabeth, many residents' coffee-colored hues, Caucasian features, blue eyes and lilting Welsh accents betray the coming of Scottish and Irish immigrants. As all living things in this zestfully fecund land, however, they have been blended into the rich racial landscape.

Later, the last of the African immigrants came as indentured plantation workers. And real Indians from India continued a migration that began about 1838. Chinese arrived, starting in 1860. The "Syrians" came as

A portrait of Jamaican youth—the "totally new breed of human being" described by Jamaican film director Perry Henzell.

itinerant peddlers and shopkeepers. Most came from the country now called Lebanon, but all Arabs are known as "Syrians" in Jamaica.

So here they all were, on this only "true" Caribbean island, the single large island surrounded by the Caribbean Sea itself. Within a few generations, they had accomplished by love what governments in some "enlightened" lands had outlawed. For here, the land began filling up with velvety skins in an exciting range of colors from ash-black to "Jamaica" white. It was a blending of stock that has produced beauties who include three Miss Worlds, athletic stars who have captured many Olympic gold medals, Rhodes Scholars, poets, painters, novelists, and musicians so original that thousands of tourists jet in for their reggae festivals. But the mix also produced some trouble.

Mixed Marriages, Spanish Blacks

English gold-seeking immigrants first peopled the southern United States beginning with Virginia in 1607. Unlike the Pilgrims who arrived in the north 13 years later, the Southerners believed that to gather profits, both hands should be free. Alexis de Tocqueville, writing in 1832, distinguished "two branches in the great Anglo-American family which have hitherto grown up without entirely co-mingling, the one in the South, the other in the North. The men sent to Virginia were ... without resources and without character." They were welcoming slavery even before cotton came.

The Spaniards who came to the Caribbean islands, a century earlier than the Virginians, were no less prone to free hands. But they did not come from what Tocqueville called the "lower orders, of which the history of the world had as yet furnished no complete examples." The Spanish had resources and character. Scores of Spanish aristocrats had belted up and stridden abroad for God and Aragon. They were not beggars who found themselves mounted in this new land. They brought their own horses; fear of the animals had helped kill the Indians. Except for their cruelties in the name of God, the Spanish had the *laissez-faire* denied the "hurry-come-up" English.

The comic army of Oliver Cromwell, the English dictator who ruled after cutting off the Catholic head of Charles the First, was for the most part made up of "common Cheats, Theeves, Cutpurses and such like Lewd persons." For mates to his colonists, that great Puritan sent out Irish girls picked

in a rush off the streets. Much could not be expected from the consequences.

In the early years, many Spanish adventurers had brought or sent for wives from Spain. But wedlock between the Spanish and blacks was neither uncommon nor did it stir controversy as long as the lady was Christian. Since it was Spanish policy that slaves be instructed into the Church, every available *señorita* of whatever hue qualified.

Intermarriage, in fact, proved beneficial to Spain. Spanish blacks, slaves and freed, fought some of the longest, toughest battles against the English invaders. Blacks even played a very visible role in Spanish exploration of the hemisphere. The group of conquistadors who accompanied Balboa when he first laid eyes upon the Pacific Ocean in 1513 included a black named Olano.

There was generally an easy relationship between blacks and whites in Spanish Jamaica. It was not so easy in English Jamaica—and this uneasiness fanned the flames in Paradise.

Quadroons, Quintroons, Fustee and Mustee

Harsh laws studded the lives of blacks and half-breeds in English Jamaica. A rainbow of new "races" was catalogued according to infusion—Quadroon, Quintroon and Octoroon, better known as *fustee*, *mustee* and *dustee* in rumshop jollity. It was equally applicable to children of both races; but, curiously, the British only used the classifications to deride blacks.

As a result, the new technology of "passing for white" became common in the Americas. To block the spread of the *rungus*, cheating, among the often undetectable Octoroons, a new color entered the kaleidoscope: every free non-white in Jamaica had to wear a blue cross sewn on the shoulder, in addition to carrying a pass.

When Jamaican slaves were emancipated in 1838, 27 years before their counterparts in the United States, plantation owners received total compensation of 6.15 million pounds sterling. But that did little to help the average planter *bakkras*. They owed more than that in mortgages and loans held by English bankers. Within a year, they were rattling the tin cup.

No sooner had Queen Victoria signed the emancipation papers at Frogmore, Windsor,

than the ex-slaves lit out for the mountains. Their ancestors had done so in centuries past when they "bushed-up" for guerrilla war against the English; this time, the war was of passive resistance and fully legal.

The mid-19th Century blacks went into the mountains for psychological and economic reasons. Year after year, prior to emancipation, they had been involved in many bloody revolts as they fought valiantly against superior weapons and trained soldiers. Most of their leaders had been caught and executed—among them, Tacky, Mansong, and "Daddy" Sharpe, whose Christmas Rebellion had started out as a strike call, the Caribbean territory's first labor union-style action.

Now, with the end of slavery, the blacks had unpleasant memories of existence on the slave savannas where they were ridiculed as "bell people" by the free people in the mountains. The plantation bell had dictated when to rise, eat, retire or appear for punishment. They intended to put distance between themselves and the bell-ringers.

Economically, the slaves' former owners had refused to sell them lands, hoping to tie them to the plantations as low-wage workers. Instead, many blacks fled into private enterprise, up the mountain to grow yams, potatoes, bananas and coffee, and to rear "small stock" like pigs and goats. Others fled to "free villages" founded by themselves and their friends, valiant abolitionist white Baptist preachers who suffered physical assaults for preaching about a God who was the father of all, black and white.

Most mixed-bloods stayed on the savannas, where they were crushingly called "Red Ibos"—in a knock at what blacks considered a sellout of the motherstock. "Red" man is the pejorative for a "white" man in Jamaica. But the mixed-bloods could hardly be blamed for electing to dig in where their chances for advancement were better. In fact, many Ibos were being looked after by their owners—who were also their fathers. Many a fair-skinned "outside *pikni*" was sent to England for education. To their credit, upon acquiring a profession or an inheritance, several dutifully saw to their mothers' declining years, even if afterwards they sought to cut all links with their heritage. They often accomplished this by "lifting" their color—marrying someone of a lighter shade. A Quadroon would look for a Quintroon and so forth. Only God and Einstein may fathom the permutations.

It seems unfair to saddle the mulattoes with the rough ride their darker-skinned brothers undoubtedly had. But their woes were many. For example, George William Gordon, the mulatto leader of peasants— who rescued his impoverished white father by saving his tiny estate from the hammer— was framed and hanged by the English governor in the 1865 Morant Bay rebellion. At independence, his countrymen made him a National Hero. While the English perfidy of giving favors to the 'Roons kept the non-whites apart, Gordon was the first in a line of mixed-bloods to whom Jamaicans know they owe a debt for more than 100 years of political leadership: all the way from Assemblyman Gordon to this generation's National Heroes, Alexander Bustamante and Norman Manley.

Color-coded Society

But something took the "par" out of "paradise." A bias in tint did it—and not only back then. Up into the 1950s, black pressure groups were demonstrating for employment of black girls in downtown offices and black kids in whites-only schools. A look down the backstretch shows where the trouble began.

The depressed economy of the sugar estates after emancipation meant that drastic cutbacks in expenses were necessary. For one, the costly importation of English overseers was out; the planters had to look elsewhere for top help. But where?

Then they noticed the "outside *piknis*," right in their own stables. They had the right color, or at least a close approximation, and this was the first requirement for authority in the color-coded society. Secondly, their loyalty would be assured. Indeed, to stay upwardly mobile, they could be counted upon to make tougher demands on blacks to work longer days for their newfangled pay. In short, these cabin children were a godsend to dad.

This was all well and good for keeping the rum punch cold (ice was brought south on sailing vessels from the U.S. or Canada), but it sure as hell heated up the cousins of darker hue.

The English-descendant planters and their city cousins, the white and Jewish merchants, did nothing to ease the growing tensions. These merchants had made fortunes selling flour and salted cod, the enduringly popular "sal'fish" which had been issued to the slave quarters since the Days of Obedience until the blacks grew sensibly fond of it. To divide and rule was a tried and proven rule in empire building, a certain path to wealth and power. The policy had failed in America because the Westminster

chaps forgot they were dealing with their own kind; but in Jamaica, the color-related decisions on job and social privileges stuck.

Accounts were better cast by men of light cast. In the stores, blacks were best at lifting bales; but it took a mulatto to cut the cloth. The "brown boy" network also worked in schools and churches: an unwritten clause obeyed by teachers and pastors ensured that the front pews and available school places were reserved for whites and "high-browns." Fifty years after 1838, only 10 percent of blacks were literate. Not that it did them much good. Up into the 1950s, a black girl in a bank teller's cage drew crowds of gapers to the door.

The police force was officered by ex-constables of the Irish Constabulary, poorly

trained by English standards. A few were only functionally literate.

The state church was Anglican. Even if he had doctorates oozing like canticles at matins, a black priest never rose above archdeacon, an honorary post usually conferred just before quitting time. The Catholics ran a similar course. Rapture engulfed the Jamaican blacks one day in 1950 when "the most educated man in Jamaica," a priest named Gladstone Wilson, was elevated to monsignor. This title of honor fell

Lucien Chen and daughter, Camille, members of Jamaica's business-minded Chinese community (above). "Ebony and ivory" skins of the Jamaica Defence Forces (right).

88

far short of a bishopric, but it *was* going up.

In their days of hardship, the Jews had been drawn to the blacks by mutual disadvantages. As usual, they were the objects of ancient accusations that in other races would be considered clever business. As the 18th Century English historian Edward Long wrote: "The rascally tricks, for which both ancient and modern Jews have always been distinguished, served to embitter the popular hatred against them." Now they were playing it quietly. Pogroms were still in the race memory.

The color curtain was everywhere. Hotels, owned by white and foreign interests and catering mostly to Americans, were believed to be very hung up on the matter; they subtly indicated that the color bar was up, contrary

white outrage was exceeded by mulatto indignation.

Little wonder that at independence, when the national motto—"Out of Many, One People"—was chosen, one young black scholar caustically proposed that if a new dispensation was truly ahead, it should read: "Out of Many, One BLACK People."

In the way of the conquered everywhere, some blacks behaved scrupulously uncensorious of the system, in the quietly desperate hope that they would be called up for their "passin' papers." This class of individuals was tagged "roast breadfruits" by their countrymen. The breadfruit, a beloved entree of Jamaican country cuisine, has a black skin when roasted but the "heart" remains white. It was introduced to the island by

to front desk declarations. The slogans fooled no locals, but visitors were straight-facedly assured they were disembarking in a happy land where "blacks and whites are in harmony like black and white piano keys." Embarrassing discord, such as the throngs of black saints rushing out of paradise to pot-wash or porter in other lands, in order to feed their families back home, was put down to the "love of travel in our people." Oddly, only the blacks among "our people" were bitten by this travel bug.

One day, the black editor of a news magazine, tired at the pretense, dove into the swimming pool of Kingston's exclusive Myrtle Bank Hotel. The splash was heard throughout Jamaica's three counties, and

Captain Bligh of *Bounty* fame as a cheap staple for the slaves.

The black and white Jamaicans led each other to the anvil. They beat each other into workable art if not the aesthetic stuff. Considering the religious, racial, economic and ideological divisions which make frontiers and holocausts of longer-settled communities, it appears that the way to go is indeed for the workable.

Jamaica had been founded on the European Plan and had never provided for its barefoot staff beyond bed-and-breakfast. The city-born, street-wise fellow worked at the hotel pool and plucked lead guitar in the mento band. In spite of two jobs, he still couldn't make ends meet. He was now queueing at the American Embassy, hoping for a green-card permit to try the American plan. In the way of the young and sardonic, he was making a wry joke of his tamarind season—the hard dry times when only the tart, mouth-puckering tamarind will fruit.

A green card or landed-immigrant visa to the States is money in the bank to many Jamaicans. Nevertheless, the rate of recidivism back to "The Rock" is high. When the U.S. government makes cushy Social Security pension payments through the local Embassy, "The Rock" is not so tough.

In a sense, high living is the reason which impels so many Jamaicans to leave "the Blessed Isle." Over centuries, the island colony had borne its role for the good of the British Empire, i.e., for the good of England. Under the Union Jack, the Caribbean was neatly divided into sugar-cane fields, timber lands, cotton fields, spice islands, and so forth. Each separate territory was dependent upon and acquired a taste for imported foods. Rice, flour, salted cod and tinned fish are still the main constituents in Jamaican shopping bags. When the overloaded economy sank under the weight of oil prices in the mid-1970s, and with the consequent increase in import prices, there was a great outcry at the cutting off of imported corn flakes. On an island ripe with oranges, pineapples, bananas, mangoes, avocados and the like, many a person will pay high prices for low-grade American apples.

Today, there are heartening signs of decline in this consumption pattern as part of a joyous rediscovery of the land and its peoples. This includes the fantastic success of "roots" music, ska and reggae; the entrance of traditional songs and ceremonies into the repertoire of the National Dance Theatre Company and the Jamaica Folk Singers; the powerful work of visual and literary artists, "self-taught" or schooled through the government's Cultural Training Centre; an exciting turn into fashion design; and an increasing number of excruciatingly attractive children who have made "baby-watching" a widespread contemplative activity.

Tales of Anansi

The English rovers who contested these seas were not of the caliber of conquistadors. Plain men at best, rogues at worst, they left law books and forts but no art or architecture, save two or three small, exquisite churches and a few Georgian houses. The island is now on the job, writing its own score out of many rhythms.

One of the most powerful of these rhythms is the *Anansi* myth, firmly rooted in Jamaican folklore. Anansi the Spiderman was brought from the west coast of Africa by the first slaves, and went into business as the only therapy for three centuries of hideousness. He took on the trappings of the tribal oral historian, with an interpretive addition.

Bra 'Nansi filled the role of story-teller, hero or villain. He was great at disguises, omniscient but nonetheless willing to be chopped to prove a moral. He was something to everyone: his indestructability, knowledge and wit were an investment in hope. The stories were usually satirical and cynical. They never had a live-happily-ever-after ending. Anansi's devotees were always on the lookout for the unexpected; everywhere were challenges that must be faced lest they come in at the back of the neck.

Nearly all Jamaicans tell bedtime 'Nansi stories to their kids, making them up as they go along. But the big story-tellers, invariably village matriarchs, are much sought after and are always warmly welcomed to the guest seat on the coffee-drying limestone terrace behind the footlights of fireflies.

Anansi's presence in politics is sequential, a bridge across the gulf that pre-election rhetoric creates. Anansi is an art that woos the loser even as it acclaims the victor.

The anti-fraud ink-dip had hardly dried on the fingers of Jamaica's honest burghers after the 1980 elections when there appeared on the streets a sight not seen since the Socialists had declared, for climate and economy, that the short-sleeved safari outfit could be worn at official functions. To the new "Conservatives," these casual clothes looked very much like Cuban apparel, not at all appropriate for a country making overtures to the United States. Immediately, phalanxes of twitching men, losers and winners alike, began appearing in the streets sweating and steaming in three-piece suits. It was Madison-Avenue-under-the-bananas. Without violence, the political statement had been made: *adios Cuba; hello, America.*

On the map, the island of Jamaica looks like a scared puppy swimming in deep water, ears laid back and feet tucked under, thrashing to escape the Cuban flail and the Florida club. "Stone a' river bottom never know sun-hot," is a Jamaican proverb sometimes cited in resentment of the insensitivity of the big political powers. Maybe Anansi the Spiderman is on the ropes somewhere up front.

Keeping the spirit of Anansi, the Spider Man, alive in stories told while fence-sitting, a popular pastime in the Jamaican countryside.

THE WORLD'S MOST BEAUTIFUL WOMEN

Down in Jamaica, they got
Lots of pretty women ...
—Stephen Bishop in *On and On*

Centuries of blending have produced a Jamaican racial stew with a spicy by-product: beautiful women. And Jamaicans celebrate that beauty with a zest unparalled in most countries. They enthusiastically choose a Miss Jamaica Universe each May and a Miss Jamaica World each September. And there are dozens of other beauty titles up for grabs around the island each year. Even Jamaican emigrants overseas carry on the tradition by choosing such representatives as Miss Jamaica United States and Miss Jamaica Canada.

The most sought-after crown is that of Miss Jamaica World. The winners of the national competition have achieved a remarkable record in the international finals for a country the size of Jamaica. Since 1963, three Miss Jamaicas have gone on to international acclaim as winners of the Miss World crown. Two others placed among the top two runners-up to Miss World.

An Annual 'Festival' of Jamaican Beauty

Jamaica's reputation as an island blessed with beautiful women began in 1963 when Carol Joan Crawford bested representatives of dozens of other countries to become Miss World. A Jamaican of Chinese descent, Patsy Yuen, brought home the Miss World crown in 1973. And just three years later, Cindy Breakspeare became Miss World 1976.

Jamaica's astonishing success in the competition has apparently prompted other countries to try to produce more deserving contestants. The island's best showings in recent years have been second runners-up in the Miss World finals—Debbie Campbell in 1979 and Sandra Cunningham in 1981. Some Jamaicans, accustomed to seeing their beauties outshine women from the rest of the world, have begun to call for a shakeup of selection procedures whenever Miss Jamaica World fails to place in the finals.

The local Miss Jamaica World pageant became such a major event that at one time the government included it as part of its annual celebration of island culture, "Festival!" But critics eventually made a strong

case against promoters of the contest for almost always winding up with a slate of queens and finalists whose skins and facial features were substantially more Caucasian than those of 95 percent of the island's population. The Michael Manley government washed its hands of the whole affair in the 1970s by removing the beauty pageant from the list of official "Festival!" activities. Since then, it has been sponsored by private concerns, mainly Kingston's Spartan Health Spa. Yet the popularity of the Miss Jamaica World pageant continues to grow.

The annual road to the Miss Jamaica World crown begins in August when judges have the unenviable task of choosing only 20 competitors from dozens of entries. Commercial sponsors like the Road Runner fast food chain and Pete's Patties then pamper the wearers of their promotional banners through a series of pageants all over the island.

The girls' faces and figures appear in Kingston's newspapers almost daily in September—in advertisements, feature stories and profiles. They are the subject of television and radio interviews. Jamaican conversation turns to the merits of one entrant's vital statistics compared to another's "personality." No doubt, many bets are placed on the outcome.

Finally, the top 20 contestants are secluded for several days in anticipation of the final showdown at the National Arena in the capital city. Long lines of spectators who have each paid 20 to 30 Jamaican dollars snake into the parking lot past legions of policemen and patrol dogs on crowning night.

The crowd heartily cheers each girl. Deafening appaluse and shouts are reserved for the top contenders. National television, most of the press, and a healthy helping of government officials look on.

As the field is narrowed to seven, then to the top five, the noise becomes ear-splitting. Judges and policemen alike hope the crowd approves of the choices. It usually does.

Tears fall. Winners and losers alike kiss and hug. A new Miss Jamaica World is crowned.

Sandra Cunningham (right)—Miss Jamaica World 1981. Contestants in the 1982 Miss Jamaica World competition line up in Ocho Rios, following pages.

THE VIBRANT SPIRITUAL SPECTRUM

It is Sunday in Jamaica. The opaque sunlight of morning falls upon little girls in bright dresses and white hats as they skip down the mountain roads and village streets of the island. Some hold the hands of their brothers, who look cranky and uncomfortable in tiny suits and ties. Old men in dark, double-breasted suits with baggy pants clutch Bibles. Big coal-skinned women dressed in white and purple stumble through stony lanes and fields in their best shoes. Throughout the country, stone churches begin to fill with these people, their fingers tapping out staccato rhythms on tambourines and their voices echoing across the hills.

Here, as in most of the Caribbean, Christianity prevails and thrives. More than 80 percent of the population professes to belong to one form of Christianity or another, the legacy of centuries of European rule and influence. Yet recent years have seen increasing numbers of Jamaicans looking to their ancestral African home for spiritual inspiration. And even within the framework of Christianity, the seductive spirits of Africa have reached out across the centuries and the seas.

Zemes and Saints

A curious footnote to the Caribbean's repute as a cradle of Christianity in the West is found in the name Jamaica. Historians generally claim that the name comes from the Arawak word *Xaymaca*, purported to mean "land of wood and water." But there was a district, in Josephus' time, in Palestine called Jamaica. And since Josephus wrote in the 1st Century A.D., it seems reasonable to assume he had not met the Arawaks. The theory that the name was chosen for its Holy Land connections is plausible, given the piety of the Spaniards who scattered saints' names all around their American conquests—including the ultimate Christian appellation, San Salvador.

A scant six years after Columbus left the Caribbean for the final time, the first three abbacies had been created, one of them on Jamaica's north coast near today's resort

Preceding pages: Christians line up for a baptism at Gunboat Beach. A girl in Sunday dress in Porus (left) and a female minister at Kingston Parish Church lectern (above).

town of Ocho Rios. From there, the Spaniards went about wiping out every other religion and massacring its adherents in the name of God. The Arawaks, like any other careful farming folk, had guardedly scattered their piety among various *zemes* (spirits) headed by the god Jocuahuma and his wife. But in a fury to plant the "true cross" in every nook and cranny of the New World, the incoming Christians put the shaft to the Indians, often en masse, after Absolution had shrived their heathen souls. Those who managed to survive were enslaved and

worked to death.

A Dominican priest named Bartolomé de Las Casas, appalled by the unholy scene, led the call for reform. Las Casas was not of the Old Country Inquisitors. His father had been with Columbus on the earlier voyages; he himself went to the Indies as a young fellow with Nicholas de Ovando, Governor of Hispaniola, in 1502. He was the first priest ordained in the West Indies in 1523. His personal liking for the Arawaks, whom he saw dying off before his eyes, moved him to suggest that to save those left, the stronger, tougher Africans should be brought in. He knew the black men well. They had lived in Spain for centuries, both as slaves and freedmen.

It was of course a jesuitic solution. After surviving in the tropics for an age, fighting off or staying ahead of the Caribs in their oceangoing canoes, the Arawaks were suddenly in Fray Bartolo's eyes incapable of standing the heat and should be moved from the hearth. In truth, Las Casas was commendably soft on Arawaks. But that left him hard on blacks.

Las Casas' dad had taken an Arawak back to Spain. The young Bartolo had taken a shine to him and acquired a sympatico for the people. As a rule, they were gentle— but not too much so when sufficiently riled, as some Spanish settlements could tell.

The blacks who came to the west from Africa brought their Islamic and animistic religions with them. Animism is an intellec-

of *obeah*, the island's peculiar brand of witchcraft and sorcery. Its influence peaked in the mid 1800s, but it is still practiced today.

The *kumina* ceremony also is practiced in modern Jamaica on rare occasions. *Kimbanda* and *kyas* drums beat out hypnotic rhythms. A queen or priestess sprinkles the drums with white rum, then fills her mouth with the liquid, spitting sheets of alcohol over the participants. The smell of white rum, cigarettes and sometimes ganja hangs over the scene. The queen calls and sings in quavering shrills mixed with ancient African words. Then a goat is hugged and petted before an executioner severs its head in sacrifice. Blood gushes out of the goat's trembling body. It is mixed with rum and fed

tually powerful doctrine burdened with a title which at first glance suggests animal worship, but which actually comes from the Latin word *anima* for "soul." It is a doctrine that encompasses the spirituality of the world's great religions, holding that life comes from a spiritual source, a soul, as distinct from matter. Like Christianity, it states that life is everywhere.

White Rum And Goat's Blood

In early Jamaica, one manifestation was *kumina*. The music and dance of the African *myal* cult were important components of its ceremonies. Practitioners used potions and entered trances to counteract the influences

to the participants.

For obvious reasons, early *kumina* rituals frightened the European conquerors of the island. British historian Edward Long wrote in 1774: "Some of these execrable wretches in Jamaica introduced what they called the 'myal dance' and established a kind of society into which they initiated all they could. The lure hung out was that every negro initiated into the myal society would be invulnerable to the white man; and, although they might in appearance be slain,

An interdenominational mass in honor of Prime Minister Seaga at Kingston Parish Church (above). An ambitiously decorated church in the country (right).

100

the obeahman could at his pleasure, restore the body to life."

Forced into accommodation with Spanish Catholicism, these early forms of African-flavored worship found no real hardship. The incense, chantings, robes and candles were not unlike the formalities of their own priests, the so-called "witch doctors." Like them, the Christians also conjured up spirits, called saints, and threatened death as a penalty for disobedience. The plaster statues in the alcoves compared favorably with their own stone and clay "dolls." It all made for a swinging, rollicking wedlock between both beliefs, and no serious damage to either.

The marvelously evocative result of this later came to be called Pocomania. In this hybrid faith, the Christian altar has become

prayers and a "tromp" or shuffling march around the table. the faithful may enter a state of grace, or trance, that lasts for several hours. Like today's "new" charismatics, healing and speaking in "unknown tongues" is in the liturgy.

Guided tours of Pocomania yards are now on the tourist circuit; it is not unknown for an American sanctuary-going *dawta*, wooed by the warm night, the flicker of stars, the rustle of coconut and banana trees, and the infectious drumming and singing, to shed her fear and join in the *poco* fun: "jumping' *and trompin' till day-O! day-O! day a-light and a time to go home!"*

The Spanish Catholics gave way to the English Protestants in 1655 and the Protestants gave way to the English Catholics at

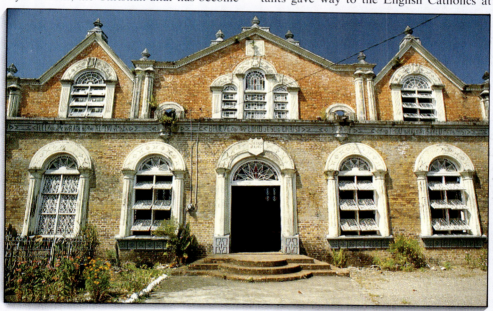

a *poco* table of a length determined by the size of the congregation. Covered with a cloth of white, the African color for solemnity and mourning, the table is fat in bowls of cooked white rice, white dove-shaped breads, and plucked white-feathered chickens. White-turbanned priests sing white Christian hymns, the tunes all but unidentifiable in their *poco* state. Bent, sprung and coiled into wondrously rhythmical shapes, they lift the old standards into a compelling tempo. What emerges is a Rock of Ages that really rocks, *te deums* without tedium.

In the ritual of ascent into total purity, Pocomania worshippers exalt God by placating the whole self, body and soul. Purified by powerful surging, singing and chanting

the time of the Restoration that brought Charles II to the English throne. Nevertheless a freedom of worship has long been established in English-speaking Jamaica. The only exceptions are short periods of persecution of Baptists and Jews, the former for being soft on slaves, the latter when they became so rich the gentiles remembered that they had killed Christ.

Only 50 to 65 Jewish families still live in Jamaica, joined in a United Congregation of Ashkenazi and Sephardic communities. The existing Kingston synagogue incorporates portions of both their rituals into its services. It also has the distinction of being one of five synagogues in the hemisphere with sand as its floor.

In the dominant Christian sphere, analysis reveals almost equal percentages of Anglicans, Baptists and members of the Church of God. Other groups include Seventh Day Adventists, Methodists, the United Church of Christ and Pentecostals. There's also a healthy smattering of Roman Catholics, mainly among the Chinese, Lebanese and East Indian communities whose ancestors came around the turn of the 20th Century.

Recent years have marked the rise of the fundamentalists, handclapping gospel-shouting sects led by voluble aggressive preachers, in whose calamitous sermons the nervous hear God's shoulder-knot creaking. American-oriented and often American-supported, they made dramatic strides during the '70s socialist administrations of Michael Manley. A generally conservative Christian group, fundamentalists share the U.S. paranoia on communism.

There are also members of the Revival Zion sect, cousins of those who shuffle through Pocomania, yet clingers to beliefs in Christian dogma. Led by head Shepherd Mallica Reynolds, better known as Kapo, they regard themselves as the national church of Jamaica. But their small numbers belie that claim.

Nowadays, except for a handful of devotees, "jumping *poco*" is a dwindling religious art form. On the other hand, the drive toward "identity" of a taproot, unentwined with and independent of white Christianity, has turned the search elsewhere. And out of this search for a Deity, whose best strokes would be in the interests of His different folks, has come the most potent socio-religious political happening since Columbus waded ashore close to where the Jamaica Hilton now sits.

Thoughts on a 'Bakkra-God'

On Sunday mornings it used to seem that God moved in a mysterious way among the white people in the front pews—secretly handing out wealth and power. The blacks at the back of the church, or in the skinny worship-sheds back in the woods, clapped and shouted and sang like crazy but to no avail. Why did He not, in the words of the reggae, *Pass the Dutchie on the left-hand-side?* Did He not know that the hungry children on this side hankered also after the Dutchie cook-pot? Maybe they were not of His family. It stood to reason. The Jesus in

Singing and dancing ignites trances during rites around a Pocomania table deep in the Clarendon parish countryside (left).

the religious pictures and plasters on the wall was Caucasian. No doubt about that. Who ever saw a blue-eyed black?

It took a while for a solution to the problem to jell. The belief that all things, including man, were an extension of and fused with the God-spirit—the principle of the African religion—had been lost under the intentional cultural destruction wrought by the slave system. The ethnic and family dislocation effectively destroyed the historic connections.

Until the advent of Moravian, Wesleyan and Baptist aggression, the religion of the "raw-eyes" was commonly discouraged from reaching the blacks' quarters. Now, then. If the whites were His children on earth, it followed that God was also a "raw-eye" *bakkra*, a blue-eyed boss man. It also followed, as the proverb put it, that "Parson christen him own *pikni* 'fore anybody else's *pikni*." Swelp me God, it was enough to vex a *bredda*!

Thoughts on a *bakkra*-God needfully gave way. Getting the *ackee*-and-*sal'*-fish into the pot was more important in a "patch-trousies" economy. In Jamaica, job anxiety has always inhibited dissent. The folk sat in the back pews and hoped. But the murmurs were mounting, especially among the young people. Hardly anybody noticed when it really towered.

Marcus Garvey And
The Roots of Ras Tafari

What towered was bizarre, as sudden as it was shocking. A handful of "crazy men" appeared in the 1930s, making absurd claims about the Emperor of Abyssinia being the Messiah: Ras Tafari, afterwards crowned as *Haile Selassie*, which translated means, "the Power of the Trinity."

Few suspected then the profound effect the movement would have on Jamaican society. Rastafarians were long-haired and bearded long before the advent of hippy fashions. If their interpretations of the Bible were outrageous, they quoted with conviction, and were ready to suffer for their beliefs—strangely sure and proud in the midst of ridicule.

The movement arrived closely on the heels of another whose impact was just winding down on the world's blacks. Founded and led by a Jamaican, Marcus Mosiah Garvey, the Universal Negro Improvement Association sought to gather ancestral Africans from a diaspora unmatched save by the scattering of the Jews.

Garvey was born at St. Ann's Bay on

Aug. 17, 1887. He was working as a printer when he founded his little organization with the grandiose name. The label turned out to be prophetic. Garvey's group did become universal. He soon found the island too small for his ideas and after visits to some Central American countries, he moved to the United States. The UNIA soon became a monolith.

Garvey called for self-reliance among "Africans at home and abroad." He advocated a "back-to-Africa" cause. He awakened a black consciousness and pride that aroused the hostility of whites as it stirred the ideas of such young black Africans as Nwamdi "Zik" Azikiwe of Nigeria, Kwame Nkrumah of Ghana, and Jomo Kenyatta of Kenya, each of whom would one day lead his country to independence.

In the United States, Garvey's work led inevitably to the defiant Montgomery bus ride that signaled the start of the civil rights movement and to the canonization of Martin Luther King Jr. Garvey attempted to establish a steamship company, the Black Star Line, an understandable corollary to a return of exiles but also a strong plank in his self-reliance platform. His steamships foundered on what is believed to have been an old-fashioned legal frame prepared for awkward blacks in ugliest America: he was ridden to the Atlanta slammer on the Mail Fraud railroad.

Garvey's honesty and integrity has never been in doubt, even among his detractors. He died in obscurity in London in 1940, but did not remain obscure for long. His body was brought home in pomp and ceremony to his native island for burial in a mausoleum befitting a man who, posthumously, has been made a national hero.

Locks, Beards and Bibles

As widely powerful overseas as Garvey's UNIA was, its local influence has been no match for Rastafarianism. A doctrine that pre-dated Black Power by two decades, it had settled into its cadence well before the tramp of Black Muslims was heard in Detroit.

Its strength is in the spiritual power it exerts, not only through its teachings, but by asserting a root-continuity of the African race through history. Its adherents are regarded as children of the *Negus*, a title of the Ethiopian kings in their descent from King Solomon and the Queen of Sheba. It is a mind-sweep warranted to steady and give hope to any godchild suffering in the Babylonian snafu into which he was kidnapped

from the Old Country. At the last, there is the ineluctable conviction of the Return from Exile—to Ethiopia.

Rastafarianism's contemplative and meditative nature, assisted by sacramental ganja smoking, drumming, Bible reading and chanting, has imbued the best of its followers with an ability to accommodate a religious, abstract-political, non-racist racialism. They also have acquired a capacity to culture ideas through music, costume, physical exercises, art, poetry and indigenous "cottage" industries like broommaking.

Reggae music developed in the "rastayards" and produced superstars like the late Bob Marley. Politicians are so conscious of Rasta influence among Jamaica's youthful

majority that as Marley lay dying of cancer in a Miami hospital, he was awarded the Jamaican Order of Merit, equivalent to a peerage in the old British Empire.

The true Rastafarian trains to desire nothing above the essentials in food and material, to stand fit and feisty, afraid of no loss save his beard and Bible. The beard is a sign of his pact with Jah and the Bible his source of knowledge, especially the prophecies of the Old Testament which he believes speak of Haile Selassie and Ethiopia. At the core

The Jamaican who inspired African pride, Marcus Garvey (above), also inspired the "Back-to-Africa" Rastafarian religion whose members zealously study the Bible (right).

104

of his faith is an absolute belief in the divinity of Ras Tafari—which renders a belief in his own divinity as a child of Jah, Jehovah, God. Selassie's physical death did not kill belief in Ras Tafari. The crucifixion at Calvary did not kill Christianity.

I-and-I And Ras Tafar-I

All this made for few apostates among the earliest adherents. Instead, they developed a heroic spiritual strength that withstood ridicule, physical assault, discrimination, and imprisonment for ignoring the "Babylonian Law" against the smoking of the sacramental herb, ganja (marijuana). *Did not the Christians take alcohol, wine, as one of their sacraments? Who made you judge over*

and interpretation for the Rastas—as they have for the many adversary readings that have set denominations at each other's throats since the Tower of Babel.

Selassie's visit to Jamaica in 1966 drew larger airport crowds than Queen Elizabeth's and incomparably more emotion. An estimated 100,000 followers braved a downpour. Skeptics of the faith delight in recalling that the Ethiopian emperor, appalled at the dreadlocked legions that swarmed around his plane, refused to exit until Jamaican authorities convinced him he would not be harmed. Rastas, in contrast, say Selassie wept at the overwhelming reception he had received.

Selassie's title, Lion of Judah, has inspired Rastafarians to adopt the lion's image as

Israel? That was the frequent defiant retort of some legally unrepresented bearded "*bredda*-man" before a colonial magistrate who had the powers to flog and incarcerate him—and often did.

The appearance of Rastafarianism has been largely attributed to three mystics. Separately and unknown to each other, aided by Holy Writ and working *inwards to the I*, the inner divinity, the id—or, as expressed in Rasta liturgy, the *I-and-I*—these mystics arrived at a realization that the King of Ethiopia was the Messiah. His imperial titles included King of Kings, Lion of Judah, Elect of God. The scriptures refer to Ethiopia and its peoples more than 40 times. They provided a rich lode of information

their own. Indeed, the animal's mane has inspired some of the most elaborately teased of the dreadlock hairstyles; and devotees copy the proud, dignified walk of the lion as they strut down Jamaican streets. The locks also hark back to Africa, the hairstyles of Masai and Galla tribesmen, and even the biblical story of the power of Samson's hair.

The doctrine has spread worldwide, wherever blacks live, and has attracted a growing minority of young whites. But the movement has also become a cover for criminals who adopt the hairstyle of their reggae idols. Their wrongdoings hand the true brethren the slick end of the stick. Rascality is not a Rasta trait. The brethren are too deeply spiritual to doubt that Jah the

Father, the inner I, will provide for all needs. That includes the sweetest smoking *sinsemilla* this side of Eden.

The Trappings of Rasta

Three major sects of Rastafarians have evolved into their own Jamaican subcultures. The older, more traditional communities of Rasta prophet Prince Emmanuel live in the hills of Bull Bay, east of Kingston. They occasionally can be seen in town, their hair rolled into turbans, cloaked in long black robes, selling brooms and booklets. The Twelve Tribes has attracted more of the young political Rastas. Bob Marley, who took the tribal name Joseph, belonged to the group. Their headquarters are near the offices of Marley's Tuff Gong recording studio in Kingston. The Ethiopian Zion Coptic Church, an entrepreneurial spin-off, has run into problems because of its dealings in the ganja trade. One of its white American leaders, Brother Louv, is serving time in a Miami prison.

Indeed, the practice of smoking the sacred ganja sacrament continues to be one of the most controversial aspects of the movement. Not all members use the herb, however. Those who do usually smoke it in a pipe, called a "chalice," made of cow or goat horn or bamboo. The ritual of preparing the chalice with water, mixing the tobacco with "herbs," and lighting it is a sacred one, accompanied by the recitation of prayers, psalms and benedictions.

The Rastafarian religion has established a working code against greed and dishonesty, sexual envy, exploitation and aberration. Yet it has accommodated the arts and a competitive edge in job efficiency, sports and games—while maintaining a strong pride in black history.

The dedication of Rasta men and women has fired the imagination of the young Jamaican. The shoulder-length ringlets, the usual mark of a "dreadlock," now bobs about everywhere—at international tennis tournaments, in the national soccer squad, or decently held under a Rasta-knit turban at important desks in commercial and government offices. The red, green and gold colors of the Ethiopian flag now adorn Jamaican clothes. The "Dread," the true Rasta, is a peaceful, careful, preferably self-employed achiever who stays within the law—save for his sacramental smoke.

In 1981, the Ethiopian Orthodox Church conducted funeral rites for reggae superstar Bob Marley, a follower of Rastafarianism.

PLACES

Get it together in Jamaica.
Soulful town, soulful people,
I see you're having fun.
Dancing to the reggae rhythm,
Oh, island in the sun! Come on and
Smile, you're in Jamaica!
      —Bob Marley from *Smile Jamaica*

Like the rhythm of a reggae song, the island of Jamaica provides a steady stream of surprises, fairly constant in mood and cadence, yet seductive and hypnotic in the way they brand themselves on your brain. Even the standard tour bus stops—Dunn's River Falls, Bamboo Avenue, Rose Hall Great House, the Blue Hole, the Rio Grande River rafting trip—provide experiences unique in the Caribbean and probably in the world. Greater rewards await the traveler who dares to turn down an unpaved country road and lose himself in the Cockpit Country, who puts on his or her hiking shoes and scales the Blue Mountains, or who saunters into a Darliston restaurant to order curry goat and breadfruit.

The travel section that follows is designed to give you a taste of both worlds: out-of-the way coves and crannies as well as the well-trodden trails. For the usual routes, you need only check with travel agencies or hotel tour desks for a list of guided tours covering such highlights. For the less-traveled byways, you will need to rent, beg or borrow a car, or join the Jamaican people on their trains, buses and mini-vans.

This section has been subdivided into three main chapters, each covering one of the counties into which the British subdivided the island. "The County of Surrey" offers a detailed look at Jamaica's business and governmental nerve center, the Kingston-lower St. Andrew corporate area. Surrey also includes a tour of the Blue Mountains and a glance at historic Port Antonio, as well as other scenic attractions that flank Jamaica's capital.

"The County of Middlesex" starts with a visit to the tourist center of Ocho Rios, a good base from which to explore Jamaica's heartland. You will travel the north coast, then head south through the hills to South Middlesex, where the two main areas of interest are historic Spanish Town and the cool, busy bauxite capital of Mandeville.

Finally, "The County of Cornwall" focuses on Jamaica's tourist capital—Montego Bay (or "MoBay")—and its coastal resort neighbors. There's also a brief dip into the mysterious Cockpit Country southeast of MoBay. The Cornwall chapter winds up the travel section with a trip to Jamaica's newest and funkiest tourist development, Negril, from which you can roam to such South Cornwall intrigues as Black River, Seaford Town and Lover's Leap.

Of course, these travel chapters cannot describe every phenomenon awaiting the adventurous traveler. As in any country, it's the human landscape that really counts. Most Jamaicans will enjoy meeting you as much as you will enjoy meeting them.

Jamaica

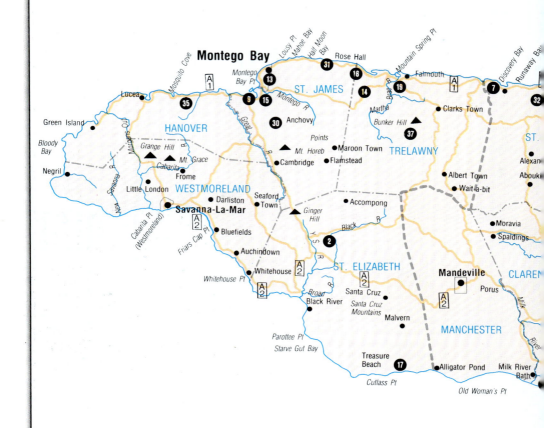

Montego Bay

Lousy Pt
Manoe Bay
Hall Moon Bay
Rose Hall
Mountain Spring Pt
Discovery Bay
Runaway Bay

31
16
Falmouth
A 1
7
32

Montego Bay Pt
13
ST. JAMES
14
19

Mosquito Cove
Lucea
A 1
35
9 **15**
Montego R.
Brae R.
Martha
Clarks Town

Green Island
30 Anchovy
Bunker Hill
37
ST.

Bloody Bay
HANOVER
Grange Hill
Points
Maroon Town
TRELAWNY
Alexan

Negril
Mt. Grace
Mt. Horeb
Flamstead
Albert Town
Abouk

Cabarita
Frome
Cambridge
Wait-a-bit

Little London
WESTMORELAND
Seaford Town
Accompong
Moravia

Savanna-La-Mar
Darliston
Ginger Hill
Spaldings

A 2
Bluefields
Black R.
2

Cabarita Pt (Westmoreland)
Friars Cap Pt
Auchindown
ST. ELIZABETH
Mandeville
CLAREN

Whitehouse
A 2
Santa Cruz
Porus

Whitehouse Pt
A 2
Broad R.
Santa Cruz Mountains
Malvern
A 2
MANCHESTER

Black River

Parottee Pt
Starve Gut Bay
Treasure Beach
17
Alligator Pond
Milk River Bath

Cutlass Pt
Old Woman's Pt

Caribbean Sea

Places of Interest

1	Bath Mineral Spa	11	Fern Gully	21	Morant Pt. Lighthouse	31	Rose Hall
2	Bamboo Avenue	12	Flat Bridge	22	Nonsuch Caves	32	Runaway Caves
3	Blue Hole (or Blue Lagoon)	13	Fort Montego	23	Paul Bogle Statue	33	Seville Nueva
4	Brimmer Hall Plantation Tour	14	Good Hope Plantation	24	Port Henderson	34	Somerset Falls
5	Caymanas Park	15	Governor's Coach	25	Portland Lighthouse	35	Tryall Water Wheel
6	Colbeck Castle	16	Greenwood Great House	26	Prospect Plantation Tour	36	White Marl Arawak Museum
7	Columbus Park	17	Lover's Leap	27	Reach Falls	37	Windsor Caves
8	Denbigh Agricultural Show Grounds	18	Marcus Garvey Statue	28	Rio Grande Rafting		
9	Doctor's Cave Beach	19	Martha Brae Rafting (Rafter's Village)	29	Roaring River Falls		
10	Dunn's River Falls	20	Milk River Spa	30	Rocklands Feeding Station		

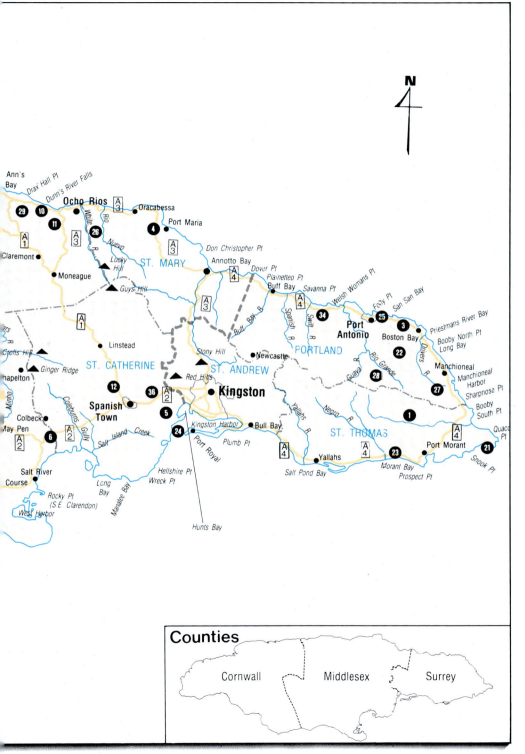

N

Ann's
Bay
Drax Hall Pt
Dunn's River Falls
Ocho Rios A3
Oracabessa
29 10
11
Port Maria
A1
A3 26
4
Claremont
Nuevo
A3
Don Christopher Pt
Lucky
Hill
Annotto Bay
Dover Pt
Moneague
ST. MARY
Plainetteo Pt
Buff Bay
Savanna Pt
Welsh Womans Pt
Guys Hill
A3
A1
Buff Bay R.
Spanish R.
A4
Folly Pt
San San Bay
Crofts Hill
34
25
Port
Antonio
3
Priestmans River Bay
Booby North Pt
Linstead
Boston Bay
Long Bay
ST. CATHERINE
Stony Hill
Newcastle
PORTLAND
22
Manchioneal
Ginger Ridge
Rio Grande
Drivers R.
Manchioneal
napelton
ST. ANDREW
28
Harbor
Sharpnose Pt
12
Red Hills
27
Colbeck
36
A2
Kingston
Guava R.
Booby
Spanish
5
South Pt
May Pen
Town
Yallahs R.
1
A2
6
A2
24
Kingston Harbor
Bull Bay
Negro R.
Quaco
Salt Island Creek
ST. THOMAS
Pt
Salt River
Port Royal
Plumb Pt
A4
A4
21
Course
Hellshire Pt
Yallahs
23
Port Morant
Snook Pt
Lcng
Wreck Pt
Salt Pond Bay
Morant Bay
Rocky Pt
Bay
Prospect Pt
(S.E. Clarendon)
Manatee Bay
West Harbor
Hunts Bay

Counties

Cornwall   Middlesex   Surrey

113

THE COUNTY OF SURREY

Jamaica's eastern protuberance packs into its 320 square miles more dramatic extremes than any other part of the island. Here in the County of Surrey, the cosmopolitan growth of modern Kingston stands shoulder to shoulder with the inaccessible reaches of the Blue Mountains. The rainy northeastern slopes of that range are scant miles away from stunted scrub forests and the elegant cactus formations of the southern coast. While daily mists descend to 3,000 feet on some parts of the mountains, coastal Kingston swelters under 60 percent sunshine annually.

Surrey embraces the parishes of **St. Thomas** and **Portland**, and the **corporate area** of **Kingston** and **St. Andrew**, comprising the capital city and surrounding areas.

The entire county throbs to the beat of unique drums, for here is centered the island's artistic and cultural life, as well as the most vital indigenous folkloric activities. Religious cults such as *kumina* flourish in St. Thomas. Portland's mountains were the stronghold of freedom-fighting Maroons whose descendants still live in villages in the area. In Kingston itself, a fusion of the traditional and the sophisticated modern takes place on the stages of theaters. Songs and rituals of Jamaica's religious groups, for instance, have been recreated in authentic fashion by the Jamaican Folk Singers and the National Dance Theatre Company.

Surrey's principal highway, Route A4, clings to a coastline of beautiful beaches—white coral sands on the northern coast, occasionally black sands on the south. But within minutes, the visitor can get away from the ennui sometimes induced by sea and sand, into the cool foothills or pine-clad slopes of the Blue Mountains. The foothills offer spectacular and diversified scenery within easy driving distance of city and towns. The mountain roads themselves are narrow and twisting and should be tackled only by those with the right spirit of adventure.

The vegetation cover, from mountains to coast, is rich and varied. Untouched wilderness flanks slopes denuded by centuries of settlement. Hill savannas choked with guinea grass, but few trees, alternate with wet forests of overgrown foliage, tree ferns and mosses. Gnarled wind-blown trees of elfin woodlands are a contour line away from acres of Caribbean Pine in commercial forestry projects. Abundant rainfall feeds cascading streams which pour into coastal marshes.

Temperatures range from around 80° F on the seacoast to 40° F at Blue Mountain Peak, just 10 miles inland. This climatic diversity has enabled Surrey residents to grow a bewildering array of vegetables, fruits and flowers from the four corners of the world. A farmer's garden might include yam vines as well as parsley, sage, rosemary and thyme, plus such decidedly tropical productions as Search-Me-Heart and Cho-cho. Peaches, strawberries, iceberg lettuce and asparagus grow on the mountain slopes.

The visitor's first stop on the island of Jamaica is frequently Kingston. And it is in the capital that this tour of Surrey will begin.

Landmarks

1 Chinese Cemetery
2 Coke Church
3 Constant Spring Golf Course
4 Devon House
5 Fort Augusta
6 Fort Charles
7 Fort Nugent
8 Gleaner Building
9 Gordon House
10 Gun court
11 Hope Botanical Gardens
12 Institute of Jamaica
13 Jamaica College
14 Jamaica House
15 Jamaica Tourist Board
16 Kings House
17 Kingston Parish Church
18 Little Theatre
19 May Pen Cemetery
20 Mico College
21 National Heroes Park
22 National Stadium
23 Railway Station
24 R.C. Cathedral
25 St Andrews Parish Church
26 St George's College
27 University of The West Indies
28 Victoria Crafts Market
29 Victoria Park
30 Ward Theatre
31 Zoo

Hotels & Discos

1 Clieveden Court Hotel
2 Courtleigh Manor Hotel
3 Epiphany Disco
4 Exodus Disco
5 Four Seasons Hotel
6 New Kingston Hotel
7 Oceana Hotel
8 Pegasus Hotel
9 Sandhurst Hotel
10 Terra Nova Hotel

Kingston

To Gordon Town & Newcastle

Skyline Dr

Widcombe Rd

Hope Tavern

13   11   31

ington Dr   Old   Hope   Rd

na Heights   Papine

erley
Hills   Mona
Reservoir   27

LONG MOUNTAIN   Gibraltar Camp Rd

Hermitage Rd

College Common

Long Mountain Rd

Hermitage

DALLAS MOUNTAIN

August Town Rd

August Town

Mounrain

Wareika Hill

St. James Rd

ens

Rockfort   A 4

7

Harbour View

Main Rd

Rd

oes Rd

Caribbean Sea

KINGSTON: THE LIVELY CAPITAL

If the expression urban sprawl had not existed, the city of Kingston would have invented it. From its founding over 300 years ago, it has made up for its lack of elegance and graciousness with the exuberance and gusto of the perpetual adolescent.

Kingston is a capital city which has defied all efforts of city fathers, planners and other do-gooders to curb it, tame it, confine it, order it, or discipline its citizens.

From every street corner, reggae music blares. Bars and betting shops jostle churches as the most ubiquitous non-residential buildings in the city. Obsolescent narrow streets are a challenge to drivers' nervous systems. Pound laws notwithstanding, animals wander at will. Street signs are usually absent. Out of this endless chaos, Kingstonians have inbred a sort of natural radar of direction and survival. They seem to find meaning or pattern in what outsiders consider so disordered.

Kingston is a city that has never caught up with itself, for it has never stopped growing. Its population is swelled daily by starry-eyed youth from the mountains who dream of hitting the big-time as reggae singers in the city. Meanwhile, they inflate the numbers of "yard" or tenement dwellers, and their dreams and hopes burgeon into the city's headaches: outgrown water supplies, public transportation, sanitation services, schools, jobs and housing.

In order to make ends meet, many of these people have turned Kingston into a city of hustlers. Hawkers (known as higglers), their bargains purchased overseas, return to Jamaica and set up their wares on the sidewalks, in direct competition with time-honored merchants who display goods indoors. The hustle on the sidewalk is known as "Ben Dung Plaza"—because you have to bend down to buy. City fathers threaten and cajole, but Ben Dung Plaza, like the rest of Kingston, rolls on with an anarchic momentum of its own.

Kingston began as a well-designed seaside town on the edge of a magnificent natural harbor. But it has voraciously gobbled up all of the Liguanea (pronounced Li-ga-nee) Plains and crept into the surrounding mountains. In the past decade, encouraged by a causeway across the western end of the harbor, Kingston has also embraced part of the promontory known as the Hellshire Hills, separating the harbor from the rest of the south coast.

A City of Views

What redeems Kingston—and makes up for the noise, the squalor, the inconveniences and the heat—is the city's setting, one of the most splendid anywhere. The readily accessible panoramic views make this evident. From Hellshire Beach at Naggo Head, the city unfolds before you, framed by the mountains. And from the hills—Beverly Drive (in Beverly Hills), Skyline Drive (on Jacks Hill), and the spectacular crest of Red Hills Road—there are incomparable views of the city, plains, mountains and sea.

From its sweeping harbor, Kingston sprawls along the fan-shaped plain, rising imperceptibly for eight miles into the foothills which surround it. Another 10 miles inland, the hills give way to the spectacular Blue Mountain Range and culminate in Blue Mountain Peak (7,402 feet).

You can orient yourself by facing the mountains, your back to Kingston Harbor. On the east, to your right, is a rocky, low-lying hill near the coast. This is **Long Mountain**, whose northern flanks are covered with the **Beverly Hills** mansions of the *nouveau riche*. Halfway up the slope is the **Martello Tower**, built of stone in 1803 to guard against French invasion. Beyond is a higher limestone hill, **Wareika** (said to be an Arawak name), and behind that is **Dallas Mountain.** The latter takes its name from a family whose descendants emigrated to the United States and achieved great prominence. One of them, George Milfin Dallas, became U.S. vice president (1845–48) and gave his name to the Texas city.

Looking westwards, the land drops slightly at the Hope River gorge and then rises sharply again in **Jacks Hill.** Skyline Drive is perched along its spine. Another dip occurs where the residential suburb of **Stony Hill** (and a major highway which leads to the north coast) are located. Then the land rises again to

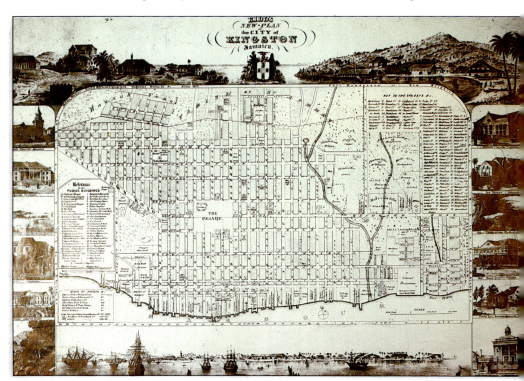

HIMANTOPUS
NIGRICOLLIS

the heights and residential areas of **Red Hills.**

'Under the Clock'

Kingston is the Americas' largest English-speaking city south of Miami. Its population, estimated at 700,000, seems to grow daily.

Old timers will proudly claim that the only true Kingstonians are those "born under the clock"—that is, the clock of the **Kingston Parish Church.** This downtown landmark at the corner of King Street and South Parade dates from the late 17th or early 18th Century: the oldest tombstone in its cemetery is dated 1699. Throughout Jamaica, during the time (before 1872) that the Church of England, or Anglican Church, prevailed as the sole official creed, the parish church was always one of the first public buildings erected in a settlement. The original Kingston Parish Church was destroyed in the 1907 earthquake; the current structure was raised in 1911 according to the same design as its predecessor.

The interior of the church contains gifts from generations of worshipers.

The high altar is flanked by statues of the Virgin Mary and St. Thomas, gifts of the Chinese and Syrian communities, respectively. Mystic Masonic emblems can be seen in the colored window in the northern chapel. A painting of the Pieta (by Susan Alexander) and stained glass windows (depicting Christ's resurrection and the Pentecost) look out on many interesting monuments within the church. Among these is the tomb of Admiral John Benbow, the English naval hero who died in Port Royal.

The square clock tower on the west side of the church was erected in memory of those who died in the First World War. Its bell is much older, having been cast in 1715. But it is many centuries since all of Kingston fell within the shadow of the clock tower. The original section of the city (bounded roughly by today's North, East and West streets and the harbor) was laid out over 300 years ago to house survivors of the earthquake which destroyed Port Royal in 1692.

The dazed survivors were glad to escape the pall of devastation across the harbor and put some solid land under

King's House, circa 1890.

their feet—even if it was a kraal (enclosure) for Colonel Barry's hogs. Fevers, starvation and disease took their toll on 3,000 to 4,000 persons in the first weeks after the exodus. But by June, the governing council agreed to purchase 200 acres of the kraal for £1,000 of public revenue.

The new city was laid out according to the rectangular grid pattern of European towns. In the north was an open square known as The Parade, the upper limit of which is marked by the **Ward Theatre.** Today the theater, across the street from **Victoria Park**, looks down on a monstrous confusion of ghetto shacks, traffic, vendors and buses.

The Ward occupies a site which has been in continuous use as a theater for centuries. The original theater on this site attracted many well-known English and American touring companies. But it was at a Kingston theater on another site (unknown today) that the famous American naval hero John Paul Jones made his debut as a professional actor. His theatrical career was brief: he took the job between ships and soon sailed off, later distinguishing himself in the U.S. War of Independence.

The Ward was a gift to the city from Colonel Ward, nephew and partner in the famous rum firm of J. Wray and Nephew Limited. In 1825, John Wray, a wheelwright, started a business as a liquor dealer in the Shakespeare Tavern next door to the theater. (Another pub occupies the site today.) Eventually, Wray went into rum-making, perfecting a superior blend. The rest, as they say, is many billion glasses of Jamaica's favorite poison later.

Theatrical activity of every description is at home in the Ward. Most popular is the annual Pantomime which opens on Boxing Day (Dec. 26) and runs for several months, usually until April-May.

But back to The Parade. It was here in colonial times that the English Redcoats, full of spit and polish, drilled for the edification and delight of the Jamaican natives. They were often joined by the Militia, an island-wide force of callow clerks and bookkeepers, paunchy merchants or dyspeptic planters, led by doddering colonels and major generals. Militia duty was compulsory for all who qualified—usually freed men between 16 and 20—and officer

LAMPORNIS
MANGO

Ward
Theatre,
below, and
John Canoe
dancer,
right.

status, which gave social advantage, was eagerly sought and bought.

The Parade also served as a promenade for the local folk and a venue for public events such as hanging prisoners or putting them in the stocks. When the island worked itself into a state of hysteria over a threatened French invasion in 1694, a fort was temporarily erected on The Parade with guns pointing down King Street.

When the British troops and Militia took their parades to Up Park Camp, The Parade lost much of its splendor. In 1870 the garden was laid out and in 1914 it was officially named Victoria Park, in honor of the queen whose statue—once a prominent landmark—faced down King Street. The statue is said to have turned around on its pedestal to face in the opposite direction during the 1907 earthquake. The north and south sections of the park are dominated by statues, executed by Jamaican Alvin Marriott, of two 20th Century Jamaican leaders, Sir Alexander Bustamante and Norman Washington Manley.

The park was officially renamed St. William Grant Park in the mid-1970s, after a labor leader of the 1930s. As with most politicians and orators of the time, Grant's main platform was the steps of the **Coke Church** on the eastern side of the park.

The present Coke Church is on the site of the first Methodist chapel erected in Jamaica. It is named for the Rev. Dr. Coke, a Wesleyan missionary who came in 1789 to establish a mission. Coke Chapel was opened in 1790 but was soon closed when a grand jury found it "injurious to the general peace and quiet of the inhabitants." Missionaries were frowned upon because of their activities among the slaves. Methodism flourished, however, and is today regarded as one of the largest organized religious groups in Jamaica.

On the Waterfront

In recent decades, the focus of urban activity in Kingston has shifted. People have increasingly deserted downtown, and the heart of the old city has been left to decay—the old 18th Century townhouses turned into tenement yards for those too poor to move upwards.

However, a bold new development scheme has begun "to put new life in

The Parade, 18th Century.

ERISMATURA
ORTYGOIDES

the old city," as the ads say. Only time will tell if the urban renewal project on the Kingston waterfront will set an example for the rest of the decaying city.

Until the 1960s, generations-old finger piers jutting into the sea were characteristic of Kingston's waterfront. But when the Kingston Waterfront Redevelopment Company was established to undertake renewal of the downtown area, a new commercial and shipping area—**Newport West**—was built from reclaimed lands on the west side of the harbor. This modern port complex, known as **Port Bustamante**, has the capacity to handle more than one million tons of cargo annually. It includes a free zone and a transshipment port.

Where the old finger piers once stood, a new waterfront has been created. Modern Ocean Boulevard embraces a complex of high-rise buildings: hotels, apartments, offices and shops, collectively known as the **Kingston Waterfront**. This is only the first phase of an ambitious long-term program to transform a much more extensive area extending to the east.

One of the waterfront's highlights is the **Crafts Market**. Straw goods, carv-

ings and embroidered goods are offered for sale along with more esoteric objects like dried calabashes. You may also find yo-yos made from *cacoon*, one of the largest seeds in the world. It grows on rampant vines found along river valleys and its pods can grow to three feet in length.

The original 19th Century Victoria Crafts Market, which stood at the foot of King Street in front of the Hotel Oceana, was one of the casualties of progress. In centuries past, this site was the location of a Sunday Market which attracted many thousands of slaves, free people and white hucksters from surrounding parishes. With the end of slavery, the market's character changed. It became known as the Christmas Grandmarket, a special attraction for children who came to buy paper hats, balloons, *fee-fees* (whistles) and toys.

In front of the market was the famous Victoria Pier, landing place for nearly all famous visitors including kings, queens and other heads of state. Among the arrivals was Maximillian, Archduke of Austria, who with his wife Carlotta made a brief stop here in 1857 on their way to Veracruz to be crowned

The Parade, circa 1983.

Emperor and Empress of Mexico.

The Roy West Building on the corner of Orange Street and Ocean Boulevard is slated to house part of the Institute of Jamaica, including the **National Gallery**. The development of a national art movement dates only to the 1930s, but since that time, Jamaica has produced a number of exciting artists. Many of their works will be on permanent show here.

Another waterfront attraction is the **Coin and Note Museum** in the Bank of Jamaica building. Although Jamaica switched to dollars and cents in 1967, older people recall and sometimes still figure in pounds, shillings and pence, the old British coinage formerly in use. The folk names for these old coins live on in song and story: *"Carry me ackee go a Linstead Market, not a quattie wut sell."* Quatties might be seen in the museum, along with souvenir coin sets, tokens, tallies, pirate pieces of eight, and other fascinating fragments of the past. Tallies, incidentally, were substitutes for coins given to task workers such as banana loaders.

The decay of downtown was hastened by the spread of the city northwards. In the '60s, a commerical revolution created North American-style shopping centers all over the city. Commerce became rapidly diffused and small shops or boutiques sprang up everywhere to capture customers. The main shopping areas are now located along Constant Spring Road, Red Hills Road, and in Liguanea, Cross Roads and Manor Park.

King Street, the downtown area's main thoroughfare, is today a sorry spectacle. In 1909, when the public buildings flanking King Street were built, they were regarded as the last word in modernity and were featured in every photograph of Jamaican "progress." They were constructed of reinforced concrete, then a relatively new material, following the destruction of most of the old wood or mortar buildings in the earthquake and fire of 1907. The public buildings house the Treasury and Law Courts and offices.

Of all the downtown area, it is probably only lower **Duke Street** which retains some of its original flavor as a business and commerical center. Once the address of all the best law firms, Duke Street is still full of attorneys'

Kingston docks, about 1900.

offices, but chambers there are no longer regarded as essential to success and prestige.

Duke Street contains some interesting buildings, among them the island's only **Jewish Synagogue** (at the corner of Charles Street). The United Congregation of Israelites represents an amalgamation in 1921 of two separate Jewish congregations—the Sephardic or Portuguese Jews and the Ashkenazi from England and Germany.

Another interesting religious structure on Duke Street is the **St. Andrew Scots Kirk.** This octagonal church was built in 1814 when Scots were prominent in the island's commercial life. Jamaica's first Presbyterian church, it was damaged in the 1907 earthquake and thereafter reduced in size.

Further up Duke Street is **Gordon House,** where Parliament meets. Its name honors patriot and martyr George William Gordon, a noted legislator branded as one of the "villains" of the 1865 Morant Bay Rebellion. He is now a National Hero.

Directly across from Gordon House, facing Beeston Street, is one of Jamaica's most historic buildings,

now undergoing extensive restoration. **Headquarters House,** so called because it was once the seat of government and the military, was built in the 18th Century by a prominent merchant and planter named Thomas Hibbert. He and three other rich merchants had a bet to see who could build the most elegant townhouse, in order to secure the attentions of a certain beautiful lady. No one knows who won, and this is the only one of the four houses still standing.

On East Street are located the Main buildings housing the **Institute of Jamaica.** Founded in 1879 for the encouragement of literature, science and art, it has since functioned as a kind of mini-Smithsonian Institution. Divisions include the National Gallery, the Cultural Training Centre (in which are located national schools of art, dance, drama, theatre), a Junior Centre (located in the building opposite the East Street headquarters), a Museums Division, an African Caribbean Institute (engaged in research on the African traditions in Jamaica and the Caribbean), and a Publications Division.

Housed at East Street are the two major collections of the Institute—the

Modern
ontainer
erminal at
Kingston's
Newport.

National Library of Jamaica (formerly the West India Reference Library), containing the largest collection of West Indian material in the world, and the Natural History Division, which includes a small museum and a large herbarium. Before the University of the West Indies or the Scientific Research Council were established, the Natural History Division was the focus of Jamaica's scientific activity. It still plays a major role in the collection and classification of flora and fauna and the publication of research findings.

The Gleaner Building on North Street is the home of Jamaica's oldest newspaper, the *Daily Gleaner*. It was founded in 1834 by Joshua and Jacob DeCordova. Jacob, a civil engineer, later emigrated to Texas, where he laid out the town of Waco and served in the state legislature.

Further along North Street, the dome of Holy Trinity Cathedral marks the focal point of Roman Catholicism. The island's largest Catholic church was once a landmark for those who arrived by sea. Established by the Spanish, Catholicism received a fresh impetus in the late 18th Century with an influx of French Catholics from nearby Haiti. The church has pioneered educational institutions throughout the island, notably the Alpha Boys School.

Ghettos of the West

As Kingston expanded, polarities developed between "uptown" and "downtown" as economically and psychologically exclusive residential areas. The stereotyped "uptowners" were relatively wealthy folk who aspired to the middle-class norms of North America and Europe. They went downtown to work or shop, but left for their uptown suburbs in the evenings. The "downtowners" were ghetto dwellers who inhabited the decaying tenements and shacks. If they worked at all, it was for the uptowners whom they envied. Yet despite the downtowners' disadvantages, it was here that two of modern Jamaica's most vibrant cultural movements established their roots: reggae and Rastafarianism.

The first songs of bondage and redemption came from an infamous settlement known as Back o'Wall. In the 1960s, this was converted into a model

Higgler stands at Kingston Parish Church.

TÓDUS VIRIDIS

community, **Tivoli Gardens.** It has become the centerpiece of the political constituency of Prime Minister Edward Seaga, who first conceptualized Tivoli Gardens while serving as Minister of Finance in the 1960s. Tivoli Gardens, with its carefully planned pattern, modern buildings, community spirit and lovingly painted murals, is an oasis of hope in an area of hopelessness and decay.

Trench Town and other ghetto areas today are referred to in Kingston as the "West." Visitors who might feel the pull of the West are advised not to do so without a guide from the area. Post-independence political confrontation has left much of the former "downtown" divided into volatile territories which are, in the interest of self-preservation, rigorously defended against outsiders.

From Horses to Heroes

Horse racing was probably the most popular sport in colonial times. There were well-patronized race courses in each parish, and race days were occasions for social splendor. In Kingston,

races were a common diversion from earliest times. The first race on Kingston Race Track was run in 1816, and from then until the outbreak of World War II, racing continued without a break. In 1953, racing was moved to **Knutsford Park**, and soon thereafter to the modern **Caymanas Park** just across the county boundary in St. Catherine.

Kingston Race Track later became George VI Memorial Park, and Kingston's war memorial or cenotaph was located there. In addition to racing, circuses and other amusements have traditionally found a home in the park. It has also been used as a tent city for refugees from natural disasters such as earthquakes. After independence in 1962, it was laid out as a shrine to the **National Heroes.** Today their monuments can be viewed inside. There is also a bust of **General Antoneo Maceo**, a Cuban hero of the independence struggles who found sanctuary in Jamaica on more than one occasion. The bust was presented by the people of Cuba in 1952.

Outside the park, in front of the Ministry of Education, is another

obile
ound
system in
owntown
ngston.

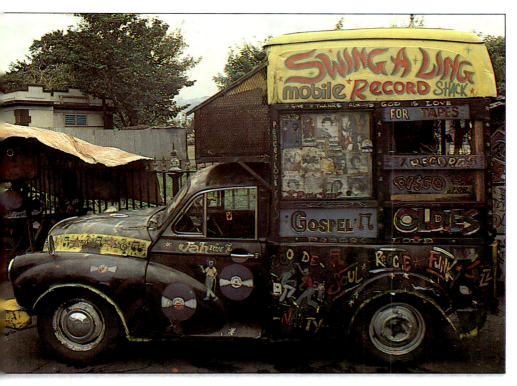

monument to a Latin American revolutionary: **Simón Bolívar**, "The Liberator." Bolivar spent seven months in Jamaica in 1817 while leading the struggles to free the Latin American colonies from Spanish rule. While here, he wrote the famous "Jamaica Letter"—regarded as one of the greatest documents of his career—and survived an assassination attempt at the boarding house where he lived at the northwest corner of Princess and Tower streets. The monument is a gift from Venezuela.

Streets of Schools
And Lignum Vitae

Wolmer's School, immediately north of National Heroes Circle, marks the northern boundary of Kingston proper. It was founded over 300 years ago with proceeds from the estate of John Wolmer, a wealthy Kingston goldsmith. It started out strictly as a boys' school; the girls' school was founded later.

Mico College, next door to Wolmer's is one of the oldest teacher-training institutions in the world. It indirectly owes its establishment to a London gentleman who refused to wed any of his aunt's six nieces, in spite of the fact that a £1,000 dowry was involved! The strings-attached inheritance which the wealthy Lady Mico had left him in her will was instead invested, and the income was later used to rescue Christians captured by Barbary pirates.

When piracy was stamped out, the Lady Mico Trust lay dormant for 200 years and grew to an enormous amount. It was used by English philanthropists to start Mico Schools throughout the West Indies to educate the soon-to-be-freed slave population. The Kingston college, established in 1834, is the only Mico institution still in existence. Now co-educational, it was originally a man's school. It has produced many of Jamaica's outstanding citizens, including the first native governor-general, Sir Clifford Campbell. At one time, Mico also trained missionaries for service in West Africa. The college was moved to its present location in 1896; the main building dates from 1909.

The street on which these schools are located—**Marescaux Road**—sometimes offers an excellent opportunity to see Jamaica's national flower. The lignum vitae is a small tree whose branches

Mobile sound system in West Kingston.

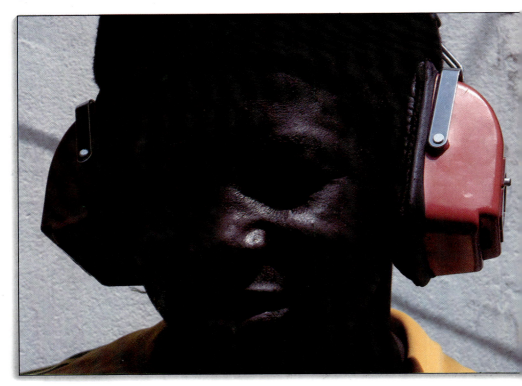

CRITHAGRA
BRASILIENSIS

might go unnoticed until they begin to flower around mid-July. At first, there is a light dusting of purple on the leaves; eventually, the tiny purple blossoms with their bright yellow stamens entirely cover the boughs. The plant has a fascination for a certain white butterfly (*Kricogonia lyside*) in some seasons, the blossoms can hardly be seen for the thousands of these creatures which set each tree shimmering.

Lignum vitae's name is Latin for "wood of life," and this gives an indication of how highly valued the plant has been in the past. As a medicine, its gum is reputed to be a cure for venereal disease and numerous other ailments. Its wood is so heavy it will sink in water, which makes it ideal for specialized purposes such as ship's propeller-shaft bearings, mortars, mallets, pulleys and policemen's batons. The attractive wood is also used to make furniture and curios.

Seeking Refuge in the 'Pens'

ingston bar ecor.

By the 18th Century, Kingston's rich merchants were discovering that it was much cooler and healthier to live in the foothills. They moved to more expansive new homes surrounded by a great deal of land. These were known as "pens," for there was now space for their horses and other livestock, and enough acreage to grow their own grass. At about 10 o'clock every morning, these merchants would leave their pens and bustle importantly into town, usually in small open carriages called "kitareens." Many place and street names in Kingston today still retain the word "pen"—as in Delacree Pen, Slipe Pen Road and Rest Pen.

One of the oldest and most splendid of these pen residences was built in 1694 and has been in continuous use since. Known as **Vale Royal**, it is now the Prime Minister's home. Located on Montrose Road off Lady Musgrave Road, it has undergone a sensitive restoration in recent years. The most notable feature of its striking facade is a rooftop lookout tower, typical of early Kingston houses. This would have been equipped with a spyglass for keeping an eye on doings in the harbor. Vale Royal was built by Simon Taylor, regarded as one of the richest men of his time.

Beyond the area of pen residences, sugar estates once covered the Liguanea Plains. The estates gave their names to many Kingston locations, including Hope, Liguanea, Constant Spring, Mona and Barbican.

Urban expansion northwards led to the creation of several important crossroads, one of which still retains that prosaic name. **Cross Roads** is a busy junction poised between uptown and downtown, though it gained significance only early in this century when the name Cross Roads became official. Prior, it was known as Montgomery's Corner after a lieutenant who was thrown from his horse at this spot. The white **Carib Theatre** for generations has been the setting for glamour and thrills born in the world of Hollywood. The clock tower here was erected in memory of Jamaican servicemen who died in the Second World War.

Not far to the east of Cross Roads is **Up Park Camp** on South Camp Road. Best known simply as "Camp," it was established in 1784 as the home of British Regiments stationed in Jamaica and is now headquarters of the Jamaica Defence Force. Duppy Gate, the southern entrance, recalls the legend of an officer of the Old West India Regiment

whose ghost regularly called out the guard there for inspection.

Kingston's Cultural Core

South Camp Road leads to **Tom Redcam Drive**, Jamaica's "cultural" street, named for a former poet laureate of Jamaica. Here are located the public library service, the Little Theatre, and the headquarters of the Anglican Church.

The library system, established in the 1950s, is highly regarded. An island-wide system of main parish libraries, branch libraries, a schools library service, and a bookmobile service is administered from here.

The **Little Theatre** was built in 1961 through the untiring efforts of Henry and Greta Fowler, who founded the Little Theatre Movement in 1942. The movement, which established the Jamaica School of Drama (now incorporated into the Cultural Training Centre), also sponsors the annual Pantomime. The Little Theatre is used by theatrical groups throughout the year, two of which have won national and international acclaim and hold annual seasons here: the National Dance Theatre Company and the Jamaican Folk Singers.

The architecturally exciting **Cultural Training Centre** on Arthur Wint Drive just around the corner from Tom Redcam Drive houses the National Schools of Dance, Drama, Art and Music. The Centre not only instructs performers; it trains teachers for the island's schools and takes in a limited number of students from other Caribbean islands. Placing all the schools in close proximity is expected to develop cross-fertilization in the arts. Students are encouraged to explore other art forms outside their own disciplines.

Arthur Wint Drive continues around the northern end of Camp to the **National Stadium.** The stadium was built for independence celebrations in 1962 and has been the venue of major sporting events since that time. The **National Arena** next door hosts other sports and more diverse activities, including a two-day National Flower Show in July. At the entrance to the stadium is a statue by sculptor Alvin Marriott, symbolic of Jamaican athletic prowess. Arthur Wint Drive is named after a famed Jamaican athlete who won a gold medal in the 400-meter run at the 1948 London Olympics, bringing international fame to his tiny island home. Wint was also a member of Jamaica's gold medal-winning 1,600-meter relay team at the 1952 Olympics in Helsinki.

A park is being developed in front of the stadium to honor outstanding Jamaicans. The first monument to be placed there was a statue in honor of reggae hero Bob Marley.

Half Way Tree

From Cross Roads, busy Half Way Tree Road leads north to Constant Spring. Aqueducts flanking the road were built in the 1770s to carry sugar to this former estate.

As early as 1696 the name **Half Way Tree** was in use, a reference to the giant kapok (silk cotton) tree which once threw its huge buttresses in all directions here. Before the tree died of old age in the 1870s, it was a resting place for market women traveling from the hills to town with their wares. Roads west to Spanish Town, north to the coast via Stony Hill, and east to the mountains via Papine all join here.

Caymanas Park races.

RALLUS CONCOLOR

A few yards south of Half Way Tree's main intersection is the **St. Andrew Parish Church**, the island's oldest. Church registers date to 1666; the first building was raised here in 1692. The foundation of the present structure was laid in 1700, though it has undergone many renovations since then.

The community of Half Way Tree is the center of government of the parish of St. Andrew. Parish law courts sit here.

East of Half Way Tree, via Hope and Trafalgar roads, **New Kingston**, built on what was once the Knutsford Park Race Track, accommodates many leading hotels including the Jamaica Pegasus and the New Kingston.

Hope Road itself leads to scenic drives in the mountains to the northeast. It contains several places of interest en route, including the stately **Devon House** at the junction of Trafalgar Road. Devon House was built in 1881 by a black Jamaican who made his fortune in South America, some say as a gold miner. George Stiebel was also a builder, so his house was harmoniously constructed. It is regarded today as the best preserved example of classical architecture in Jamaica. Each room is a

Vale Royal.

period piece of exclusive style.

The government bought and restored the house in the 1960s and opened it to the public. Former stables surrounding the building have been converted to craft shops and a popular bar and restaurant known as the Grog Shop. For a time, Devon House was the home of the National Gallery; but with the removal of the gallery to downtown Kingston, Devon House has reverted to its original concept.

The modern **Jamaica House**, further north, was built in the 1960s as the residence of the Prime Minister. It served that purpose only for a short time, and was soon converted into the Prime Minister's office instead.

At the Kingsgate traffic lights is **Kings House**, official residence of the Governor-General. This was originally residence of the Bishop of Jamaica. The building was wrecked in the 1907 earthquake and rebuilt to a design of Sir Charles Nicholson. Visitors may view the attractive 200-acre grounds.

The studio built by reggae star Bob Marley, **Tuff Gong International**, is unmistakable just beyond the Lady Musgrave intersection. It flies the Ethiopian

flag and has renderings of hit Marley records painted on the wall in front.

Matilda's Corner And Hope Gardens

The busy intersection further north is known as **Matilda's Corner**, probably after a French Haitian refugee who settled here. The official name for the wider area is Liguanea, a name which may derive from the iguana, the large lizard much esteemed by the Arawaks.

Hope Road leads to **Hope Gardens** and the campus of the **University of the West Indies.** Major Richard Hope, who came here with the conquering British Army in 1655, gave his name to this area. Hope's land grant, which extended from the hills at Newcastle to the harbor, was one of the most progressive estates on the island. By 1758, his **descendants** built stone aqueducts to carry water from the Hope River to turn the estate mills. The city's first public water supply came from this source and sections of the aqueduct are still in use in the vicinity of Hope Gardens and Mona Heights.

Hope Gardens have been a favorite sanctuary for sweethearts and amateur photographers since their establishment over a century ago. The gardens were laid out in 1881 on 200 acres acquired by the government from Hope Estate. They were officially designated the Royal Botanical Gardens in 1953, on the occasion of a visit by Queen Elizabeth II. The gardens have been somewhat neglected in recent years, but efforts are now being made to revitalize the complex, which includes a small zoo. Children are also attracted on weekends to **Coconut Park**, a small funland.

University of the West Indies

The lovely campus of the University of the West Indies (UWI), called "You-wee" by initiates, is wedged in the hills between Long Mountain and Dallas Mountain. From small beginnings in 1948 with 33 medical students, the university has grown to embrace three campuses—in Jamaica, Barbados and Trinidad—and university centers in the other Caribbean territories which support it. This is a regional institution and the crests of all its member states can be

Half Way Tree, about 1890.

seen inside the **Chapel.**

Located near the main entrance, the Chapel is the foremost visitor attraction on campus. The old cutstone building of classically simple lines was formerly the sugar warehouse of Gales Valley estate in Trelawny. It was pulled down and reassembled here stone by stone as directed by its last owner. The original owner and the date of construction— "Edward Morant Gale: 1799"—are written at the top of the pediment just under the roof. This is by no means the university's only connection with sugar. The campus embraces parts of the old Mona and Papine estates, and ruined aqueducts and sugar works can be seen throughout the grounds.

The **Gordon Town Road** beyond Papine travels along the gorge of the Hope River for some miles, climbing to the **Blue Mountain Inn**—regarded as Jamaica's most romantic dining place if not its most expensive. Established in 1754 as a plantation coffee house, it is set at the foot of waterfalls where the Mammee River joins the Hope. A left turn above the inn leads eventually to **Newcastle**; a right turn goes to **Gordon Town**, **Mavis Bank** and other hill vil-

lages, and ultimately to the **Blue Mountain Peak** walking trail.

The Hope gained fame at the turn of the 20th Century as the "Healing Stream" of the self-proclaimed Prophet Bedward, who attracted thousands of followers to his church at **August Town**, below the university. Bedward's much-publicized announcement that he would fly to heaven on a certain day was not fulfilled, but that did not dampen the ardor of his followers. Support did fall off, however, when authorities decided to confine him to an insane asylum. Nonetheless, there are faithful Bedwardites to this day, and some scholars see a political element in his activities.

The Hellshire Hills

Southwest of Kingston, off Marcus Garvey Drive and across the causeway on the west side of the harbor, are the city's bedroom communities and some of its favorite beaches.

In a few short years, the Hellshire area has gone from uninhabited headland to urban extension of Kingston. **Portmore**, at the entrance to the region, is now home to 80,000 Jamaicans, with

Devon House in oils.

an additional 70,000 to be accomodated by expansion into the Hellshire Hills. Long-range plans for the 45-square-mile promontory include provisions for natural areas and forest parks; but much of its original character is disappearing beneath the demands of a burgeoning population.

As you drive across the causeway, look to the west toward Caymanas Park and an area called **Passage Fort.** Formerly on the mouth of the Rio Cobre river (which has since shifted course), Passage Fort was the island's principal shipping port in Spanish Town's early years as capital, before the development of Kingston Harbour. It was here that a British fleet landed in 1655, later marching six miles inland to capture Spanish Town and end Spanish rule on Jamaica. The imposing structure on the left is **Fort Augusta** prison; it was originally constructed in the mid-18th Century as the major fortification on the western side of the harbor.

Port Henderson

Where the road forks, proceed left through Portmore. At the end of this community are remains of the charming old 18th Century village of **Port Henderson.** Six of the original buildings have been restored by the Jamaica National Trust Commission. Among them is **Rodney's Arms**, a bar and restaurant.

Port Henderson was established as a port and later became a holiday resort for the fashionably rich, including the governor. A mineral spring which was the spa's main attraction disappeared after a hurricane in 1951, and the hamlet became a virtual ghost town. The modern high-rise building which contrasts so sharply with the beautiful 18th and 19th Century architecture is now used for government purposes, but was formerly the Forum Hotel.

For the visitor, the main attraction of the Hellshire Hills is its beaches. These begin several miles beyond the housing developments. The Hellshire coastline consists of a series of coves containing charming white-sand beaches, unlike most other south coast beaches where the sand is black. Two are readily accessible. **Fort Clarence** is a "developed" beach-entertainment center with parking lot, security, changing facilities, and frequent entertainment including reg-

gae. But true beach aficionados head for the fisherman's beach beyond it, at **Naggo Head.**

This is regarded by many as the most relaxed and *iriest* beach in all Jamaica. Naggo Head is packed on weekends and public holidays, and all levels of society rub shoulders here: rich man, poor man, Rasta man, fisherman, diplomat, Miss Jamaica beauty queen and grandmother. The atmosphere is relaxed and hassle-free. A spirit of mutual coexistence, harmony and tolerance prevails between the resident fishermen (who live in colorful castaway-type shacks); their canoes (with names like "Try for All"); the bathers; the women who come each day to the bamboo shacks on the beach to cook the best fried fish on the island; and the ubiquitous goats, always looking miraculously well-fed despite a total absence of vegetation. The beach is threatened with development, but the fishermen and their allies, the seekers after the natural life, are resisting, not to mention the goats.

For the naturalist, Hellshire also offers a great deal of zoological and botanical interest. In the past, most of it has been little disturbed by man.

SYLVICOLA PENSILIS

Twin Sisters' Cave near Hellshire Beach, below. A sister's salute at the beach, right.

138

Port Royal: Lair
Of The Buccaneers

The quiet fishing 'village of **Port Royal**, resting at the tip of the seven-mile-long Palisadoes spit, sleeps on a turbulent past.

Famed as the principal port of the pirates of the Caribbean in the late 17th Century, it also was once the regional headquarters for the British Royal Navy—at a time when seapower controlled the world.

Today, little remains of Port Royal's glorious past. But a large-scale restoration is planned to make the town one of the truly significant historic attractions of the Americas. Archaeologists are at work on land and sea, and dreamers of treasure have intensified their explorations of surrounding waters.

The name Port Royal evokes tales and legends of fabulous wealth beneath the ocean waves. The sea floor, in fact, is where most of the town ended up when it was destroyed by a devastating earthquake and tidal wave in 1692.

Underwater searches so far have revealed little actual treasure, but many fascinating and historically valuable artifacts have been recovered. Some of these can be seen at the **Archaeological Museum**, located in the former naval hospital (built in 1819).

Port Royal's booty was the property of the buccaneers, who carried it here from every city they sacked and every ship they robbed on the high seas. These "Brethren of the Coast" had the long-standing approval of British authorities since they were acting against the Englishmen's deadly enemies: the Spaniards.

The buccaneers themselves hardly ever got rich. There were too many temptations in Port Royal. The pirates were soon parted from their pieces of eight by the taverns (at one time, there were 40) and friendly women who inhabited the city. Port Royal soon gained a reputation as "the wickedest city in the world." Christian moralists said it could not go unpunished, and pointed to the ruinous 1692 quake as retribution.

But the town refused to die. Some of the survivors returned to rebuild their houses, and though Port Royal could

Giddy
House near
Fort Charles,
Port Royal.

ERTHIOLA
FLAVEOLA

Modern
buccaneers
haul in
Kingston
Harbour
catch.

never be the same again, it achieved a different character as a naval port.

The great British Admiral Horatio Nelson once trod the streets of Port Royal, and visitors can still follow in his footsteps at **Fort Charles.** As a 20-year-old officer in the Royal Navy, Nelson was left in charge of the fort's batteries in 1779 when a French invasion was feared. The attack never came, probably because the fort's 104-gun complement was the strongest in the British Caribbean, but Nelson spent many anxious hours pacing up and down the deck. Today the platform is known as **Nelson's Quarterdeck.**

Fort Charles was Port Royal's original structure, its foundations having been laid by the British shortly after their capture of Jamaica in 1655. Today it houses a small **Maritime Museum.**

Another attraction in Port Royal is the **Giddy House,** so-called because it leans at an apparently impossible angle. An old artillery store, it was tilted by the 1907 quake.

A fascinating reminder of the 1692 quake is found in the epitaph on **Galdy's Tomb** in St. Peter's churchyard. Mr. Galdy was swallowed up by the earth during the tremor, but there must have been something unappetizing about him—for he was spewed out again, living to a ripe old age to tell and retell the tale.

The highway from Kingston to Port Royal skims across **The Palisadoes,** an alluvial strip created by centuries of sand, gravel and debris deposits from mountain streams. The alluvium joined a string of small islets, of which Port Royal was one. The spit encloses Kingston Harbour and acts as an ideal natural breakwater.

The road was built in 1936. Previously, a ferry—still operating from the foot of King Street—was the only form of transportation between Kingston and Port Royal. The highway cuts through what was once a flourishing coconut plantation, but has now reverted to its indigenous vegetation, including many native species of cacti and mangrove.

The broadest part of the Palisadoes is occupied today by the **Norman Manley International Airport,** Kingston's principal port of entry. It began as a landing strip during World War II; previously, seaplanes had set down in Kingston Harbour.

143

High in The Blue Mountains

The majestic **Blue Mountains** range from Kingston's northern suburbs to the north coast. They encompass the tallest mountain on the island, a high-altitude botanical garden, a national park and bird sanctuary, old plantations, great houses, and magnificent hill walks.

At least three days can be devoted to exploring the Blue Mountains. A sturdy, preferably compact vehicle such as a Volkswagen is recommended for covering the rugged roads. Those from Kingston to Mavis Bank via Guava Ridge and Kingston to Section via Hardwar Gap are paved and passable in all weather. But unpaved roads connecting Content Gap and Section and the Yallahs Crossing can be difficult during or immediately after heavy rains.

Route B1 follows Hope Road from Half Way Tree to Papine. Your last chance to gas up is at the Papine Service Station. At Papine, B1 passes left round the little park and becomes Gordon Town Road. It follows the Hope River Valley past **Blue Mountain Inn**, the restaurant that was formerly the "great house" of a coffee plantation. The coffee produced was shipped in wooden casks, made up the road at **The Cooperage** by imported Irish coopers, who were quartered farther up the Mammee River Road at the village still called **Irish Town**.

At Cooperage, the road forks. Continue straight ahead to a village called **Industry**, a slightly incongruous name in view of the normal level of activity there. Three miles from Papine, 1,200 feet up the valley, stands **Gordon Town**, a metropolis by Blue Mountain standards. It boasts a police station, a courthouse (typical local crimes include "cussin' bad words" and "stone-throwing"), a post office, two schools, a convent and its share of bars.

Gordon Town was the site of Jamaica's first botanical garden, established by Hinton East in 1770 at **Spring Garden**. East introduced hundreds of foreign plant species from places as diverse as China and Sweden. Many of his imports—including hibiscus, azalea, cassia, magnolia, oleander, croton and

jasmine—permanently altered the Jamaican scene. Nothing survives of the original garden except the profusion of attractive plant life that engulfs Gordon Town.

Higglers and Hairpins

The road to **Guava Ridge** leaves the town square from the police station, crosses a narrow bridge over the Hope River, and climbs above the town along the side of the river valley. As the road twists and turns in and out of a succession of valleys, the red roofs of the Newcastle army camp constantly appear then recede from view, 4,000 feet up across the valley, straggling down the mountainside. From here, Newcastle looks like some lost Inca city in the Andes, especially in low-hanging clouds.

A succession of tiny houses dot this route. Some cling precariously to the hillside, a small patch of banana, coffee, and vegetables around them. Down below the road, many more can be seen scattered over the valley floor. Such small holdings supply most of Kingston's vegetables and fruit needs. As the weekend approaches, the road fills up with brightly painted market trucks carrying unbelievable loads of higglers with their baskets of produce to sell at city markets. This was the free land settled by the newly emancipated slaves in 1834. The pattern of their agricultural life has not changed significantly since then.

Two hairpin bends straddle the 11-mile post as the road climbs steadily around the sides of the mountains. Shortly before the 13-mile post on the left hand side is "**World's End.**" Here, some of Jamaica's most famous liqueurs and rums are produced under the **Sangster's "Old Jamaica"** label. Dr. Ian Sangster, an immigrant from Scotland, started production in 1973.

This attractive little factory straddles five levels as it descends the side of the valley to a visitor's terrace which commands a fine view of Newcastle. Factory tours (including product sampling) are available.

A Hotel in the Pines

A junction beside the bus shelter beyond "World's End" at an elevation of 3,000 feet forks right through the scattered township of Guava Ridge and descends via **Mavis Bank** to the Yallahs River at 1,700 feet. The left fork ascends after a mile to the gates of **Pine Grove Hotel**, owned and run by Ronnie and Marcia Thwaites. In addition to spectacular panoramic views over Kingston and around the mountains, the hotel offers chalet accommodation, a limited selection of typical Jamaican food, and bar service.

Pine Grove is the best central point from which to explore the Blue Mountains. Sit here in the evening with the mountains all around, while the sky changes from blue through turquoise to pink and the lights of the capital gradually come to life far below.

After Pine Grove, the road passes **Valda** at 3,758 feet, then drops steadily to **Content Gap**, a village connected by footpath to Gordon Town, four miles and 1,800 feet below. At the round water tank the left-hand track offers an easy one-mile walk up to **Charlottenburg House**, a well-preserved Great House furnished with antique Jamaican furniture. Former slave quarters, dating from coffee plantation days, still stand adjacent to the house. The durable and

Blue Mountain coffee beans on the bush.

orting
eans at
avis Bank
offee
actory.

attractive hardwood used in the construction is local cedar, cut from the plantation when it was cleared for coffee.

Past **St. Peters**, there is a junction with the road to **Clydesdale**, a picturesque forestry station on the River Clyde, 1½ miles up a bumpy little road. This also was once a coffee plantation. It still has coffee-drying barbecues and an old water wheel. The Forestry Department rents the two-bedroomed main house at Clydesdale. Linen, towels and essentials are not provided. The house looks down on Clydesdale town from its location above thousands of massed tiny conifer seedlings, standing in serried ranks. The entrance road is to the left of the seedlings beds.

A Flowery High

A worthwhile side-trip from Clydesdale takes you to the **Cinchona Botanical Gardens**. Follow the descending road on the right which passes below the old wooden coffee-mill house. About 100 yards later the dirt road divides. The branch on the right leads two miles up to **Top Mountain**, where a

very rough Jeep road on the left side (if you come to some houses of the Yallahs Valley Land Authority, you've gone too far) leads slowly, if scenically, up to **Cinchona**. If you don't have a Jeep, park at Top Mountain for a breathtaking if strenuous walk of more than 1,000 feet in less than two miles.

The "main" road at Top Mountain junction leads on to **Westphalia**; from here, a bridle road beside the water tanks leads one mile up to the lower end of Cinchona. The left hand fork from Clydesdale passes a picnic rondel on the left en route to Cinchona. It is quite steep, but is by far the easiest route.

The Cinchona Botanical Gardens cling to a magnificent stretch of ridge which plummets from 5,500 to 4,500 feet high above the valleys of the Yallahs, Clyde and Green rivers. Cinchona may have the most inspiring site of any botanical garden in the world. It was founded in 1868 as a center for the cultivation of Assam tea and cinchona trees, whose bark was in great demand as a source of quinine for the treatment of malaria.

The cinchona is a native of the high Andes. Its medicinal properties were

passed to the Spaniards by the Quechua, descendants of the Incas. An experimental few hundred acres were planted around Cinchona and proved initially profitable. Later, however, large-scale production in India proved to be cheaper, and the Jamaican plantations of both cinchona and tea failed. The plantation shrank to an expatriate's dream, a "European Garden," established by an English gardener to supply Kingston with flowers and vegetables. As a result of its success, the trade remains an important source of income for local people.

Cinchona affords views in all directions, with John Crow Peak and St. John's Peak to the north, the main ridge of the Blue Mountains stretching east (and viewed spectacularly from the **Panorama Walk** on the east side of the gardens), and Kingston and the sea shimmering away to the hot south.

The uninhabited Great House was formerly the home of Jamaica's Superintendent of Gardens. Well-tended lawns bordered by a profusion of flowers front the house. Around the lawns is a veritable labyrinth of paths and walks that lead through the loosely arranged trees. These include many imported types: some huge specimens of eucalyptus, easily recognizable by their spear-shaped leaves and peeling whitish barks; juniper; cork oak, whose bark is in fact cork; Chinese cypress; ferns and tree ferns; rubber trees, whose leaves when plucked emit a white latex; and some fine examples of Blue Mountain yacca, a tall tree with tiny dagger-shaped leaves and reddish marks on its smooth trunk.

Follow the main route half a mile after the Clydesdale detour to a small road on the right that leads to **Silver Hill Coffee Factory**. Between September and February, you can see workers picking the red coffee berries. They remove outer pulp from the two inner green beans to prepare them for drying, husking and roasting.

In the Blue Mountains, optimum soil and climatic conditions combine to produce coffee of exceptionally fine flavor, believed to be the most expensive and sought-after in the world. After the introduction of coffee in 1728, its cultivation spread through the Blue Mountains. Most of the Great Houses here were plantation homes built during the

Newcastle.

RETTA NIVEA

halcyon years 1800 to 1840, when coffee exports rose to 17,000 tons per year. After emancipation, the large plantations declined and were split up among small farmers. That system has never produced more than a fraction of the earlier tonnages. Silver Hill is one of four coffee factories that operate in the Blue Mountains.

Misty Roads and Militiamen

At **Section** the road joins route B1, which connects Kingston to the north coast at **Buff Bay**. The partially paved road on the right drops north through the mountains via villages with engaging names like **Birnamwood** and **Tranquility**, to Buff Bay. Bear left instead to **Hardwar Gap**, the highest paved road in Jamaica at 4,000 feet. The hills around the Gap constitute **Hollywell Forest Park**, a fine example of montane mist forest. The area has an annual rainfall of over 100 inches a year, with wet clinging mists an almost daily occurrence.

In the almost constant moisture, the flora is quite distinct even from that of Newcastle, only two miles away. Pine trees predominate among the many tree types, while a striking feature is the profusion of a wide selection of Jamaica's 550 types of fern, including the high tree ferns, *Cyathea arborea*. Some of the trees grow to over 30 feet and many support epiphytes, climbing plants and even orchids. The bird songs that fill the forest include the harsh cry of the red-headed Jamaican woodpecker and the hauntingly plaintive call of the solitaire thrush. Picnic rondavels with views of Kingston speckle the hillside. The Forestry Department rents several log cabins at reasonable rates.

From **Hardwar Gap**, follow B1 to **Newcastle** along the contours of **Mount Horeb**, with views over the Mammee River valley. Newcastle is a military camp built between the 3,500 and 4,500-foot levels on the mountainside. The road passes right through the parade ground and you may find yourself in the middle of a military march.

General Sir William Gomm established the camp in 1841 in an attempt to reduce the fearfully high death rate from yellow fever that occurred at lower altitudes.

The Jamaica Defence Forces now

Military graveyard at Newcastle.

command Newcastle. Visitors may use the bar and facilities of the Sergeants' Mess, located in the building above the parade ground. The army also rents out a series of comfortable cottages a mile above the camp.

The Japanese Connection

From Newcastle, the road drops steadily to the few houses of **Irish Town**, passing the signposted entrance drive up to **Craighton Great House**. This old property was purchased in 1981 by the UCC Coffee Company of Japan to expand production of Blue Mountain coffee for the Japanese market, which virtually absorbs the total Jamaican production.

At the 13-mile marker, a signposted road leads to **Bamboo Lodge**, a small attractive hotel which was formerly a British Naval Hospital claiming association with Admiral Nelson, commander of Port Royal in 1799.

Below Bamboo Lodge is **Belancita**, home of the late Sir Alexander Bustamante. His widow, Lady Bustamante, still lives here. The road continues down the mountainside to the Mammee River, whose course it then follows to the Blue Mountain Inn at Cooperage Junction and where you turn south for Kingston.

The most popular approach to **Blue Mountain Peak** itself begins from Guava Ridge. The road descends through pine woods along the broad valley of the Falls River to Mavis Bank. After one of the bends, a panoramic view of the Grand Ridge including the Blue Mountain Peak suddenly unfolds. The Peak, not a sharp, discreet cone in the Matterhorn style, is a rather rounded hump amid a series of others almost equally high.

Shortly before Mavis Bank, where the main road bears left over a bridge, a dirt road leads into the local **Central Coffee Factory** where the preparation and roasting of Blue Mountain coffee beans may be seen. The factory is owned and operated by former government minister Keble Munn, who said it processes about 12,000 bushels annually. The raw coffee is purchased from some 4,000 small to large Blue Mountain farms.

Munn noted that the most prized coffee is a form called "rat-bite." Rats literally chew the biggest, juiciest beans

off the trees and when farmers round up the beans before they start to ferment, they can grind them into a variety of coffee that is in great demand.

The main road passes above the coffee factory before reaching Mavis Bank, a small township that nevertheless boasts both a police station and a post office. A broad dirt track continues straight through the Yallahs River at **Mahogany Vale**, then climbs steeply to **Hagley Gap**, the nearest village to the Peak. Here at the tiny square in front of the village store, take the dirt road to the left. Climb for one mile to **Farm Hill**, bear right and continue for half a mile to **Whitfield Hall**, five miles and 3,200 feet below the Peak. The house is clean and homey, if somewhat ascetic, and resembles a European youth hostel. Your hike should start from here.

Scaling Blue Mountain

Only the hardy will succeed in reaching the summit of Blue Mountain Peak, a three-hour scramble up a rough track. The climb begins in montane mist forest, a rare remnant of Jamaica's original forest. Its name derives from the characteristic mist which often lies on the peaks between 10 a.m. and 4 p.m. This reduces the incidental sunlight greatly, thus affecting the flora.

The **Elfin Woodland** starts about 5,500 feet, petering out in windswept scrub on the summit. It is an open woodland of mainly short, twisted, gnarled trees, often laden with lichens, epiphytes, mosses and ferns. The greenish gray moss which festoons most trees combines with a swirling mist to give the landscape an eerie aspect. This is accentuated by the dwarf species of orchid found here. Other flowers which grow well are honeysuckle, rhododendron, ginger lilies and the lesser known *merianias* (called "Jamaica Rose"), whose hanging rose-like blossoms appear to be lit from within when bathed in sunlight.

Once on the Peak, tired but triumphant, there is little to do but wallow in the incredible view over most of Jamaica. In clear weather, especially in the dawn hours, you can see as far north as Cuba. It can be cold, so a sweater and a swig of rum or brandy help to deaden the chill. There is a small house with toilet and cooking facilities but this must be booked in advance.

Port Antonio and Country Comforts

North of the Blue Mountains, Jamaica slopes gently back to the Caribbean. Surrey's coastline, carved out by volcanic activity, boasts the most ruggedly beautiful scenery on the island. This is Country, as Jamaicans call any region that lies outside Kingston.

Route A4 winds and twists through local fishing villages and hidden coves of jagged rock and secret sandspits. The seas swell in on northern fronts and currents crash against cliff and sand in some of the island's biggest breakers. From Surrey's western boundary below Annotto Bay east around the coast through Port Antonio, Morant Bay and Yallahs back to Kingston, the discriminating visitor will discover some of the most breathtaking vistas in all the Caribbean.

The heart of this region is **Port Antonio**, once the cradle of Jamaica's tourist trade. In the 1890s, visitors arriving by ship marveled at the little town perched above the twin harbors. Poet Ella Wheeler called it "the most exquisite harbor on earth." She said: "There were five distinct colors in the waters of the bay; there was tropical verdure everywhere and summer, and joy, and life was good."

Most first-time visitors who don't arrive by cruise ship come by car from the north coast resorts in the west or from Kingston. The popular, sight-saturated approach from Kingston is via Route A3, usually just called the Junction.

Follow Constant Spring Road north out of Kingston. Bear right onto Long Lane after negotiating the Manor Park Roundabout. The road will swing north again and become Stony Hill Road, Route A3. A detour on Gibson Road past the red slate-roofed **Stony Hill Hotel** provides spectacular views of Kingston and an insight into the lives of Jamaica's elite, who live behind barred gates guarded by security dogs in the mansions on the hillcrest.

The main route takes you through the bustling center of **Stony Hill** through smaller towns like **Golden Spring**. Drivers should take care around the increasingly hairpin corners and narrowing roads. Buses and trucks rarely slow down when slipping through them.

Castleton Gardens on the boundary of Surrey and Middlesex Counties begs a visit. Established in 1862, it has blossomed over the years into a showcase of exotic Jamaican flora. The highway bisects its 15 acres. Huge trees provide shade and cool rest spots in the upper half. The lower part runs along the bank of the **Wag Water River** with which the road plays tag from this point on. For a tip, guides willingly introduce you to fascinating plants like the *strychnos*—from which strychnine poisons and medicine are derived. Feathery, inviting bamboo lines the river, usually a mere trickle that exposes enormous, water-worn boulders.

The road worsens, but the views become more spectacular beyond the gardens. There's a graceful suspension bridge at boulder-crested **Mahoe Hill**. Again, local youths will escort you over the bridge to a quaint old school for a Jamaica dollar or two. The road eventually winds down out of the Wag Water ravine into broad plains of sugar cane reminiscent of those on the Big Island of Hawaii.

Turn east when the road dead-ends

The "Junction" Road to Portland, left. Plant with exotic characteristics at Castleton.

at the Caribbean. **Annotto Bay** takes its name from an orange dye made from a Central American tree that presumably once grew in the area. The town, like most in north-coast Surrey, has a weather-beaten **train station** that hasn't been used since Hurricane Allen shredded Portland's railroad tracks in 1980. There's also an imaginatively structured **Baptist chapel** built in 1894, just beyond the market square.

You cross back into Surrey and the parish of Portland at **Windsor Castle**. Further east at **Buff Bay** is the junction with the sensational but torturous back route from Kingston. This road climbs up through Newcastle, then plummets 4,500 feet from Hardwar Gap to the Buff Bay River gorge.

Of Rats and Rafts

The road winds east, turning inland into thick, wet foliage, beyond **Spring Garden**. William Bancroft Espeut lived on an estate here where he introduced the mongoose in 1872. Plagued by cane-piece rats that annually damaged some 45,000 pounds worth of his sugar crop, Espeut imported nine mongooses from India. Although they ate the rats, they also preyed on birds, crabs, lizards, domestic stock and fruit and became as much of a pest as the rats. Wildlife experts blame the mongoose for nearly decimating the populations of coney and Jamaican iguana.

The only evidence of recent volcanic activity on the island is a low ridge about 600 feet high just beyond **Orange Bay**. It was formed by lava believed to have poured from a fissure in the earth.

You can take a dip in the cool clear waters of Somerset Falls near **Hope Bay**. There's a small admission charge here, a restaurant and changing facilities. Swim or take a boat beyond the small trickles at the top of the stair for a look at bigger, more secluded waterfalls in a blue-green grotto.

Another road swings inland at Hope Bay. It provides spectacular views of the Blue Mountains before rejoining the coast road at **St. Margaret's Bay**. Here, on the old **Burlington Estate** grounds, a tree exemplifies the region's fertility by growing out of the factory chimney.

A bridge crosses the **Rio Grande**, the island's largest river. Maroons and

Cruising the Rio Grande.

TANAGRELLA
RUFICOLLIS

other residents once floated bananas down the stream on long rafts. In the 1940s, Port Antonio's most notorious resident, movie idol Errol Flynn, arrived and began organizing raft races. The Earl of Mansfield later built the landing site, shops and restaurant at **Rafters Rest**.

A swift ride on a 30 foot-long raft has been one of Jamaica's major tourist attractions ever since. Licensed raftsmen, some of whom spent up to 10 years as apprentices, guide your craft through gentle rapids with long poles. The 2½ hour trip begins at **Berrydale**, north of Port Antonio off Red Hassel Road. About 150 rafts work the river, but it rarely appears crowded. The sight of mothers washing children or clothes, or kids swinging from vines along the banks, makes the trip an exotic adventure through time for most visitors.

The Rio Grande rises nearly 3,000 feet up into the mountainous interior of Portland. Torrential rainfalls often swell it beyond its banks. Portland's wet reputation results from the meeting of the moist northeast trade winds with the Blue Mountains. The winds, forced to rise, mix with ever-cooler air and form pregnant clouds. They drop most of their load here, leaving leeward areas like Kingston parched. As much as 300 inches of rain falls annually in parts of inland Portland.

Twin Harbors

Portland's rugged terrain long deterred settlement of this part of the island. Here, nature was so unbridled that early settlers may have felt threatened by its very presence. Even the Arawak Indians seem to have shunned Portland. No signs of their presence have been found here.

The first Europeans on the scene were the Spaniards. They named the Rio Grande and the twin harbors just east of it—Puerto San Francisco and Puerto Anton, from which Portland's principal city got its name. They are now known prosaically as **West Harbour** and **East Harbour**.

The Spaniards carved a few *hatos*, cattle ranches, out of the jungle, but made no serious strides toward settlement. Portland remained virtually unknown territory long after the British settled the rest of the island.

Port Antonio gateway.

The British created the parish of Portland in 1723. Fifty years later, Port Antonio had no more than 20 houses. The government offered free land and slaves, to prospective settlers, as well as seven years' freedom from land taxes, arrests or prosecutions. Two barrels of beef and one of flour would be given to everyone until they reaped their first crop. But only the most desperate took up the challenge, discouraged by heavy tropical downpours, the dense jungles, and the swampy, mosquito-infested coastline. Raids by the feared mountain Maroons also deterred pioneers.

To combat the invasions from Maroons or Spaniards, the British began building **Fort George** in 1729 on the peninsular bluff that juts into the harbors. Its 10-foot-thick masoned walls had spaces for 22 guns. The old barracks have now been turned into classrooms, and the parade grounds have become a playfield for the **Titchfield School** compound. The existing cannons date from a later period but are mounted on the original emplacements.

The island north of the school, originally intended as the site of the town, was also acquired by the British military. The navy established a formidable installation there, but only the name, **Navy Island**, lingers. The island became more famous when it was purchased in the 1940s by lusty Errol Flynn, whom Jamaicans fondly recall as having staged wild Hollywood parties there. The likes of Clara Bow, Bette Davis and Ginger Rogers became part of the Port Antonio scene.

Flynn is long gone and Port Antonio has settled back into its serene setting as a resort for visitors wanting to get away from the commercial tourist scenes at Ocho Rios and Montego Bay. Just south of Titchfield School on the peninsula is one of their favorite haunts, pink-and-purple-painted **DeMontevin Lodge**. Built circa 1898 at the corner of Fort George Street and Musgrave, the property is now operated by Mr. and Mrs. J. Mullings. If you don't intend to stay, you should at least sample one of Mrs. Mulling's authentic Jamaican meals of suckling pig, codfish and ackee, or lobster. Mrs. Mullings was once Flynn's cook. Phone in your order before you are ready to eat, however.

DeMontevin Lodge sits on "The

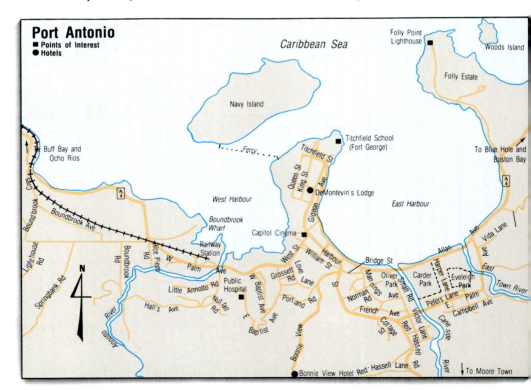

CYANOPTERUS
INORNATUS

Hill,'' once an exclusive residential area restricted by race, class and wealth. The British named the town Titchfield after the English estate of the Duke of Portland. The Hill became Upper Titchfield. The common people lived in Lower Titchfield along the seashore.

After the signing of a treaty with the Maroons in 1739, Titchfield grew more rapidly with the influx of sugar-cane money. By the end of the 18th Century, Portland had 38 large estates and more than 100 smaller ones. But while sugar readily grew in most of Jamaica's soil and climate, heavy rain took its toll. By 1854, only four estates remained; all had vanished by the turn of the century.

But another green crop saved Port Antonio from economic ruin. As the large estates dwindled, Jamaicans carved them into smaller plots where peasants began to grow yams and other ''ground provisions'' as root crops are called. They also began to grow bananas.

'Hey, Mr. Tallyman...'

The empty wharves and vacant warehouses of modern Port Antonio provide little evidence that this city was once the world's banana capital, the very stereotype of Harry Belafonte's Tallyman Town where men and women carried heavy banana bunches on their heads as they swayed and sang, ''Day-O.''

If you time your trip right, you may still see bananas being loaded at **Boundbrook Wharf** near the railroad crossing when you drive into town from the west. But they will have been packaged elsewhere, and will be loaded into the ships mechanically.

The Spanish brought the banana to the West Indies from the Canary Islands in 1516. The trade later was founded on a large, sweet, creamy fruit called the *Gros Michel* (and pronounced ''Gross Mitchell'' by Jamaicans). It can still be bought in the markets or on the roadside, but is no longer exported.

For the first 350 years after it arrived, the banana was disparaged as animal food. But canny Yankee sea captains loaded them green, watched them ripen on board ship, and found they could sell them for a profit on the eastern seaboard of the United States. Captain George Busch carried the first bunch of

Early view of Port Antonio.

bananas from Port Maria, west of Port Antonio, in 1869. Captain Lorenzo Dow Baker turned bananas into an industry in 1871 when he sold 1,450 stems at a US$2,000 profit in Boston. Baker organized Jamaicans to set up planting, collection and marketing systems among the peasants in Portland's interior. His effort grew into the Boston Fruit Company, later acquired by the giant United Fruit conglomerate.

With fleets of empty banana boats traveling to Jamaica to pick up bananas, the enterprising Baker filled them with tourists seeking refuge from harsh winters, simultaneously touching off Port Antonio's tourist trade. He built the first Titchfield Hotel on "The Hill" in 1905.

Bananas became big business in Port Antonio. In the town's heyday, weekly sailings of banana boats were said to exceed weekly departures from the big British port in Liverpool. One American writer, visiting in 1920, said he "chanced to reach Port Antonio at the very height of a banana war. The two powerful older companies had determined to annihilate a new one by that simple little method of starving it to death."

The arrival of a ship in those days was signalled by the blowing of a conch shell. All hands rushed to the fields to cut down mature fruit with machetes. Then they wrapped it in banana "trash," or dried leaves, for its journey to the docks.

The banana plant is a giant herb with a stem formed by overlapping leaf bases. The mature plant sends out a large purple bud which reveals rows of tiny flowers when it opens. The flowers fall off, leaving behind small "fingers." Each one grows into a banana. A cluster of fingers forms a "hand," and several hands make up a bunch.

When bananas were unloaded from trucks, a long line of workers would carry them past two checkers who took a "stem count" of each bunch. Nine hands or more were considered a "bunch;" eight hands were a three-quarter bunch; seven hands were half a bunch. Anything less was rejected. "Six hand, seven hand, eight hand, bunch!" as the song says. When a carrier walked the line, he received a metal disc showing the bunch count. This was redeemable later. Another long human chain,

ACANTHYLIS
COLLARIS

View toward Titchfield from DeMontevin's Lodge, below; and banana man.

this one mainly female, carried the bunches aboard the truck. Here the famed "tallyman" of song gave each carrier a "tally" to be redeemed.

The plaintive songs of banana workers were very real reflections on their lives. "Mi back dis a bruck with the bare exhaustion," they sang as they carried heavy loads from dawn to dusk, earning only 25 to 70 cents per day. Portland-born Evan Jones, screenwriter of *Funeral in Berlin* and other movies, wrote in his poem "Song of the Banana Man":

Thank God and this big right hand
I will live and die a banana man.

Devastating hurricanes and Panama Disease eventually crippled the banana industry. The trade passed temporarily into the hands of large operators who had the means to control the disease; today, it is back in the hands of small to medium-sized growers. The government controls marketing and shipping. Bananas continue to be a major crop, but the days of "Come Mr. Tallyman, tally me banana" have ended.

Many varieties of the banana and its fat cousin, the plantain, can be sampled at the **Town Market**. Just follow your nose and the crowds to the clutter and color opposite the cenotaph on West Street. Port Antonio's best food market days are Thursday and Saturday.

The Bonnie View From Bonnie View

From ground level, particularly around the market, Port Antonio displays a dingy, dusty, lived-in look. But a drive up Richmond Hill changes all that. Follow the signs to the **Bonnie View Hotel**. Built in 1943 as a honeymoon retreat, the hotel's chief attraction has always been its view. Here, the noise of the city vanishes in the hill air, and gives way to sweeping panoramas of Port Antonio, its twin harbors, Navy Island and Portland.

Some consider it charming, others annoying, that Port Antonio lacks a synthetic infrastructure to stimulate its tourist trade. There is a rejuvenation program in the works, however, calling for the creation of a pedestrian mall for artists and craftsmen, a new market, and a fountain in the square to be donated by Patrice Wymore Flynn in memory of her late husband.

Mrs. Flynn balked at allowing her

Maroons in Moore Town, about 1920.

160

Anglican
Churchyard,
Moore
Town.

husband's remains to be buried in Port Antonio as he had wished, to the dismay of Jamaicans who still delight in relating tales about the star. He was buried instead in Forest Lawn cemetery in Hollywood.

But Mrs. Flynn later returned to the area and has lived ever since at the Flynn ranch. Situated on Priestman's River near Boston Bay, the ranch is surrounded by fields of coconuts, pineapples, pimentos, bananas and about 2,000 head of cattle. She is considering opening the ranch to the public and creating a museum of memorabilia from her husband's movies, letters and photographs.

The Maroons of Moore Town

One worthwhile side trip from Port Antonio takes you to **Moore Town**, the capital of the Windward Maroons' community. Before you go, try to contact Col. C.L.G. Harris, the leader of this proud, secretive people, or the trip could prove pointless. If he agrees to meet you and introduce you to Moore Town and his people's fabled history, prepare for a rocky, 10-mile ride up a steep, winding dirt road into the John Crow Mountains.

Take Sommers Town Road behind Port Antonio. Watch for Maroons carrying bananas in the traditional headsling. Turn left at the town of **Fellowship**. Through **Newington** and **Windsor**, you will be struck by the wild blends of river, vegetation and mountains. Turn left again at **Seaman's Valley**. The last small dirt road leads to Moore Town.

As you enter on your left, there's an **Anglican Church** fronted by a serene graveyard. The church, one of seven in Moore Town, is the community's oldest building.

A bridge crosses the **Wildcane (Negro) River**. Col. Harris lives in the one-story cement house on the right, next to the Post Office. He is a full-blooded Maroon, educated in Moore Town's All-Age School and a graduate of Kingston's Mico College. He retired from teaching in 1980, but to many Maroons he will always be "Teacher Harris" as well as Colonel.

Moore Town's school is the low rambling set of buildings on your left. More than a century old, it has an enrollment of about 300 children aged six to 15 years. **Bump Grave** is across from the school, a simple stone monument where lies the body of national hero Nanny, the founder of the town and legendary chieftainess of the Windward Maroons. Here, the flagpole flies the Maroon flag next to the Jamaican flag. **Cornwall Barracks**, another Maroon settlement under the Colonel's jurisdiction, lies across the river.

Maroons from throughout the region—from Comfort Castle, Ginger House and Seaman's Valley—travel to Moore Town annually to celebrate Nanny's canonization as a National Hero in 1975. The *abeng* horns and Coromantee drums call them here. *Kumina* dances last long into the night and stories of old are told. Colonel Harris will point out a trapezoid-shaped bump, high up on the Blue Mountain Ridge to the northwest, believed to be the site of the legendary **Nanny Town**.

A Rich Man's Folly

Brooding **Christ Church** on Port Antonio's Harbour Street is a neo-Romanesque style Anglican Church built in 1840 by English architect

Annesley Voysey. The Boston Fruit Company donated its lectern in 1900.

East of East Harbour rises another fascinating bit of Parthenon-type architecture now simply called **Folly**. It is the subject of a favorite romantic legend. As the story goes, a rich man built the mansion for his bride. He stocked its gardens with flowers, birds and animals—all of them white—then brought his lady to Jamaica for the honeymoon. Just as he carried her over the threshold, the concrete that had been foolishly mixed with sea water began to crumble. So did the rich man's dreams. His bride burst into tears at the omen and fled, never to return to him or his mansion.

In reality, a Connecticut jeweler named Alfred Mitchell built the mansion in 1905 and lived there occasionally with his family until his death in 1912. His wife, one of the Tiffanys of New York, was already a grandmother when they moved in. The building began to fall apart in the 1930s. Salt air rusted the steel reinforcement rods and the roof caved in.

What local people are already calling **Folly II** stands unfinished and uninha-

bited just east of Port Antonio. The castle-like mansion was begun several years ago by a European baroness who reportedly has encountered some financial problems.

The Price of Paradise

East of Port Antonio, several high-priced hotels have cloaked themselves in some of Jamaica's most splendid scenery. You will first pass the **Trident**, an elaborate reincarnation of a regional favorite that succumbed to Hurricane Allen. This new hotel sprawls along the rocky, volcanic coast offering luxurious suites and villas and a four-room chateau that rents for US $2,000 per day. Owner Earl Levy plans to open a seven-bedroom castle nearby that will rent for substantially more.

Port Antonio's old reputation as a playground for the rich and famous was built on the likes of Errol Flynn, Rudyard Kipling, William Randolph Hearst, Jazz king Paul Whiteman and billionaire J.P Morgan, who came here each year on his *Corsair II*.

In 1956, Canadian biscuit heir Garfield Weston opened a resort that

EGRETT
RUFICOL

Folly,
below.
Cannon at
French-
man's
Cove, right

further enhanced this area's elite aura. **Frenchman's Cove**, tucked back from the road in a magnificent setting on the lava rock cliff, is a cottage-style colony. In its glory days, the luxury cottage rented for £1,000 a week, a fortune in the '50s. For that price, everything a vacationer could possibly want—and then some—was included: personal servants, all food and drink, sports equipment and activities, a golf cart for zipping around the expansive grounds, caviar flown in from Russia, French champagne, and free airplane rides up and down the coast. Author V.S. Naipaul spent several days here in 1962 and wrote in *The Middle Passage*: "Within 24 hours my interest in food and drink disappeared. Everything was at the end of the telephone, and it was my duty to have exactly what I wanted. But how could I be sure what I wanted best?"

The glory didn't last. Frenchman's Cove eventually went bankrupt. Part of it has been reopened at modest rates.

As you round a bend along the water beyond Frenchman's Cove, you will see the kind of picturesque island you thought existed only in the movies.

Monkey Island, also called Pellew Island, no longer has any monkeys. But you can swim or boat to it across the unimaginably blue waters of **San San Bay** but beware of sea urchins.

Just a half-mile further, bear left past palatial private villas to the **Blue Hole** a.k.a. Blue Lagoon. Its intense natural color is a result of the depth of the lagoon, estimated by realists at 210 feet and by romanticists as bottomless. The area is good for swimming, snorkeling or picnicking. A glass-bottomed boat operates from the cove. Fine hotels here include **Dragon Bay**, with its lily ponds, almond trees, dragon fountain and private beach, and **Jamaica Hill**, back from the beach but with a glorious clifftop view.

Spelunkers can wander up into the hills beyond **Sherwood Forest** to the **Nonsuch Caves**. They are dry and easily negotiated with the aid of guides.

Boston Bay beyond the Blue Hole is a "must" stop for gourmands of uniquely Jamaican cuisine. Here the local people make what is reputed to be the island's best Jerk Pork. This delicacy was the creation of Maroons who seasoned a pig with wild herbs, pimento or allspice and

MELLISUGA
HUMILIS

Monkey
Island, San
San Bay.

pit-barbecued it on an aromatic green sapling. Jerking takes several hours, so you probably won't be able to buy any before mid-morning. And most will have been eaten by mid-afternoon.

Mrs. Flynn's **Priestman's River Plantation** lies a few miles east of Boston Bay. From here, the road winds around rocky cliffs slapped by waves, through small villages full of wide-eyed people, and past outcroppings of dense rainforest, all reminiscent of Maui's Hana Coast. Enjoy the scenery until you reach **Manchioneal**.

From here, you can also reach **Reach Falls**. Take the turnoff just before the Driver's River bridge, then continue a mile or two inland until you come to a fork in the rocky road. A hand-scrawled sign will direct you to the spot. It's a tricky walk down stone stairs carved into a cliff to the bottom. Few tourists venture to this out-of-the-way spot, so except for the inevitable local guides and a free-lance mento drummer, you are likely to have the lovely cool water and falls all to yourself. Climb up into the caves under the falls for a look.

When the United Nations drew up a "national physical plan" for Jamaica in 1970, the committee members found the Manchioneal area so magnificent that the establishment of a coastal wilderness area was recommended.

Quakers and Africans

On top of the hill east of Manchioneal is the **Happy Grove School**, founded by Quakers for East Indian sugar workers in 1898. Soon after, you leave the parish of Portland and cross into St. Thomas. The transition is appropriate, as the scenery begins to change. The plains at the island's eastern tip are laden with palm and sugar cane, an impressive view of which is available as the road winds down **Quaw Hill**.

Turn off at **Golden Grove** onto a long road that leads to **Morant Point Lighthouse**. Built in 1841, the 100-foot-high cast-iron structure is listed by the Jamaica National Trust as a historic monument. Engineer George Grove is better known to musicians as the author of *Grove's Dictionary of Music and Musicians*.

Labor for the lighthouse construction was provided by Kru men from Africa. They were among the 11,400 free Afri-

Villas on the Blue Hole.

cans who were brought to Jamaica after emancipation. Many landed in Morant Bay and settled in the St. Thomas hinterland, especially around the Plantain Garden River Valley.

Jamaicans today regard St. Thomas as the parish where the African heritage is strongest. Here, the ancestor worship cult of *kumina* flourishes.

The Settling of St. Thomas

Among St. Thomas' many historical relics are the overgrown ruins of the oldest house in Jamaica—**Stokes Hall**, slightly off the highway near Golden Grove. In 1656, Government Luke Stokes, seeking colonists, attracted 1,000 settlers from the Leeward islands of Nevis and St. Kitts. Less than three months later, Stokes and his wife died, along with two-thirds of the other pioneers. The disease-ridden Morant swamps had taken their toll. But Stokes' three sons survived, and although all were under age 15 at the time, they prospered. One is believed to have erected Stokes Hall. Like many plantation houses, it was built with loopholes through which guns could be fired in case of attack, a grim reminder of those hard times.

Continue on A4 to **Bowden** and **Port Morant**, both busy harbors in the days of sugar and bananas. Port Morant was guarded by **Fort Lindsay** (now in ruins) on Morant Point and **Fort William** on the other side. Bowden, on the eastern end of the harbor, gave its name to the **Bowden Formation**, which has yielded extensive fossil remains from the late Miocene geological period. Several hundred species of marine shells have been discovered in this formation.

The Legacy of Morant Bay

At Port Morant beaches like **Lyssons** and **Roselle**, you can mingle with the people of St. Thomas. The shores swing toward Kingston in soft undulating curves quite different from the jagged beauty of the Portland coast.

The parish capital at **Morant Bay** was the site of the famous rebellion of 1865. The bloody reprisals in which national heroes Paul Bogle and George William Gordon were executed, along with hundreds of other residents, live on in a dramatic **Statue of Bogle** that

Rugged Portland Coast near Manchioneal.

166

MERULA
JAMAICENSIS

dominates the town square. Created by Edna Manley, the sculpture depicts a defiant Bogle clutching a machete in a crucifix pose.

The statue stands in front of the **Courthouse**, a reconstruction of the one burned out during the rebellion. Gordon and 18 others were hanged from a boom in front of the courthouse, while Bogle and his brother were hanged from the center arch of the gutted building.

Seventy-nine skeletons were found behind the wall of the old **Morant Bay Fort**, behind the courthouse, during excavations in 1965. A mass grave and monument have been installed under the fort cannons. The fort dates to 1773, but the three cannons were installed early in the 19th Century. The **Parish Church** nearby was built in 1881.

Today, Morant Bay has turned into a quiet town with unusual street names like Soul Street and Debtor's Lane.

Curing a 'Depraved Appetite'

For a pleasant side trip into inland St. Thomas, take the road from Morant Bay through **Airy Castle** to the Bath Spa

and Botanic Gardens. The mineral bath opened in 1699 after a runaway slave discovered it and claimed it had cured chronic ulcers on his legs. The government bought the spring and 1,300 acres of surrounding land, and immediately it began to record cases of cures. A Mr. Watson had a "dry bellyache eased by the first draught of the water," and a Mr. Gordon was cured of "lowness of spirit and a depraved appetite."

The mineral baths do have therapeutic value for treating rheumatic ailments and skin diseases. Hot water reaching 128° F and "cold" water at 115° F miraculously pour from the same igneous rocks above the Sulphur River, and are mixed in the baths to proper bathing temperature. They contain high percentages of lime and sulfur.

Once known as the Bath of St. Thomas the Apostle, little of the spa's early splendor remains today. But the spring continues to attract health addicts from around the world. Nearby is the Western Hemisphere's second oldest botanical garden, established in 1779. The breadfruit trees in one corner are offsprings of those brought from Tahiti in 1793 by Captain William Bligh of

Former Holland Estate in St. Thomas near Morant Point, 19th Century.

Bounty fame.

From Morant Bay, the highway traverses Jamaica's longest span, **Busta-mante Bridge** across the Morant River. The arid district of **Yallahs** provides a dusty change of scenery. The huge **Yal-lahs Ponds**, south of the highway, are separated from the sea by an arm of land. They have twice the salinity of sea water and provided salty supplies for early settlers.

Jamaican folklore claims two of the three ponds were formed years ago, when two brothers argued so fiercely over how to divide a piece of land that their plots sank and filled with sea wa-ter. At times, the water turns red and gives off an overpowering stench. Legend blames it on the blood of slaves once drowned in the ponds. Scientists attribute the mystery to a bacteria in-fected by virus.

The **Yallahs River** is usually a mere riverbed filled with enormous boulders. But it can become a raging torrent during the rainy season, since its source lies 4,500 feet up in the Blue Moun-tains. A huge landslip upriver occurred when a mountain fell into the valley during the 1692 earthquake. A 1,000-foot escarpment left behind is called **Judgment Cliff** because the rubble buried a plantation belonging to a wick-ed Dutchman—or so say the locals. The best view of the cliff is from **Easington**.

The road soon bends back into beautiful valleys, the foothills of the Blue Mountains. At the hamlet of **Eleven Miles**, look for the roadside marker commemorating Three Finger Jack. This Jamaican Robin Hood was courtly to ladies and the poor, but cruel to male travelers and British soldiers. He pillaged until his death at the hands of the Maroons in 1781. The Maroons cut off the head and the famous hand that gave Three Finger Jack his name. They preserved them in rum, then car-ried their gruesome trophies back to Kingston to claim a reward.

Evening light falls upon these moun-tain roads like a sprinkle of dew. The road bottoms out at **Bull Bay**, home of a community of fervent Rastafarians. A road from the city leads up to the small but lovely **Cane River Falls**.

Wickie Wackie and **Copacabana Beach** are disappointing dirt slivers. Harbour View's popular drive-in and Kingston lie just beyond.

SYLVICOLA
PANNOSA

Town square, Morant Bay below. Eye contact at Reach Falls, right.

THE COUNTY OF MIDDLESEX

Middlesex, as its name implies, spans the heartland of the island. Its attractions run the gamut of the Jamaican experience: from the commercial tourism center of Ocho Rios to history-rich Spanish Town, from industrial hubs like May Pen and Mandeville to sparsely-inhabited strips of wild terrain around Alligator Pond and Gut River.

There are also the "Northern Reaches, Sandy Beaches" of the parishes of **St. Mary** and **St. Ann**. Coastal towns here rely heavily on the influx of foreign visitors. On these tourist-oriented stretches, Jamaicans no longer blink at the sight of pale-skinned people surging through the streets in Bermuda shorts and flowered shirts. But inland a few miles, the hotels and their trappings vanish. Cows and sugar cane take over a landscape studded with intriguingly named places like Walker's Wood and Golden Grove and Cave Valley.

"Spanish Town and South Middlesex" are another matter. The only hotels here are small local establishments. Otherwise, it's a wide-open land of unexplored enchantments where you can spy on the gentle giant of the sea, the manatee, and bathe in a spa more radioactive than any in Europe. Children peddle pouches of delicious raw cashew nuts along the railway tracks near Old Harbour. Fishermen will sell you enormous lobsters just caught off the dusty beach at Rocky Point.

Three parishes comprise the southern part of Middlesex: **St. Catherine**, where Spanish Town looks much as it did in the days when the British still ruled; **Clarendon**, rich in the traditions of Pocomania around its capital of May Pen; and **Manchester**, spread out across a rolling mountain plateau pock-marked by bauxite mines. Acres of sugar cane and citrus bind these parishes together and sustain them.

Northern Reaches, Sandy Beaches

The northern region of the county of Middlesex reflects two sides of Jamaica. There is the beach-fringed coast where fishing villages huddle between the major tourist resorts and modern hotels. Then, there is the interior, tourist-free small towns and hamlets where Jamaicans earn a simple, but seemingly adequate, living from the soil.

Both sides of this intriguing heartland can be explored on solid roads. Routes A1 and A3 skirt the coast and Route B11 winds inland almost parallel to this coast. A tangle of crossroads connect the routes, so you can drive any portion of the region without having to double back. Along the coast, you will find tourist meccas and Columbus country, as well as the town where James Bond, Agent 007, was born. The inland roads offer glimpses into typical Jamaican lifestyles and hills full of raw scenery.

At the core of this part of the county lies one of Jamaica's premier travel destinations, **Ocho Rios**. You may wish to make your "base camp" in one of its plush hotels or villas, or perhaps in more modest accommodations, as you wander into other parts of northern Middlesex on jaunts of a day or two.

The most popular route to Ocho Rios from Kingston follows A1 through Spanish Town, along the lovely Rio Cobre river, through Linstead and Ewarton with its massive Alcan bauxite complex, then up **Mount Diablo** and down into the parish of St. Ann. At the crest of the mountain, you will look into an enormous red earthen sea, one of the unfortunate legacies of a bauxite-mining industry that has otherwise brought a measure of prosperity to the lives of many Jamaicans. Just before, you will come to a wide-open tract that is a popular spot to stop, stretch your legs, and fill your belly with saltfish, yams, corn and fresh fruit from roadside chefs and vendors.

Past **Moneague**, where Route A1 forks west to an inland route covered later in this chapter, you follow A3 into **Walker's Wood**. This area lives up to its name with a Tolkienesque setting of rounded hills, pastures and valleys criss-

Preceding pages: Falling flowers near Walker's Wood; Ocho Rios. Below, Fern Gully.

SEIURUS
OVEBORACENSIS

crossed by stone walls. The British countryside couldn't look more British. Take the road to **Friendship Farm**. It offers a routine farm tour, but also incomparable views of the storybook scenery from its handsome Great House and swimming pool.

Two miles past the farm on A3, you suddenly plunge from daylight into semi-darkness down the roller-coaster ride of **Fern Gully**. Once a river bed, dense growths of ferns and trees blanket the road and block the sun. But don't allow the surreal scene to distract you from the tricky drive. The road is often slippery and its corners are sharp, so low gear is recommended. Its fern population has diminished some, probably because of vandals and car exhaust fumes, but Fern Gully still pleases the senses.

Ocho Rios: Cruise Capital

Billboards announcing the American chain hotels and Kentucky Fried Chicken fast-food franchises bring you out of Fern Gully and back to 20th Century reality. You have entered Ocho Rios, the navel of island tourism. Ocho Rios

is hardly a town; it is more like a village mugged by tourist development. Its hotels, houses and shops are haphazardly strung out along the coastal strip.

Ocho Rios' name is not what it purports to be. There are not eight rivers in the town, although its Spanish translation might suggest that. In fact, its original name in *español* was *Las Chorreras*, "the waterfalls," obviously a reference to the magnificent Dunn's River cascades just west of town. Apparently, English settlers heard wrong and applied elementary Spanish. It's been called Ocho Rios ever since.

Ocho Rios' only historical claim to fame is as the lair of pirate John Davis. Rich area planters were said to have subsidized Davis' rape-and-plunder expeditions, which included sacking the city of St. Augustine in Florida. The only reminder of those days are the walls and cannon of an old fort, buried in dust from the Reynolds bauxite terminal next to it.

The town's growth as a magnet for tourists began in the 1950s. That reputation has accelerated in recent years: Ocho Rios has surpassed Montego Bay and Port Antonio to become Jamaica's

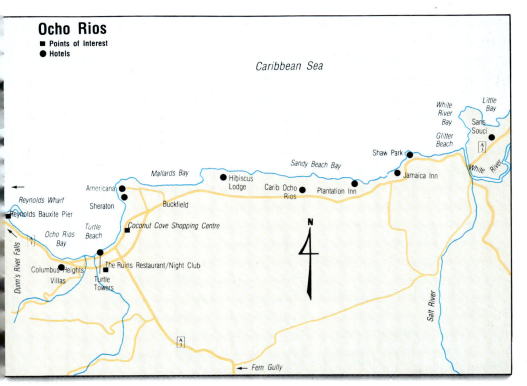

top cruise ship destination. It's an attraction in itself to rise early in the morning to watch the enormous luxury liners taxiing into a berth at the wharf near the bauxite terminal. Passengers are usually greeted in "Love Boat" style by an old mento or calypso band and dancers. Two of the monstrous ships often moor in Ocho Rios Bay at the same time. Their arrival turns sleepy Ocho Rios into an anthill of activity. Higglers, craftsmen, taxi drivers and mini-van operators all jockey for good positions from which to be the first to offer their wares or services to free-spending cruise passengers.

Scaling the Falls

For a John Crow's view of Ocho Rios, try **Shaw Park Gardens** up the hill to the west of A3 as you enter town from Fern Gully. These landscaped grounds were once the setting for the old Shaw Park Hotel, since closed but resurrected as the Shaw Park Beach far below these heights. There are also a variety of trees and flowers, a rushing stream and waterfalls.

But the premier attraction of Ocho

Rios—and probably of the entire island—drops 600 feet to the seacoast in a series of cascades two miles west of the town center. **Dunn's River Falls** have been delighting visitors since the Spanish arrived. They are the most spectacular of a series of waterfalls that gush from lush, wooded limestone cliffs along this ridge. A large park, full of snack bars, souvenir stands and wood-carvers' shops, has grown up around these falls. But the tradition at Dunn's River Falls is to climb them.

Stairs lead downhill through a tunnel under Route A1 to a beach where you can check your clothes and valuables in a locker. You must purchase a ticket; this entitles you to climb with (or without) an official guide. It's a common sight to see a guide, his dreadlocks dangling among the dozens of cameras strung around his neck, leading a daisy chain of tourists up the rocks, through the falls to the top.

Take the climb slowly, checking your footing. The rocks are slick in spots and the torrents of water powerful enough to send you plummeting backwards. There are several spots along the way where you can exit back to dry land if

"Love Boat," Mallard's Beach.

the climb becomes too tiring.

A smaller but much less crowded spot for showering in a waterfall is located less than a mile west of Dunn's River by the hydroelectric station. The best section of **Roaring River** falls on a private property called **Laughing Waters**. Scenes for the first of the James Bond secret agent epics, *Dr. No*, were shot here.

Rum and Jasmine

The other prime draw in Ocho Rios is its strand of white sand. **Turtle Beach** turns into **Mallard's Beach** at the high-rise **Sheraton** and **Americana** hotels. At night, you can reggae with Jamaicans at the **Decade** disco or indulge in the romantic setting of **The Ruins** night club, where music plays against the background of a waterfall.

Route A3 twists and turns east through Ocho Rios' most pleasant area. Here, hotels like the **Plantation Inn**, **Carib Ocho Rios** and the **Sans Souci** nestle amid the trees and nudge the rocky coast. One of the grandest old lodgings is the **Jamaica Inn** perched on a cliff above a secluded slice of beach.

Here, time has stopped. Waiters in white coats serve you rum punch; trade winds trickle through the trees; and the scent of jasmine fills the air.

Continue east to the **White River**. Once lined with handsome Jamaica tall palms, the mysterious Lethal Yellowing disease has taken its toll. Only the trunks of the trees remain. They look like warped telephone poles, their crowns of palms lopped off by the disease. The frondless trunks now give the river an eerie appearance. Jamaicans are replacing their rapidly dwindling tall palm population with the sturdier, but less attractive, Malayan Dwarf. The stumps of dead trees are being processed into parquet flooring.

Tuesday and Saturday nights, exotic torches burn along the bank for "A Night on the White River." Guests get a romantic cruise down the stream to a clearing where there is a dinner, drinks, a show and dancing.

A signposted road near the river leads inland one mile to the grounds of **Prospect Estate**. It opens daily for tours of its banana plantation and cassava crop, the White River gorge, **Sir Harold's Viewpoint** over the coast, and

Dunn's River
Falls "daisy
chain."

a lane of memorial trees planted by such notables as Winston Churchill, Noel Coward, Charlie Chaplin and Canadian Prime Minister Pierre Trudeau. Prospect Estate takes young men from poor backgrounds and trains them as "cadets" who live and work on the estate while learning useful skills.

East of White River, Annabella Ogden has handsomely restored **Harmony Hall** great house. Inside, you will find a bar, a restaurant and a gallery where you can buy work by some of Jamaica's leading artists and craftsmen.

Couples, for Couples

Across the road, commanding another nice beach on the turquoise waters of the Caribbean, rises **Couples**, formerly the Tower Isle Hotel. Couples boasts the distinction of having the highest year-round hotel occupancy in Jamaica, an astounding rate of more than 95 percent. Its popularity stems from its club-style plan: one reasonable price includes accommodations, all meals and snacks, side trips, the use of water sports equipment, entertainment, even all drinks and cigarettes.

Unlike its Negril affiliate, Hedonism II, however, only couples are permitted here. A marriage certificate is not necessary, although the management will supply wedding services as part of its package for those who impulsively decide to tie the knot. Ceremonies are performed on the tiny offshore island with the tower—after suntanning hours. During the day, the island is strictly reserved for those who prefer to swim and sunbathe in the nude. Couples earned a flurry of publicity when it opened with its advertising poster of two lions, one a well-endowed female, mating.

From Couples, Route A3 continues down the increasingly scenic coast. **Rio Nueva** is the spot where Great Britain finalized its claim on Jamaica in June 1658 by routing Spanish guerrilla leader Ysassi and his men from a stockade above the river mouth. A small monument marks the site of the last battle.

A side road that leads south from here, Route B13, provides a picturesque tour past banana plantations up the Rio Nuevo valley to **Retreat**, where a suspension footbridge straddles the river. The beautiful old **Holy Trinity**

The view from Noel Coward's room at Firefly.

Church and an abandoned sugar mill lie further on. The road climbs to **Gayle** and **Guy's Hill**, where there's a junction with a road to **Highgate**.

James Bond, Bird-watcher

East of Rio Nueva, Route A3 enters Jamaica's most lovely coastal country. The gorgeous seascapes extend all the way to Manchioneal at the eastern end of the island. The first point of interest is in **Oracabessa**, "Golden Head"— from the Spanish words *oro* for gold and *cabeza* for head. Opposite an Esso gas station north of the main road is a small lane leading to a beach lined with traditional dugout canoes. Imposing gateposts, surmounted by black wood-carved pineapples, mark the entrance to an old home that gave birth to the world's most famous, albeit fictional secret agent: "007," otherwise known as James Bond.

The home is called **Goldeneye**. For many years, it was owned by Ian Fleming, author of the 13 James Bond novels that have sold more than 18 million copies in 23 languages. Fleming wintered here from 1946 until his death in 1964. Ironically, he borrowed the name for his secret agent from a most unlikely source. In *Ian Fleming Introduces Jamaica*, he explained:

I was looking for a name for my hero—nothing like Peregrine Carruthers or "Standfast" Maltravers—and I found it, on the cover of one of my Jamaican bibles, *Birds of the West Indies* by James Bond, an ornithological classic. ... Would these books have been born if I had not been living in the gorgeous vacuum of a Jamaican holiday? I doubt it.

You too can drink in the inspirations that fueled the Fleming imagination by renting the three-bedroom Goldeneye (from Mrs. Braham in Port Maria, telephone 994–2282) and sitting at the very desk where it all happened. Celebrities the likes of Truman Capote, Graham Greene, Stephen Spender and Evelyn Waugh have done the same.

The literary juices of yet another famous author and playwright flowed just down the coast from Oracabessa near the city of Port Maria. Watch for the sign that directs you off A3 and up a rutted dirt road to **Firefly**. Here, the master of dry British wit, Noel Coward, spent many of the last 23 years of his life. This modest house commands a priceless hilltop panorama that inspired Coward's song, "A Room With a View."

The house is now maintained by the National Trust. Coward's butler, Miguel Fraser, will show you books, records, manuscripts and paintings that litter the small rooms much as they did when Coward died here on March 26, 1973. During his years at Firefly, Coward entertained the likes of the Queen Mother of England and her daughter, Princess Margaret. He is buried in a simple grave protected by a huge white cage in an idyllic spot on the crest behind the house.

From Port to Plantation

A few yards below Firefly is a derelict limestone building reputed to have been a "pirate kitchen" for Sir Henry Morgan. It has musket-firing slits and an escape tunnel that suggest some military use.

East of Firefly, **Port Maria** springs up after you round a rocky cliff. It has the standard town trappings—a courthouse built in 1820 and a church that dates

Relaxing on Port Maria monument.

from 1861. A bridge joins a noisy shopping section of town to a quiet residential area. A sign at the church gates points you to the **Tacky Monument** that commemorates the leader of the Easter slave rebellion of 1760.

One worthwhile side trip from Port Maria leads up Route B13 to **Brimmer Hall** and its plantation tour. Here, you can ride a tour wagon through acres of banana, coconut, pimento and other crops. You can also tour the great house, have a Jamaican lunch of curry goat or ackee and sal' fish, and take a swim in the pool.

Beyond Port Maria, A3 curves back inland through thick rainforests. Look for the shop near **Whitehall** where a Rastaman sells solid cast-iron pots. Whitehall also marks the junction with Route B2, an off-the-beaten track drive through the country to Bog Walk and then back to Kingston or Ocho Rios. Alternatively, you can take the Junction Road that breaks off to Kingston just before reaching Annotto Bay; or you can continue east on to Portland and Port Antonio. The road west from Ocho Rios passes Dunn's River Falls and Roaring River.

West of Ocho Rios

Take Route A3 west past the **Eden 2 Hotel**, with a ceiling in its round bar that is festooned with all sizes and shapes of straw hats, then swing by **Drax Hall**, the north coast's polo center. Polo was, of course, imported by the British colonial elite. In fact, Prince Charles still plays here—or at the Caymanas Polo Field in Kingston on occasion. Now the game is open to any Jamaican who has a horse, however.

Prior to reaching **St. Ann's Bay**, the road transits plantations of elegant coconut palms that have thus far managed to resist the blight of Lethal Yellowing. These palms mark the approaches to **Seville Nueva**, the first Spanish settlement in Jamaica.

We are now entering Columbus Country. In fact, foreign research scientists are working with the Jamaican government to find the hulks of the last two caravels abandoned here by Columbus in 1504. The government also plans to reconstruct Spanish townsite ruins with an archaeological park at the **Seville Estate**.

EUPHONI
JAMAICA

Port Maria
as it looked
about 1830.

The modern history of Jamaica began near present-day St. Ann's Bay, just north of the junction of routes A1 and A3. The town has been bypassed by the new trunk road (the **A.G.R. Byfield Highways**), but it makes for a worthwhile detour to this pleasant parish capital.

The **Courthouse** on the main street, next to the **Parish Church**, was built about 1866. Beyond the town on the landward side of the road is a **Statue of Columbus**, cast in his native town of Genoa, Italy. Behind the statue is a **Catholic Church**. It was built in 1939 of stones from a variety of local sources, including those from the ruins of the original Spanish Church of Peter Martyr, which stood slightly west of the present church. Peter Martyr of Anghiera was a 16th Century soldier-turned-priest who authored a book about the New World—but never set foot in Jamaica.

A more fitting island tribute is the **Marcus Garvey Monument** fronting the town library. Garvey was born in St. Ann's Bay in 1887 and has been elevated to National Hero status because of his work in developing among black people a sense of pride and identity in their African heritage.

Route A1 swings south into the mountains from St. Ann's Bay to **Claremont**, a bauxite center once called Finger Post. It proceeds to Moneague, where roads connect to Kingston or Ocho Rios.

A detour from Claremont leads some five miles to the town of **Pedro**, where Jamaica's most macabre ruin stands. In the hill tower of **Edinburgh Castle** lived Lewis Hutchinson, a sadistic red-haired Scotsman. In the 1760s, this ex-medical student murdered more than 40 travelers by shooting them from the slit windows of his tower. The bodies were robbed and decapitated; they are thought to have been thrown down a nearby sinkhole. Hutchinson was captured while trying to board a ship offshore. He was unrepentant. Before being hanged, he left £100 for the erection of a monument to himself with the requested inscription to read: "Their sentence, pride and malice I defy. Despise their power, and like a Roman I die." The monument was not erected.

The ruins of the first Spanish settlement in Jamaica at Seville Nueva lie just

Brimmer
Hall
Plantation.

west of St. Ann's Bay. After crossing the river, take the dirt road behind the gate that crosses the seaward side of the main road. Castle ruins have been discovered to the right of the road, while the remains of a Spanish sugar mill, surely the island's first, are strewn to the left of the road. These buildings are believed to have been some of the few structures constructed in the settlement before the Spanish decided to pack up and relocate their capital at Villa de la Vega, the modern-day Spanish Town. Beyond this cradle of modern Jamaican history, Route Al continues through the sugar cane country of **Priory** and the **Llandovery Central Factory** to **Laughlands**.

Runaway Bay, so-called because the last Spaniards allegedly left Jamaica from here after their final defeat by the British, is a booming tourist area. On entering, you'll find a settlement of small conical habitations, like a Hottentot housing scheme. This is **Club Caribbean**, tourist accommodations with individual cottages arranged around a central clubhouse that contains a restaurant and bar. Next is the **Jamaica, Jamaica! Hotel**, one of the most expensive in the area. It has an 18-hole golf course, followed by a string of smaller hotels and guest houses. **Eaton Hall** is notable for being built on the foundations of an old English fort, complete with an underground passage to the cliffs. The **Jack Tar Village** is a lively newcomer to Runaway Bay.

Beaches and hotels are Runaway Bay's claim to fame. As a town, it is non-existent. Much of it occupies **Cardiff Hall**, a vast estate granted to one of Jamaica's first British settlers.

Well-signposted beyond are the **Runaway Caves** and **Green Grotto**, the most accessible of Jamaica's large limestone caves. Guided tours take in some of the $1\frac{1}{2}$ miles of caverns, and include a sail across an eerie grotto 120 feet below the earth's surface. Discreet lighting brings out the grotesque beauty of the stalactites and stalagmites. A fascinating property of some formations is that they are hollow. The guide, by cunningly striking them with a stick, coaxes primitive music from them! Outside the caves is a 160-foot-deep lagoon.

Discovery Bay, five miles further on is slowly developing under the stimulus of

Marcus Garvey, St. Ann's son, left. Polo at Drax Hall about 1920, right.

YPSELUS NIGER

Carreras
tobacco
farm.

the Kaiser bauxite operation. But many tourists are put off by the presence of the great, dusty **Port Rhodes** bauxite shipping terminal in the middle of the bay. Guided tours of the mine and plant are combined with a stop at **Armadale Approved School**, where you can listen to traditional songs.

Beyond the bauxite terminal, with its huge green storage dome, is **Columbus Park**, a pleasant open-air museum on the cliff with a panoramic view over the bay. Cannons and sugar-mill fragments (including a water wheel and the old cast-iron pans used for boiling juice down to sugar) are on display. You will also find a stone crest of the Clan Campbell of Argyll dated 1774, taken from Knapdale in St. Ann parish.

Discovery Bay's name comes from the claim that Columbus first landed here in 1494. He called it *Puerto Seco*, "dry harbor," because of its lack of water. Today **Puerto Seco** beach is open to visitors and has restaurant facilities. Opposite is **Columbus Plaza**, containing a bank, bar, supermarket, and other modern amenities.

The road crosses the Rio Bueno river by the **Bengal Bridge**—a stylish stone

structure of 1798 which serves as a boundary marker between St. Ann and Trelawny parishes. It is an interesting combination of bridge and hill: its eastern end is much higher than its western end.

Rio Bueno, in a bay at the mouth of the river of the same name, also has claims to being Columbus' landing site. It is an unspoiled fishing village, the main street of which has some old stone houses. **Gallery Jo James** (right), with its little jetty behind, serves light though expensive meals. **St. Mark's Church** at the water's edge, fronted by its walled churchyard, is photogenic. Inside, a J.B. Kidd print shows how Rio Bueno looked in the 1830s. At the far end of town was **Fort Dundas**, built in 1778 to command both sea and bay.

From Brown's Town
To Marley's Tomb

Route B3 from Runaway Bay, and a smaller road from Puerto Seco, both lead south into the main structures on the enormous **Orange Valley Estate** property. If you can arrange a tour of this private estate, you will see a sugar-

works factory that looks much as it did 200 years ago.

Another lovely estate that looks like a slice of the British countryside is **Minard**, behind imposing gateposts south of Orange Valley. Drive up the dirt road and peek over the fence at the acres of Brahman bulls on the property. The first handsome home you see looming on the grounds is **New Hope**, now the private residence of farm manager John Allen. Further on is the unoccupied great house of Minard, once the private residence of Lord Wimborne of England. Do not leave your car for a close look, unless you want a pack of vicious security dogs attaching themselves to your legs.

Minard's first owner was a man named Brown. It is for him that the next community on this route, **Brown's Town**, is named. A quaint and picturesque country town, it is built up and down the sides of hills and valleys.

Facing the central market, an arresting example of 19th Century Gothic architecture, is **St. Mark's Church**. It was completed in 1895. The main street also features a twin post office and police station, each with stone arches,

and balconies and tile roofs that give them a Spanish look. Above these two structures is a Georgian courthouse, well-built in cut stone with a pillared portico. Brown's Town's many-tiered layout gives it a Mediterranean flavor that is good for camera buffs but hard on the legs.

At the fork in the middle of town, you can take Route B11 east through a small town with the unlikely name of **Philadelphia**, then continue to Claremont. Or you can proceed south on B3 through splendid hills and dales to **Alexandria**.

Reggae fans will want to ask directions here to the tomb of Jamaica's international superstar, Bob Marley. Marley was born near the village of **Nine Miles**. Crowning one hillside deep in the bush is a small chapel, its stained-glass windows displaying the Ethiopian Lion of Judah. **Marley's Tomb** inside is festooned with flowers and portraits of the messiah of Rastafarianism, Emperor Haile Selassie. A few ganja plants decorate the garden. Fans and reggae stars make a pilgrimage to this site on Marley's birthday in February, when they play his music long into the night.

SPERMOPHILA
BICOLOR

Brown's Town market, below. Typical rural scene, right

OTUNICULUS
TIXICURUS

Spanish Town And South Middlesex

The southern half of Middlesex County is a land of enormous variety. Sites of great historical importance—including Spanish Town, Jamaica's original capital, and caves once inhabited by the ancient Arawaks—are part of a landscape that encompasses bauxite-filled plateau country, green rolling "English" hills, and undeveloped coastal grasslands.

Most visitors are introduced to the region at **Spanish Town**, just 14 miles west of Kingston on Route Al. The approach leads across the **Ferry River**, which until the early years of this century was still important as the last staging post for horses and carriages traveling from Kingston to the western part of the island. The original 17th Century inn can still be seen. It is in poor repair but is earmarked for restoration.

Rodney Memorial, Spanish Town.

Three miles outside of Spanish Town, is the **White Marl Arawak Museum.** Located on the site of a large Arawak

village of centuries past, the building is said to be a replica of an Arawak hut. Important archaeological finds have been made in this area.

A short distance further on, the main highway passes an **Iron Bridge** regarded as a national monument. Indeed, this span over the Rio Cobre, while no longer in use, is the oldest surviving cast-iron bridge in this part of the world.

From the time of its founding by the Spanish in 1523, until the British moved the capital to Kingston in 1872, Spanish Town was the seat of Jamaican government. The Spaniards called it *Villa de la Vega*, "the town on the plain," while the English (after their 1655 conquest) preferred St. Jago, in honor of St. James of Compostella, the patron saint of Spain. But gradually people simply began to call it Spanish Town, even though all of its Spanish buildings had disappeared by the 18th Century.

In the center of Spanish Town is the **Square**, surrounded on all sides by Georgian-style buildings constructed during the heyday of sugar. On the east side is the **Parish Council Office**, formerly the House of Assembly. Built in 1762, it is notable for the superb brickwork of its long, shady colonnade and the pillared wooden balcony above. Opposite, on the west side of the square, are the remains of **King's House**, also dating from 1762. It was gutted by fire in 1925, leaving only the grand portico and facade. An interesting archaeological museum, displaying artifacts found here, has been established on the site. Demanding a closer look is the **Jamaican Peoples Museum of Craft and Technology**, located in the adjacent former stables. Its collection features a variety of relics from years past—everything from home furnishings to a village store.

On the south side of the Square is the **Court House**, built in 1819. Still in active use by parish magistrates, it attracts a vociferous throng of defendants, witnesses and onlookers outside its doors when court is in session. The building's upstairs floor contains the **Town Hall**, where concerts, plays and other public entertainments are performed.

The **Rodney Memorial** at the north end of the Square was sculpted in Italian marble by the noted English artist John Bacon. It was erected in the late

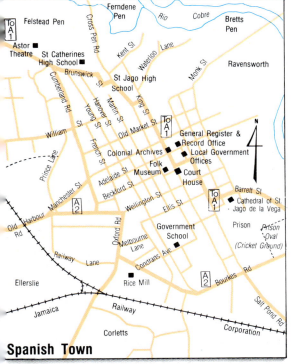

Spanish Town

18th Century in gratitude to Admiral George Rodney for saving the West Indies from French domination with his famous victory at sea over the Count de Grasse in 1782. Rodney is depicted in the dress of a Roman emperor; apparently, this was the artistic convention of the day. The statue is missing a hand and a few additional chips, the result of a feud between the residents of Spanish Town and Kingston. When it was removed to Kingston with the island administration, Spanish Town citizens were outraged and went to reclaim the statue. It has remained in Spanish Town ever since.

Behind Rodney's statue is the **Archives Office**, where many historical documents are kept, and the **Records Office**, where legal records for the entire nation are stored, from birth certificates and wills to deeds of title to land. Among the old records still on hand is the last will and testament of Sir Henry Morgan, the buccaneer-turned-governor of the 17th Century.

A short five-block walk back in the direction of Kingston on Barrett Street will take you to the **Cathedral Church of St. James**, also known as the Cathedral of St. Jago de la Vega. When originally constructed in 1523, this small house of worship was the first cathedral in the New World. The British replaced it 1666, and the current structure was raised in 1714 after its predecessor was destroyed by a hurricane.

The church is built of brick in the form of a cross. The wooden steeple was added in 1831. In and around the structure are tombs and memorials to 17th Century settlers and notables of later centuries. Since 1843, it has been the cathedral of the Jamaica diocese of the Church of England.

Take the St. John's road north out of Spanish Town. After passing through **Guanaboa Vale**, site of a famous colonial mutiny in 1660, keep an eye out for a signpost directing you to the **Mountain River Cave.** Leave your car here; a local guide will take you up a rough path and through a streambed to this natural museum of Arawak cave drawings. They have been cleaned and protected by the Archaeological Society of Jamaica, and are under the jurisdiction of the National Trust Commission.

Most of the cave drawings are on the underside of flat limestone surfaces,

Rio Cobre river, circa 1800.

TANAGRA
NIGRICEPHALA

sheltered from wind and water erosion. Drawings of hunters, turtles and various birds are similar to those found in the Dominican Republic and Puerto Rico, and resemble prehistoric African art. The Smithsonian Institute is sending a team to research the cave art, which some feel may be as old as 1,300 years.

Beyond here, a left-hand fork in the road continues about 10 miles through Point Hill to **Lluidas Vale.** This emerald gem amidst the hills is the home of the **Worthy Park Estate**, a three-century-old sugar plantation.

The right-hand fork leads to **Bog Walk**, on the main A1 highway between Spanish Town and St. Ann's Bay. Bog Walk is one of the oldest settlements in Jamaica, a rest stop for cattle wagons carrying hogsheads of sugar from nearby estates to ships waiting at Passage Fort. Today, Bog Walk is a railway junction and the site of a milk condensery, sugar factory and citrus packing plant.

North of Bog Walk, A1 continues through the town of **Linstead**, whose market (beneath the little square clock tower) is the subject of a famous folk song. Seven miles further is **Ewarton.**

Alcan has a major alumina factory here; bauxite is supplied by ropeway from a mining area six miles north, processed, then shipped by rail to Port Esquivel.

The return to Spanish Town from Bog Walk follows the Rio Cobre river to **Flat Bridge**, a Spanish relic set just a few feet above water level between towering vertical walls of limestone. Heavy rains frequently make this bridge impassable. A high-water mark of 1933 is indicated on the rock face, 25 feet above the bridge.

Route A2 begins in Spanish Town and continues west through Mandeville to Savanna-la-Mar. Twelve miles down this route is **Old Harbour**, best known for its iron Victorian clock tower. Such towers can be found all over the island, having been constructed mainly between 1890 and 1930. This one is unusual: it has been maintained in excellent condition, and keeps accurate time.

Colbeck Castle is located two miles north of Old Harbour on a side road. Once perhaps the largest building in the Caribbean, it is generally thought to have been built in the late 17th Century by an English settler named Col, John Colbeck, as protection against Maroon

Rio Cobre river, circa 1983.

attacks and possible invasion by the French. The main walls of this huge brick mansion are still erect, although the roof and floors are gone. Beam slots in the higher walls give an idea of the size of beams used in construction. Four underground slave quarters can be seen at each corner of the castle. The building is in the midst of what is now a large tobacco farm.

A short distance west of Old Harbour on A2 is the **Bodles Agricultural Station**, where some of Jamaica's finest dairy cattle are bred. The Jamaica Hope, the world's first tropically adapted dairy cow, was developed here by Dr. T.P. Lecky as a cross between the Jersey and Brahmin breeds. It is hardy and heat-tolerant. Crosses of Holstein and Frisian breeds have also been successful.

Opposite Bodles, beside a railway crossing, is the entrance road to **Port Esquivel.** This is the deepwater port of the Alcan Jamaica Company. From here, alumina is shipped to smelters in British Columbia and Scandinavia. You can visit the port by calling the firm's Kingston office in advance; they will arrange to have a pass waiting for you at the gate.

In Old Harbour Bay, beyond Port Esquivel, lie the two **Goat Islands.** Great Goat Island was an American naval base during the Second World War. Some of the old fortifications, barracks and ammunitions stores can still be seen, although the island now is used only by occasional fishermen. Further down the coast in Vere is the site of another former U.S. base, Fort Symonds. Now known as **Vernam Field**, it is the scene of occasional motor-racing events.

Crocodiles and Sugar

At **Freetown**, Route B12 branches south toward Lionel Town and Milk River. It first passes through mangrove swamps, a last refuge for Jamaica's declining crocodile population, then enters **Salt River.** This was once a major port for shipping sugar, despite its lack of deep-water facilities. The estates on the surrounding plains of Vere can still be seen, although many have been amalgamated under the influence of Tate and Lyle and its Jamaican subsidiary, the West Indies Sugar Company (Wisco).

A small road leads south to **Rocky**

Point, a scattered fishing village where the local delicacy is turtle eggs in red wine. North of this hamlet is the interesting town of **Alley**, with its sugar factory windmill-turned-library and its 18th Century St. Peter's Church, surrounded by old tombstones and huge kapok (silk cotton) trees.

May Pen, the halfway point between Spanish Town and Mandeville, is the market center for Clarendon, Jamaica's largest parish. Fridays and Saturdays are market days; May Pen's downtown area becomes colorful, crowded and chaotic. The Clarendon capital, along with the parish church and hospital is actually at Chapelton, north of here, but May Pen is far more active commercially. The famous Trout Hall citrus products are canned here under the direction of the Sharpe family, developers of the ugli fruit.

A visit to **Trout Hall** and its surrounding citrus orchards is very rewarding. Let the Sharpes know of your planned visit by telephoning the May Pen or Kingston office of the Citrus Company of Jamaica, then head north on B3 out of May Pen.

After passing through the old sugar

CORVUS
JAMAICENSIS

Old Harbour
clock tower.

capital of **Chapelton**, now notable chiefly for its war memorial clock tower, parish church and hospital, you'll travel up the Rio Minho valley. The citrus plantation is located at the junction of routes B3 and B4.

From Trout Hall, you can continue north to Runaway Bay, passing en route through **Cave Valley**, site of a Saturday morning donkey, mule and horse market. Or you can proceed west through Frankfield and Guinea Corn to the town of **Spaldings.**

On the boundary of Clarendon and Manchester parishes, Spaldings is famous for its co-educational **Knox College**, founded in 1947 by the Church of Scotland and the Presbyterian Church of Jamaica. This boarding school is based on the progressive concept that education must extend beyond the classroom. It offers a wide curriculum of academic subjects; a printery, farm and meat-processing plant make it almost self-sufficient.

Spaldings sits at about 3,000 feet elevation, giving it a cool year-round climate. The ginger grown in this region is said to be the best in the world.

Returning to Route A2, a few miles west of May Pen are the **Denbigh Agricultural Show Grounds.** The island's biggest show is held here annually over the long Independence Day weekend in early August. Just south of May Pen is the **Halse Hall** alumina plant, owned by Alcoa Minerals of Jamaica. It takes its name from the Halse Hall great house, the focal point of the company's operations. Halse Hall has been beautifully restored. Contact Alcoa's Kingston office ahead of time if you wish to visit.

At Toll Gate, eight miles west of May Pen, Route B12 branches south toward Milk River. **Milk River Bath**, not far from the river's mouth, is the island's leading spa. The spring waters here, known since the 17th Century, are the most radioactive on earth: three times more than Karlsbad in Czechoslovakia, and 50 times more than Vichy in France! The minerals in the water are said to have curative powers for those suffering from gout, sciatica, lumbago, rheumatism, neuralgia, eczema, and liver and kidney complaints. The baths have recently been refurbished, and the Milk River Bath Hotel is ideal for weekends of bathing, swimming and fishing.

Touring
Colbeck
Castle.

Beyond Toll Gate, Route A2 crosses the Manchester parish line and enters **Porus**, a thriving market town for citrus, coffee and other cash crops of the region. Leave this mini-metropolis via **Melrose Hill**, which climbs about 2,000 feet in five miles; you can rest and admire the view from roadside shops which sell delicious roast corn and yams to weary travelers.

Jamaica's 'Last Resort'

A new highway winds into clean, cool **Mandeville** town, cradled in a hollow at about 2,000 feet elevation. Often called "the most English town in Jamaica," it now boasts a resident population heavy in North Americans employed in the bauxite industry.

Mandeville is the capital of the parish of Manchester, created in 1814 from pieces of other parishes. The parish was named after the Jamaican governor, the Duke of Manchester, and the town after the duke's heir, the Earl of Mandeville. Mandeville's pleasant climate (in the 70s in the summer, 60s in the winter) appealed to many English colonialists, who came to think of it as their "last resort," but while some retired here, many more stayed only long enough to make their fortunes in coffee and pimento before heading home 'to the British Isles.

There are few points of particular interest in Mandeville itself. The Georgian courthouse and stone parish church were built around the central green soon after the town was founded. The oldest golf course on the island, the nine-hole **Manchester Club**, is located a half-mile from the town center. The major hotels include the Mandeville, built on the site of the 18th Century British garrison's hill station barracks; and the Hotel Astra. The latter can arrange overnight visits to **Marshall's Pen**, an 18th Century great house set on a 300-acre cattle farm.

The mayor of Mandeville is a former sno-cone salesman named Cecil C. Charlton, Esq. Charlton lives in a huge octagonal house atop **Huntingdon Summit**, $1\frac{1}{2}$ miles south of town. Set amidst Buckingham Palace-replica furniture in the living room is an indoor pond, connected through an underground tunnel to the outdoor swimming pool!

The countryside around Mandeville is rich in citrus fruits, particularly oranges and tangerines, grown on small farms by independent cultivators. An odd but tasty fruit called the "ortanique," a unique natural cross of the orange and tangerine, was discovered here and propagated by Charles Jackson.

The Mining of Bauxite

Jamaica is the world's largest producer of bauxite, and a visit to a mining operation and alumina factory is something that should be included on any itinerary. Most hotels can arrange tours, or permission can be obtained from head offices in major towns.

Perhaps the most easily reached operation is Alcan's **Kirkvine Works**, just off the new highway on the northeast approach to Mandeville. You can't miss its red bauxite "lake" at the foot of Shooter's Hill. This was Jamaica's first alumina plant (completed in 1957, although mining began in 1952) and is still the country's largest.

Alcan (more properly, the Canadian Aluminum Corporation) is the largest of four multination firms working in Jamaica. The other three are American: Alcoa, Kaiser and Reynolds. Between

Country Commentary.

PYRRHULA
VIOLACEA

them, they annually claim well over 10 million tons of bauxite from Jamaican soil.

Bauxite is an iron-rich mineral containing approximately 50 percent aluminum oxide. Most commerically exploitable bauxite lies close to the earth's surface; thus it is mined in open pits. The ore is then transported to a processing plant, where it is crushed, washed, kiln-dried, powdered, and shipped to another factory for refining into alumina. This product is ultimately smelted into aluminum. Four to six tons of bauxite ore will yield a single ton of aluminum.

Most of the valley northeast of Mandeville belongs to Alcan. This includes **Shooter's Hill**, on the top of the which is the tomb of Alexander Woodburn Heron, the original owner of the property. Heron's tomb and an adjacent lookout are preserved by Alcan. The view across the island is fantastic: on clear days, Blue Mountain Peak, 60 miles to the east, is easily seen.

Another attraction at the base of Shooter's Hill is of more interest to gourmets. At the crossroads where Route B4, B5 and B6 converge is the famous **Pickapepper factory.** This sauce, sold throughout the world, is similar to Worcestershire Sauce. Jamaicans insist it is much tastier.

Proceeding north on B5, the road passes through **Walderston**, founded by a Moravian missionary who bought the land and sold it in parcels to free slaves. His descendants still live in the village. The road continues through lovely mountain vegetation to the **Villa Bella** hotel, and on to **Christiana**, a trading center for ginger, bananas, Irish potatoes, and other hill-country crops. You can return to Mandeville via **Mile Gully**, notable for its lovely early 19th Century church, and **Grove Place**, site of the island's largest livestock breeding research station.

South to the Coast

From Mandeville, there is easy access to Jamaica's south coast. Start west, via Route A2. At the top of a steep descent down **Spur Tree Hill**, turn into the Alpart (Aluminium Partners of Jamaica) Farm parking lot and gaze across a 2,000-foot dropoff into eastern St. Elizabeth parish. Directly in front of you are the Malvern Hills. To your

Country bus at Alligator Pond.

right, or north, lie the peat-rich swamps of the Black River, the ganja-rich plains of Elim, and the rum-rich Appleton Estate. To your left, or south, is the world's largest open-field bauxite mine at Nain. It is an eyesore in the daytime, but is a fairlyland of lights at night.

The steep descent to appropriately named **Gutters** has seemingly endless hairpin bends. But tiny cookshops selling "curry goat" line the route, providing energy to continue. Turn south at Gutters and proceed through Downs to Alligator Pond on the south coast. (Another route from Mandeville winds through Newport, Rudds Corner and Plowden Hill to Alligator Pond.)

Alligator Pond is a quiet fishing village, outside the influence of the tourist industry. The early-morning fish market attracts mainly local people, and the proliferation of bars caters primarily to fishermen. Accommodation is limited to a few small cottages.

An 18-mile dirt road follows the Long Bay coastline through Gut River to Milk River. The latter portion of the route is almost impassable without a four-wheel-drive vehicle. Vegetation along the rutted road changes from tall grass and palms to treeless rocks and cacti. It seems more like Africa than the Caribbean. But the ancient Arawaks must have found the terrain hospitable, for numerous artifacts and rock carvings have been found here.

The road passes close to **God's Well**, a 160-foot-deep limestone sinkhole with clear turquoise water. It was named by a man who claimed to have been cured of a terminal illness by bathing in its waters.

The chief attraction of this coastline is the colony of manatees which make it their home. At **Cano Valley**, local conservationists will meet your car and guide you to a lookout. The manatee, sometimes called "sea cow," is a sluggish marine vegetarian that frequents shallow coastal waters and estuaries. Adults range from eight to 15 feet in length, and attain weights up to 1,500 pounds. Once common throughout the Caribbean, man has hunted this seal-like mammal for its meat, hide and fat until it has become rare. You may be lucky enough to see a family of manatees. They neither see nor hear well, so they communicate primarily by nuzzling one another.

PIAYA PULVIAL

Bulldozing for bauxite, below. Bauxite-rich earth near Mandeville, right.

The County of Cornwall

Cornwall and its English namesake have at least one thing in common: a beautiful seacoast setting. But while Cornwall in the United Kingdom is a land of rocky terrain, frequent rain and sea mists, Cornwall in Jamaica is one of the Caribbean's foremost centers for tourism and sugar (and rum!) production.

Montego Bay and its immediate surroundings attract a seemingly endless invasion of sun seekers to their sandy beaches. Direct flights connect major cities on North America's east coast with Montego Bay and its famed hotel strip. Exclusive restaurants and night clubs, and endless daytime recreational opportunities, keep visitors returning year after year. Off the beaches, old legends like that of the White Witch of Rose Hall blend with newer sensations like the Reggae Sunsplash festival to give the north coast of Cornwall a flavor all its own.

At the western point of Cornwall county, and indeed of the entire island of Jamaica, is Negril Beach, the most popular destination for young ganja-smoking, nude-bathing foreigners. A journey through south Cornwall leads from here through the sugar estates of the Westmoreland Plain around Savanna-la-Mar and Frome, into the hill country with its old German settlement of Seaford Town, past the lovely beaches of Bluefields Bay to the fishing town of Black River, into rum-making and ganja-growing country north of Santa Cruz, and finally to the tranquility of Lover's Leap and Treasure Beach, far from the beaten tourist track.

Five parishes comprise Cornwall county: St. Elizabeth and Westmoreland in the south; Hanover, St. James and Trelawny in the north. The isolated reaches of the fabled Cockpit Country, parts of which remain unexplored even today, comprise a large percentage of Trelawny and parts of both St. James and St. Elizabeth. This stronghold of the Maroon culture maintains an autonomy from the rest of Jamaica. It is the most traditional and to many the most fascinating part of an amazing country.

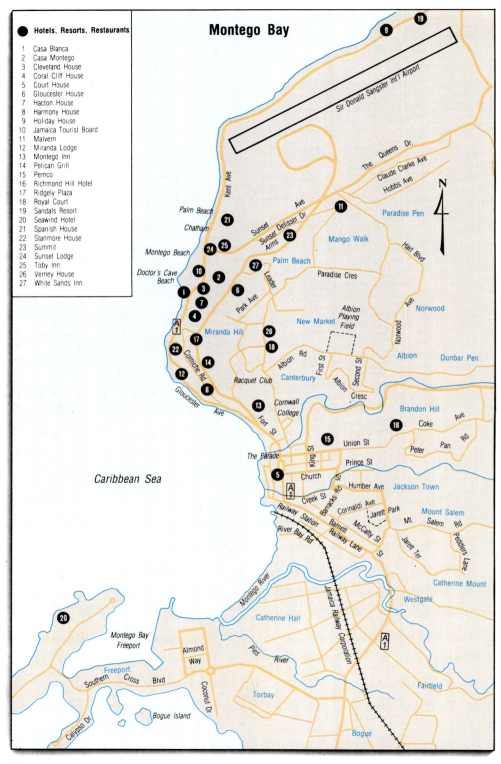

Montego Bay

● Hotels, Resorts, Restaurants

1 Casa Blanca
2 Casa Montego
3 Cleveland House
4 Coral Cliff House
5 Court House
6 Gloucester House
7 Hacton House
8 Harmony House
9 Holiday House
10 Jamaica Tourist Board
11 Malvern
12 Miranda Lodge
13 Montego Inn
14 Pelican Grill
15 Pemco
16 Richmond Hill Hotel
17 Ridgely Plaza
18 Royal Court
19 Sandals Resort
20 Seawind Hotel
21 Spanish House
22 Stanmore House
23 Summit
24 Sunset Lodge
25 Toby Inn
26 Verney House
27 White Sands Inn

Caribbean Sea

200

DOWN THE WAY AT MONTEGO BAY

In many ways, Montego Bay and its north coast suburbs are the least Jamaican part of Jamaica—an "Independent Republic of Montego Bay" built almost exclusively around the annual invasion of hundreds of thousands of sun worshippers. The phenomenon has resulted in a riotous clash of cultures where well-dressed, bejeweled young men with their hair in dreadlocks walk arm-in-arm with visiting coeds from New York; where Chicago businessmen chat up bikini-clad Jamaican girls; where retired couples chase goats off the golf greens before putting; where waistcoated waiters serve champagne and caviar in plush hilltop restaurants overlooking valleys of wooden shacks and poverty.

Other than Kingston, Montego Bay is Jamaica's only city, a helter-skelter development without distinct boundaries that has slowly swallowed up the coastline as far east as Rose Hall, as far west

Preceding pages: Rose Hall; Doctor's Cave Beach. Below, riding the wind over Montego Bay.

as the Tryall Club, and as far north into the Caribbean as sailboats, windsurfers and Jet-skis will take you. Beyond, Jamaica itself slowly resurfaces in such historic hamlets as Falmouth and Lucea and in small towns like Green Island, Anchovy and Duncans. Thus, visitors can spend daytime hours exploring Jamaica—and return home to Montego Bay at night.

'Lard Bay'

To modern man, **Montego Bay** means soft beaches, transparent waters, exotic living. To the first European visitors, it meant lard. Historians believe the word "montego" evolved from *manteca*, Spanish for lard or butter. The early Spanish occupants used the bay for shipping fat from wild and domesticated pigs and cattle. Now most people simply call it MoBay.

Christopher Columbus anchored in the bay, a crescent of beach that rolls into gentle hills, during his first visit to Jamaica in 1494. He found Arawak villages onshore; stories claim Columbus recruited one of the Indians as a crew member. But the Spanish did not

establish a settlement here until about 1655.

Ten years after that, the British established the parish of St. James, named for King James II, but settlers trickled in slowly during the latter part of the 17th and early 18th centuries. Potential residents feared the bay's vulnerability to attacks from pirates and from Maroons living in the nearby Cockpit Country. But by 1773, Montego Bay boasted the island's only newspaper outside Kingston, the *Cornwall Chronicle*, and even a regular theatrical season.

Fires destroyed chunks of the town in 1795 and 1811. And "Daddy" Sam Sharpe led area slaves in revolt during the winter of 1831–32. British authorities reacted by hanging him in The Parade on May 23, 1832, and by murdering an estimated 500 of his followers. Then, MoBay lapsed into a period of decline until the seeds of its tourist industry were planted around the turn of the 20th Century.

Its main attraction was its best beach, **Doctor's Cave Beach**, which still draws the tourists of today. The beach took its name from Dr. Alexander McCatty, who owned it and turned it into a semi-public bathing club in 1906. A small nearby cave no longer exists. Another doctor, British osteopath Sir Herbert Baker, further heightened the allure of the beach in the 1920s by claiming its waters could cure a variety of ailments.

The subsequent development of a series of hotels along Kent and Gloucester avenues have created MoBay's **Strip**, a scaled-down version of Waikiki or Miami Beach. There's still a small fee charged for use of the beach and its facilities.

Arriving in MoBay

Most travelers get their first look at Montego Bay from the window of an airplane. **Sir Donald Sangster International Airport** serves destinations in the United States, Europe and the rest of the Caribbean, and has connections to Kingston's Norman Manley International Airport. The loveliest drive into MoBay is west up **Queen's Drive**, which skirts the cliff above the beach strip.

Queen's Drive bends back down **Miranda Hill** past the remnants of **Fort**

19th Century Montego Bay.

SPERMOPHILA
ANOXANTHA

Montego. Three of its 17 original cannons remain pointed seaward. Its massive powder magazine lies landward. No one is sure when the fortification was built, but historians first described it in 1752.

Fort Montego's contribution to the struggle for power in the Caribbean was negligible at most. It only fired its guns twice: once to celebrate the surrender of Havana (a defective cannon exploded and killed a gunner); and the second time in 1795 when soldiers fired at what they believed to be a French privateer entering the harbor. They missed, fortunately. The privateer turned out to be a British ship.

At the roundabout you can swing back north along Gloucester Avenue to the Strip beaches. To the south, the roads converge into **St. James Street**, the main thoroughfare through town. It leads to the inevitable town square. Formerly known as Charles Square and The Parade, it is now called **Sam Sharpe Square.**

The square is a miniature version of The Parade in Kingston, a jumble of tacky new buildings and crumbling old structures, dusted by fumes from auto-

mobiles and buses. In its northwest corner is an attractive little building called **The Cage.** As its name implies, it was once used for imprisoning runaway slaves. Any blacks found on the streets after 3 p.m. on Sunday were considered runaways. The Cage dates to 1806. At the corner of Union and East streets is another reminder of that grim era, **The Slave Ring**, a decaying stone amphitheater once believed to have been used as a slave market and later the scene of cockfights.

Church Street, which crosses St. James Street west of the square, has a fine old plantation house-turned-Town House Restaurant at No. 16. **St. James Parish Church** rises opposite it on Church and St. Claver streets. The church, built from limestone, is a fine example of modified Georgian architecture. Its foundation stone was laid in 1775. Artist James Hakewill called it "the handsomest church in the island" at that time. The elegant monuments inside include a tribute to Rosa Palmer sculpted by Britain's John Bacon, who also executed the Rodney Memorial in Spanish Town. The lady draped over the urn has faint purple markings in the

The high life at Richmond Hill Hotel.

marble around her neck and nostrils. These markings have contributed to the theory that Rosa Palmer may have actually been the legendary, but probably fictional, "White Witch of Rose Hall" who murdered several husbands and lovers until she was strangled by a slave.

Poverty and Elegance

For a good view of Montego Bay and a startling look at the gap between its affluent visitors and poor residents, take Church Street back to Union then head east up the steep hill to **Richmond Hill Hotel.** Peek into the valley called **Canterbury** which is not very well hidden by the stone wall in the parking lot. Thousands of small wooden dwellings cling precariously to a hillside devoid of paved streets and other modern amenities. Here live many of the poorly paid personnel who wait on you in hotels and restaurants and try to sell you souvenirs along the streets of MoBay. Their homes are made from plywood, cardboard, corrugated tin, concrete and any other building materials residents can lay their hands on. The steady din of life

hovers above the whole surrealistic scene. Yet you're only steps away from the comfort and Old World elegance of Richmond Hill Hotel, formerly the 18th Century Spanish-style residence of a local plantation owner.

Back down Union Street, take Dome Street to its junction with Creek Street. The small, unimportant-looking structure in the intersection is called **The Dome.** In the 18th Century it controlled distribution of the small river called **The Creek,** once the main source of water for MoBay. Its architectural style might be called "Creek Orthodox."

Reggae Sunsplash

Continue east on Humbers Avenue around the corner to Cottage Park Road. Behind the wall west of the road lies **Jarrett Park,** once the home of the world's biggest reggae music festival, Reggae Sunsplash. Sunsplash is a marvelous concept that has brought mainly young people of all creeds and colors together for a week-long celebration of Jamaican life and rhythms. Unfortunately, it has been marred in the past by organizational problems. Up to 40,000

MoBay crafts market.

people have bludgeoned their way through only four small gates, then have endured delays, long lapses between performers and lack of proper sanitation facilities. An endless roster of mediocre reggae groups are trotted out from midnight until dawn; then the superb, top-name groups finally take the stage to sluggish applause from an exhausted, dwindling crowd.

Reggae Sunsplash has had its highlight, however. In 1981, American superstar Stevie Wonder sang a moving tribute to Jamaican superstar Bob Marley, who died of cancer earlier that year. The government plans to move the shows to more modern, spacious facilities in Montego Freeport at the edge of the Caribbean. There has also been talk of tightening up the shows to make Reggae Sunsplash the genuine showcase of Jamaican talent that it deserves to be.

For all its problems, Reggae Sunsplash has become one of the world's premier musical events, ready to take its place among giants like the Newport Jazz Festival. Attendance, especially among foreign visitors, has increased steadily since the first splash in 1978.

Even when Sunsplash is not in session, MoBay offers a variety of day and nightlife. When you finish para-sailing above coral waters, you can dance to the latest reggae and funk at **Disco Inferno** (in the shopping center across from the Holiday Inn) or at the aptly-named **Cave** at the Seawind Resort in Freeport. Here you bend down to enter a dark catacomb of a dance hall, where you pay for your drinks with tiny plastic bananas that you can snap together and string around your neck.

Haggling With Higglers

Another attraction in the city proper is **Harbour Street.** Its wharves still hum with activity when fishermen come ashore with their daily catch, and MoBay still snips its share of fruit, produce and other goods from the port area. The local **Crafts Market** is located along Harbour Street. Here, you can haggle over prices for sack-cloth clothing, Bob Marley T-shirts, or fruit from a higgler's head basket. You can even have your hair turned into a mass of African-style braids and beads.

For a look at a genuine Jamaican

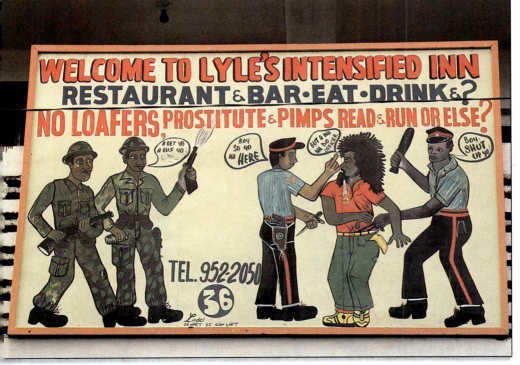

market, however, head for the **Fustic Street Market** off Barnett Street. The women higglers reign supreme here. The practice dates back to early colonial times when slaves brought their sales practices from West Africa. Here, as in Africa, the "Market Mammy" is an important person.

Markets first bloomed on the sugar estates or at busy crossroads where slaves and free persons alike met to trade and barter. Each slave received a plot of land for cultivation. What he didn't eat, he traded. Some also crafted baskets or *bankra*, clay bowls called *Yabbas*, and "jackass rope," tobacco twisted and rolled into long ropes for traveling.

The men usually did the cultivating and manufacturing. The women became salespeople. They controlled the money. Often, the peasant women walked as many as 20 miles loaded with goods to sell at the market. Today, higglers remain the queens of the trade. Young ones dress in contemporary fashions, but older women cling to the age-old uniform of a large apron worn over a green dress with huge pockets. They wear head ties and keep their money buried in their bosoms in cloth "threadbags."

It's a tough life. Higglers have developed a reputation for being loud and quarrelsome. But approach them with a smile and a query, and you will find most warm up to you quickly.

Visitors interested in taking a look at the inland towns and villages from which come the profusion of goods and people to the Fustic Street Market can try the **Governor's Coach Tour.** A diesel rail car makes a run each morning 40 miles inland to such towns as Catadupa, Cambridge and Ipswich. It also makes a stop at a working Appleton rum distillery.

Route A1 east of Montego follows Queen's Drive past another shanty village and an airport runway. The junction turns right to **Sandals Resort**, another of the popular "club-style" complexes where one price includes all accommodations, entertainment, food and beverage. Couples only are allowed. Next door to Sandals is the atmospheric **Holiday House Resort.** Its studio apartments are entirely crafted out of hand-cut Jamaican coal stone in various pastel hues. No two rooms are

NYCTIRIUS
PALLIOUS

Rose Hall
Great
House.

the same, but all have tasteful mahoe and wicker furniture and overlook a lagoon-like sea-water pool. The pool leads out under a stone arch right into the Caribbean.

Further east lie more hotels, from the inevitable **Holiday Inn** to the plush **Half-Moon Club.** Considered one of the island's top three hotels, the Half-Moon takes its name from the shape of its perfect beach. It has 360 acres of gardens and manicured lawns, a championship golf course designed by Robert Trent Jones, tennis courts, saunas and prices to match.

'The White Witch of Rose Hall'

Looming mightily on a ridge just east of the Half-Moon is one of Jamaica's premier attractions, **Rose Hall Great House.** Drive up the road and pay the stiff admission charge for a look at this plantation house built about 1770 by John Palmer, when he served as the custos (queen's representative) of the parish of St. James. It was restored by American millionaire John Rollins, a former governor of Delaware.

Although most of the interior decorations have been imported from other parts of the island as well as foreign countries, Rollins and his wife have attempted to recreate the typical grandeur of an 18th Century plantation house. Its antiques and art treasures are museum-quality pieces dating to the 17th Century.

Still, Rose Hall's trappings and restoration remain overshadowed by its famous legend. One of the many versions of the story says Annie was an English woman tutored in the black arts of voodoo by a Haitian priestess. She came to Jamaica and supposedly, at age 18, married John Palmer. Three years later, Palmer died, reportedly poisoned by the petite and pretty but sadistic, Annie. She later stabbed a second husband to death and strangled a third. She also took slaves as lovers and murdered them when she got bored. Finally, the slaves rebelled and murdered Annie in her bed in 1833.

Naturally, Rose Hall is now said to be haunted by the ghost of the "White Witch." In fact, one Friday the 13th in 1979, 8,000 people turned up to watch a group of U.S. and Jamaican psychics attempt to call up her ghost. An inter-

Modest dwelling near Rose Hall.

ORTYGOMETRA
MINUTA

nationally renowned Greek Cypriot resident of Jamaica, named Bambos, claimed to have actually communicated with Annie's spirit. This led him to discover a huge termite's nest behind Rose Hall, within which was a tarnished brass urn. Inside was a voodoo doll dressed in a gown and a paper-thin black material: the charred remains of Annie, Bambos said.

The legend of the White Witch of Rose Hall makes a great story, but probably is more fictional than factual. There *was* an Annie Palmer at Rose Hall. But she wasn't Irish, she had only one husband, and she died a respected citizen in 1846. Rosa Palmer of Rose Hall did have Irish connections and four husbands. But she kept the last one for 23 years. He buried her at the age of 72 in the Montego Bay churchyard.

A side road leads from the main road past the right corner of Rose Hall to the walled burial ground of the Moulton Barrett family, 200 yards below the 19th Century Great House. The Barrett family, which produced poetess Elizabeth Barrett Browning, lived in the **Cinnamon Hill Great House** further up the road. It has since been modernized

and restored, and purchased by American country-and-western star Johnny Cash. Cash and his family make yearly visits to his Jamaican hideaway, and he has become a valued patron of the Montego Bay SOS Children's Village, which provides family-type homes for destitute and abandoned children.

Beyond the house, free-lance guides will be happy (for a fee) to take you across the golf course fairways to a waterfall where scenes for the James Bond movie *Live and Let Die* were filmed. They will also point out an underground tunnel that they said was once used by Annie Palmer to leave Rose Hall for clandestine meetings in the woods with her slave lovers.

Route A1 continues east past souvenir stands chockablock with conch shells to yet another great house. **Greenwood Great House** was also built by the Barrett family between 1780 and 1800. It's now owned and operated by Bob and Ann Betton. Like Rose Hall, it has been decked out with antiques that include giant musical boxes and even a court jester's chair.

The next major town, **Falmouth**, virtually dates *in toto* from the time the

Falmouth
square,
below.
North coast
artist, left.

famous Barrett family roamed Jamaica. It developed as a sugar port during a period of wealth and good taste—the end of the 18th Century. The good taste is reflected in its broad streets and well-built stone and wooden houses.

The Georgian heritage here is better preserved than elsewhere on the island. The greatest concentration of Georgian buildings is on **Market Street**, west of the central **Water Square** with its small ornamental fountain. The **Post Office** has a well-balanced upper window pattern that sits boldly on a support of semicircular arches. At the bottom of the street is the **Methodist Manse**, built in 1799 by the Barretts, a stone-and-wood house with elegant wrought-iron balconies and fine Adam-style doorways and friezes.

Adjacent to Water Square is the 1815-era **Courthouse**, one of the finest Georgian buildings in Jamaica despite a poor restoration attempt after a fire in 1926. A double exterior staircase leads up to a portico with a pediment supported by four doric columns. The building now houses the offices of the town council. On leaving town via Upper Harbour Street, you pass by the 1801 **Phoenix Foundary**, one of Jamaica's earliest.

Like Port Antonio in the east, Falmouth has its rafting river, the **Martha Brae.** There's a **Rafter's Village** a mile upriver at the neck of an oxbow in the stream. It has a restaurant, bar, and boutiques. The trip downriver takes an hour and a half; you will be driven back to the village afterwards.

East of Falmouth on A1, there is a phosphorescent lagoon at **Rock.** At night, microscopic organisms glisten when the water is agitated with a stick or a stone. A seafood restaurant in front of the lagoon serves good fresh food at reasonable prices, but you may have to nudge the waiters and owners into action. You can also charter deep-sea fishing boats here to try your luck at catching a marlin, kingfish, wahoo or barracuda.

An impressive ruin, **Stewart Castle**, can be reached a mile up a dirt road from the main highway past Rock. The structure appears to be a large home that was fortified with thick stone walls perforated with musket and cannonade firing slits. It appears to date from the early 18th Century when large landowners constructed such dwellings to pro-

tect themselves from attacks by Maroons, slaves or pirates. Designated a national monument, Stewart Castle is slated for renovation.

At **Silver Sands**, an excellent beach, you can head south up Route B10 for a look at the **Long Pond Sugar Factory and Distillery**, where Gold Label Rum is made. Then head back west at **Clark's Town** on Route B11, or continue south to **Duanvale** and **Sherwood Content** on the fringes of the **Cockpit Country.**

West of MoBay

West of MoBay, a spur road off A1 leads to a shopping complex designed to cater for cruise ships. Its products are in-bond (duty-free) as well as out-of-bond. Beyond are the twin towers of the **Seawind Hotel** complex and a yacht marina.

West of **Reading** is a junction with a road that jogs across the island to Savanna-la-Mar on the south coast. The road climbs up **Long Hill**, providing views over town and coast. Two miles up, a signpost indicates Rock Pleasant. A bird sanctuary operated by Lisa Sal-

SYLVICOLA EO

Country dominoes match.

mon, is one-half mile along.

Bird-watchers carrying their bird society cards are welcome all day, but for the general public **Rocklands** bird feeding starts daily at 3 p.m. Miss Salmon, who insists that Rocklands is a "bird-feeding station" as opposed to a sanctuary, calls many of the feathered visitors by name. Even the skittish doctor birds have become so tame they feed from your hand. Miss Salmon established the station in 1958.

The road continues to **Anchovy**, then to the town of **Montpelier**, center of the local dairy and beef cattle industry. The road's right-hand fork proceeds to Savanna-la-Mar via Ramble.

West on A1 beyond Reading, the scene is graced by some large and elegant homes, many owned by wealthy winter visitors. Shortly after crossing the parish boundary into Hanover at **Great River**, round, beehive-like gateposts on the right seaward side indicate the **Round Hill Hotel**, one of the most exclusive and expensive in Jamaica. It is also one of the most beautiful, enjoying an incomparable setting on its own private beach. A list of guest names over the years resembles "Who's Who" and includes rock star Paul McCartney and U.S. Senator Edward Kennedy. Fashion designer Ralph Lauren of "Polo" fame owns the estate west of Round Hill.

Sugar and Golf at Tryall

Four miles later on the left is the magnificent **Tryall water wheel** and ruins. The wheel is still turned by water carried via aqueduct from the **Flint River.** Its brick chimney was rebuilt in 1834 after the old sugar works were destroyed during Sam Sharpe's slave rebellion of 1831. The water wheel turned the single three-roll crushing mill. In the old days, the mill could also be turned by wind power (the island is dotted with old sugar towers which carried sails), animal power or even human power. On the right is picturesque Tryall championship golf course. Above on the hill is the small but exclusive **Tryall Hotel.**

Beyond **Sandy Bay** are perhaps the finest sugar-estate ruins in Jamaica, **Kenilworth Estate**. The sugar factory buildings, a mile south of the main road, were built on a far grander scale and more durably than the adjacent

Tryall Water Wheel, below.

Great House. The first block is the sugar mill, with long, deep, rectangular housing for the water wheel (which probably looked like the one at Tryall). The two-story building is beautifully constructed of limestone in two shades, with oval Palladian windows trimmed in light stone and an arched front doorway reached by a semicircular flight of steps. The second block, the sugar-boiling house and distillery, is constructed in the form of a long central room with two wings. The sloped hillside accommodates the furnaces on a lower level.

About 25 miles beyond Montego Bay is the quiet little town of **Lucea**, administrative center of Hanover parish. Once a busy port for the shipment of sugar, its economy now is based around bananas and molasses. Pimento, ginger and yams grown in the surrounding districts are also important. The new **Town Centre** was dedicated by Queen Elizabeth II during her 1966 visit to Jamaica. Lucea's 19th Century **Courthouse** is an attractive stone and wood structure with a clock tower supported by columns in corinthian style.

Fort Charlotte, behind the school and the Public Works Department, is another Jamaican fort which never fired a cannonball in anger. Named after George III's queen, this octagonal structure had ports for 20 guns; three remain. It commands a lovely little turquoise harbor, an obsolete reminder of Jamaica's turbulent past.

Backtrack to the main road which continues west in and out of little nooks like **Cousins Cove**, **Davis Cove** andd **Negro Bay**. A paved road from Davis Cove leads two miles inland to Blenheim, birthplace of national hero and Jamaica's first prime minister, Alexander Bustamante. Bustamante's father, Robert Clarke, was an overseer on Blenheim Estate. His famous son was born in the overseer's home. The house has been reconstructed on its original site as a national monument.

The next town on the main road is **Green Island**, with a fishing-village flavor and an old Presbyterian chapel. There are several junctions in Green Island with roads that spiderweb up into the hills toward Savanna-la-Mar. Route A1, meanwhile, cuts a steady course down the coast to Jamaica's growing center of hedonism, **Negril.**

HIRUNDO EUCHRYSEA

Damp Scamper in Green Island.

CONQUERING THE COCKPIT COUNTRY

One of the most mysterious and intriguing blemishes in the Jamaican landscape is the Cockpit Country, a pot-holed limestone plateau that cuts into its mountainous surroundings like a missing piece from a giant jigsaw puzzle. It's a land that begs to be explored, a land that looks much like it did when mighty Maroon warriors first staked their claim to its sinkholes, valleys and caves some four centuries ago.

An automobile will take you only along its outer fringes. A four-wheel-drive vehicle won't go much further. The best view of the eerie landscape is from an airplane or helicopter. Otherwise, you must mount a small expedition and hike into the Cockpit Country.

Maroon Town, on the northwestern edge of the Cockpit Country, is as good as any to begin a brief automobile tour of the surroundings. Maroons settled here long ago, but no longer live in the village.

A side road off the main track slices through banana plantations to **Flagstaff**, formerly a Maroon settlement called Trelawny Town.

You must backtrack to the main road from here, then head south past **Elderslie** where a sign will point you to the Maroon capital of the Cockpit Country, **Accompong**. The village is scattered over several miles, but has a square flanked by shops, a church and a school. Cudjoe Day is celebrated here on Jan. 6.

Backtrack again to the main road. It dead-ends in the town of **Quick Step**, in the **District of Look Behind**. Communities along the eastern rim road bear equally interesting names: **Burnt Hill**, **Barbecue Bottom** and **Good Design**. You can swing back west again on **Route B11** to **Sherwood Content**. A side road here darts back into the Cockpits from here to **Windsor Cave.**

The cave's first two chambers can be easily negotiated. Step carefully through the layers of "rat bat" manure. More advanced spelunkers will find the cave plunges to uncharted depths.

Beyond Sherwood Content and Windsor Cave, much of the Cockpit Country is said to remain unexplored.

Melvin Pearson displays grave of British soldier of 1846 near Maroon Town, left. Shelter from Cockpit Country storm, below.

216

JOURNEY THROUGH SOUTH CORNWALL

Beaches and sugar: these are the main calling cards of southern Cornwall county. But lest the visitor be misled, there is much more to found here. The parishes of Westmoreland and St. Elizabeth also feature mountains, swamps, the island's longest river, an avenue lined with bamboo, major agricultural and industrial areas, and important historical sites.

Chances are you'll start your wanderings at **Negril's** famous seven-mile beach, Jamaica's westernmost escape. Many regard this strand as a home for hedonism and bacchanalia, a nook for nude bathing, sun and sin.

But Negril is not restricted to swinging singles and 1980s hippies. More than any other resort area in Jamaica, accommodation here ranges over all levels of price and quality. Hotels stretch along the full length of the beach, interspersed with local homes, fishermen's huts, patches of indigenous flora, stretches of coconut trees and deserted sand. Local residents mix with the tourist population in a manner not possible elsewhere.

Food shops are almost infinite in number and variety, ranging from small "supper shops" selling hot pepper-fried fish and hard-dough bread, to establishments like "Miss Brown's" specializing in psilocybin mushroom omelets; to higher-class seafood restaurants. Clothing varies as well, from none at all (a not-uncommon sight on Negril Beach), to shapeless, unisex flourbag pants and tops, to sophisticated dress in better hotels and eating spots.

There are many fascinating places to sleep and dine Rita Hojan's **Sundowner Inn** is a quiet hideout to which artist Norman Rockwell often fled. The **Rock House** consists of a series of thatch-roofed, clifftop bungalows with a birds-eye view of waves crashing against the rugged shoreline. The **Awaeemaway** offers water beds and hammocks, free bananas, a communal kitchen—but no electricity. At **Rick's Cafe**, diners come not only for the seafood—fish chowder, river perch, red snapper and lobster—but also to see local youths diving 100

feet from the clifftop into the crystal water below. Beyond is the **Negril Lighthouse** near South Negril Point; west of here there is nothing but 600 miles of ocean to the Yucatan.

Negril's most famous inn is **Hedonism II**, which offers all-inclusive week-long holidays at reasonable rates. Accommodation, food, entertainment (including an all-night disco), sports facilities, and unlimited liquor and cigarettes come to about US $850 per person per week. Scuba diving and snorkeling, sailing and parasailing, windsurfing and waterskiing, volleyball and horseback riding are part of the daily activities.

Hedonism II (formerly the Negril Beach Village) is located on a 22-acre resort fronting **Bloody Bay**, where pirate "Calico Jack" Rackham and his colleagues Anne Bonney and Mary Read were captured in 1720. Bloody Bay was not named for the pirates, though. It got its name from passing whalers who disemboweled their catch here, often leaving the waters red with blood.

One of the best ways to see Negril's waters is by Polynesian catamaran. The 40-foot *Reggae II* leaves the harbor daily at 4 p.m. for a sunset party cruise along Long Bay's beautiful cliffs. At the northern end of the bay, take a glance at **Booby Cay**, a small island used for filming scenes in the movie version of Jules Verne's *20,000 Leagues Under the Sea*. The awkward booby, a species of gannet, flies to these cays to breed.

On the east side of the Negril Beach road is the **Great Morass** of Westmoreland. (There is another one in St. Elizabeth.) This two-mile-wide mosquito breeding ground is the habitat of an interesting variety of rare birds and plants. It can be explored by airboat: the *Swamp Dragon* tours the bog between 9 a.m. and 5 p.m. daily. In its advertisements, the *Swamp Dragon* offers visitors a chance to "see an illegal clandestine airstrip deep in the Morass used to smuggle marijuana back to the U.S. (3 crashed aircraft on site)."

The Petroleum Corporation of Jamaica is conducting experiments in extracting peat from beneath the water of the Morass. More than 7,000 acres of peat here form a potentially valuable asset for Jamaica's future. Scientists are concerned, however, that unless the

Rick's Cafe scene, left. Below, need an oil change?

MERULA
LEUCOGENYS

peat can be reaped without harming the swamp's valuable vegetation, the ecology might be so severely damaged that the entire region could become a wasteland of stagnant water. At the moment, the Morass is like a giant sponge, holding water from the mountains to the east, releasing it a little at a time into the sea.

Through Canefields
To Savanna-la-Mar

The highway east from Negril crosses several miles of swampland before emerging onto the vast Westmoreland Plain with its miles of canefields and pastureland.

At **New Hope Estate**, note the fanciful 1920s oriental gateways. Then continue to **Little London**, which is nothing like its British namesake. In fact, many feel it would be best renamed "Little Southall" for the numbers of East Indians who make it their home. Descendants of indentured laborers who were transported from South Asia to Jamaica after the abolition of slavery in the mid 19th Century, many of them still work in the sugar industry.

Hot limbo at
Hedonism II.

The capital and chief city of Westmoreland parish is **Savanna-la-Mar**, best known as "Sav-la-Mar" to its friends. Its name means literally "the plain by the sea." That plain has not always been kind to the town. Since its establishment in 1703, it has been devastated by hurricanes in 1748 and 1912, and by a tidal wave in 1780. The 20th Century storm left a schooner stranded in the middle of **Great George Street**— with the crew still aboard!

Great George Street is the longest city street in Jamaica. At its seaward end is the **Old Fort**, the surviving stone walls of which form a swimming and bathing pool for local citizens. Among the interesting buildings further up the same street is the **Courthouse**, with its ornate cast-iron drinking fountain dating from the 19th Century. Note the admonition on all four sides of the fountain to "Keep the pavement dry."

Savanna-la-Mar was established as a sugar port, and that is still its most important function. The bustling wharf is near the end of Great George Street, next to the Old Fort. Watch as raw brown sugar is loaded onto barges and carried to ships, to be transported to

refineries abroad.

Most of the sugar comes from factories around **Frome**, six miles north of Sav-la-Mar on Route B9 toward Lucea. The **Frome Central Sugar Factory** processes cane from estates throughout Westmoreland and Hanover parishes.

Sugar-coated Riots

Sugar cane is in fact a type of grass that grows to 10 or more feet in height. Within the hard rind of its stalk is contained a soft sugary fiber. Between mid-November and June, this cane is harvested and transported by truck or rail to the mill. Here, a double series of rollers crushes out the juice, which contains about 13 percent pure sugar. At first a cloudy green in color, this cane juice is then clarified, evaporated and separated in centrifugal machines into golden sugar crystals and cane molasses. One of the end products of the molasses, of course, is Jamaica's famed rum.

In 1938, Frome was the site of riots which led to the rise of Alexander Bustamante as a national labor leader. The sugar mill, then the largest West Indies Sugar Company plant in the country, had just been built. Thousands of unemployed Jamaicans converged on Frome in the hope of finding work, but instead most were turned away. Police were called in to quell the property destruction and canefield burning that followed. The disorder spread to other parts of Jamaica, leading to the formation of the island's first lasting unions and of political parties linked with those unions. Bustamante, of course, became a leader in Jamaica's drive toward independence, and the free nation's first prime minister.

Not far from Frome, at the Shrewsbury Estate, is the source of the **Roaring River**. Seemingly from nowhere, the river emerges in full flow from a subterranean course. Swimmers, spelunkers and mere picnickers enjoy the strange phenomenon and its beautiful surroundings.

East of Savanna-la-Mar, Route A2 meanders cross-country for 123 miles before reaching its terminus in Spanish Town. Just five miles from Sav-la-Mar, at **Ferris Cross**, is **Paradise Park**, a 1,000-acre 18th Century plantation. Book a week in advance, and take a

Seaford Town's people.

PYRRHULA
ROBINSON

horseback tour of the jungle, cattle ranch, tropical farm, bird sanctuary and botanical garden.

The Inland Route

Ferris Cross is the junction of Route B8 to Montego Bay. It is also the starting point for an interesting inland tour.

The Montego Bay road passes through **Haddo** about six miles north of Ferris Cross. At the turn of the 20th Century, the Haddo store was the home of the clairvoyant "Prophet of Haddo," a man named Charles Stewart. His visionary refuge in the neighboring hills was a place of worship for many of the region's common folk.

Two miles before Haddo, at the hamlet of **Whithorn**, turn right (east) toward **Darliston**. The winding five-mile climb up **Frame Hill** offers grand views across the sugar plains. Darliston itself is a tobacco-growing center where cheap local cigars are a popular purchase.

At **Struie** is a roadside landmark called the **Soldier Stone**. The inscription is almost illegible, but local folklore tells of an infantryman named Obediah Bell Chambers who rode out on muleback to do battle with rebellious slaves and had his head severed. Struie residents returning from market at night often claim to hear the clash of steel as they pass the Soldier Stone.

After passing through another village with the unlikely name of **Rat Trap**, you'll enter **Seaford Town**, the island's best-known German-descended community. In fact, although many of the residents have fair skins, blue eyes and German surnames, they have preserved virtually no traces of their European language or culture. Instead, this is a sadly inbred group of "poor whites."

The Roman Catholic priest of Seaford Town, Father Francis Friesen, will tell you the town's history if you visit his home across the street from the old stone **Sacred Heart Catholic Church**. Friesen, a Dutchman who is compiling a history of the town, displays some of the memorabilia he has collected at the **Historical Museum** next to the church.

Seaford Town was founded in 1835 by peasant farmers from northern Germany. Their economy depended at first on sugar cultivation, and later on bananas. As late as the 1960s, the population was close to 500; today it is nearer 200,

Black River hopping center.

many townspeople having emigrated to Canada.

From Seaford Town, Route B6 continues to Mandeville via Maggotty. There are also easy routes north to Montego Bay and east to the Cockpit Country.

Pirates and Fishermen

Our route reverts to Ferris Cross and follows A2 down the south coast to **Bluefields Bay**. It was from this wide curving bay, now popular as a swimming area, that Henry Morgan sailed in 1670 to sack Panama. This is believed to have been the location of the early Spanish settlement of Oristan, although no remains have been discovered.

At **Bluefields House**, near the Bluefields police station, naturalist Philip Gosse gathered materials for two classic reference books: *Birds of Jamaica* and *A Naturalist's Sojourn in Jamaica*. He lived here for 18 months in 1844 and 1845. A breadfruit tree on the lawn of the house is reputed to be the oldest in Jamaica; Captain Bligh may have anchored his *Providence* in the bay in 1793.

Auchindown Farm has its entrance on the north side of A2 just above Banister Bay. A working pimento property, its grounds include a fascinating ruined castle which rumor says was built to house the deposed Emperor Napoleon. That claim is disputed. The castle was certainly built early in the 19th Century by Archibald Campbell, a descendant of the noted Campbell clan of Glengoe, Scotland. An underground passage running to the castle from pimento barbecues at Orange Grove may have been used by smugglers.

The main road passes through **Whitehouse** village. Most of the north coast hotels get their supplies of seafood here. Every morning, weather permitting, local fishermen sell their previous night's catch on the beach. It is cheap and fresh, having been kept overnight on ice taken to sea in the boats.

At **Black River**, you enter the first sizeable town since leaving Sav-la-Mar. The capital of St. Elizabeth, it is nevertheless a sleepy settlement strung along the shore of Black River Bay at the river's mouth. Many Georgian-style buildings remain from days long past when logwood and fustic—both dye-

Black River, about 1830.

NAS MAXIMA

producing trees—and the ubiquitous sugar gave a strong base to the local economy.

Around the turn of the 20th Century, Black River was a bustling port. In 1893, it became the first community on the island to have electric light, generated and sold by two local merchants, the Leyden brothers; and in 1903 there were already motor cars being driven on the streets of town. The **Parish Church of St. John the Evangelist** was founded in 1837. The famous **Black River Spa** just outside town has not been maintained, in spite of the therapeutic value of its water; at present, it is little more than a watering hole for animals.

The Black River itself is the longest in Jamaica. It follows a winding course of 44 miles from the mountains of southern Trelawny parish. There is good fishing for both freshwater and sea fish on the broadwater about a mile from the mouth.

Much of the Black River's lower course takes it through the Great Morass, a huge freshwater swamp that constitutes the largest remaining crocodile refuge in Jamaica. Slaughter by sportsmen and farmers has reduced the croc population to a fraction of what it once was.

At the upper end of the Morass, eight miles from Black River, is the little village of **Middlequarters**. Should you stop your vehicle here, you'll be set upon by women vendors urging you to try the savory local shrimp. Hot and peppery, these morsels should be taken with some hard-dough bread and a bottle of beer lest the unsuspecting visitor's throat be set on fire.

Close to where A2 crosses the oddly labeled **Y.S. River** (whose name may have been adapted from the Welsh word *wyess* for "winding"), the **Holland Estate** and sugar factory stand just off the roadside. This small mill, no longer in operation, was once owned by John Gladstone, father of the famous Victorian prime minister of Great Britain. Gladstone made his fortune in the colonies, trading out of Liverpool.

A three-mile stretch of road between Holland Estate and Lacovia is known as **Bamboo Avenue**. One of the most-photographed locations in Jamaica, it is easy to see why it is so well known and loved. Entering the avenue is like walking into a giant cathedral whose nave

Black River "gingerbread" house.

disappears in the distance. Bamboo was planted on both sides of the road in the 19th Century by local landowners appreciative of the shade as they traveled the road. The Hope Botanical Gardens now maintains the bamboo, assisted by local citizens who are swift to raise the alarm if anyone is discovered interfering with the plants.

At the eastern end of Bamboo Avenue is **Lacovia**, one of the longest villages in Jamaica. Divided into West Lacovia, East Lacovia and Lacovia Tombstone, it sprawls along A2 for some two miles on either side of the Black River bridge. Originally a Jewish settlement, it was an inland port for the shipping of sugar, logwood and fustic downriver.

Logwood and fustic dyes were so important in days before the development of synthetic dyes that even the ermine robes of English Lords were stained in logwood. Although Jamaica's dye factories closed down in the 1950s, recent discoveries indicate that natural dyes are in fact brighter and longer lasting than synthetic ones!

Today, Lacovia is a center for the growing of cashew nuts.

Lacovia Tombstone is so named for two tombs in the middle of the road. Beneath are the bones of two young men, one of them just 15, who died following a tavern brawl in 1723. Tombstone is the junction for a road leading inland to **Maggotty**, where it connects with Route B6.

Cecil Baugh, one of Jamaica's leading pottery artisans, maintains his workshop in Maggotty, a seven-mile excursion. Reynolds Jamaica Mines have established their **Revere Works** bauxite operation a short distance north of the town. From Maggotty, there is a road heading north to the Maroon village of Accompong in the Cockpit Country. B6 heads west to Seaford Town and east through Appleton and Siloah to Mandeville.

Rum and Ganja

Appleton is best known as the home of Jamaica's most famous and popular rum. The **Appleton Sugar Factory and Distillery** is picturesquely located alongside the Black River in a lovely green valley, surrounded by canefields and framed by mountains. It was founded in

ZENAIDA PLUM

A bouncy ride down Bamboo Avenue.

the 19th Century by a former St. Ann wheelwright named John Wray, who acquired this plantation after perfecting his blend of rum in a small shop on the site of Kingston's Ward Theatre.

Route A2, meanwhile, proceeds through Lacovia to **Santa Cruz**, St. Elizabeth's bustling market center. Traditionally an area of horses and livestock, Santa Cruz once provided mules for all of the British army's garrison troops, as well as for parish councils and public works departments throughout the island. **Gilnock Hall**, just outside the town, still has a polo field in use. Next to the hall is **St. Andrew's Church**, an Anglican house of worship built in the 1840s by Duncan Robertson, chief of the Scottish Clan Robertson of Struan.

The **Braes River**, **Elim** and **Barton Isles** districts northeast of Santa Cruz are noted for their prolific ganja farms. Rice and cattle farming, for beef and for dairy products, are more legitimate economic mainstays.

It is another seven miles on A2 from Wilton to Gutters at the Middlesex county line, and another 14 miles into Mandeville. At **Goshen**, the Ministry of Agriculture has established a **Dairy Industry Training Centre**. In addition to dairy cattle, a special ovine breed known as the St. Elizabeth Sheep has been developed here. It lambs twice a year, and while its coat is too hairy to be wool and too woolly to be hair, it may someday form the basis of an unusual new fabric.

A Jewel of a Beach

Those looking for a south coast beach would be best advised to head for **Treasure Beach**. This out-of-the-way but lovely stretch of sand is an "in" spot for young Jamaicans. It can be reached from Black River via Fullerswood or from Mandeville via Downs, but the most direct approach is from Santa Cruz.

The route is extremely picturesque. It first winds uphill to **Malvern**, an old resort town 2,400 feet up in the Santa Cruz Mountains. The climate is cool— seldom over 80°F—and dry. Today it is a quiet village. Its continued existence is due largely to the three fine schools located within a few miles of one another along the ridge. These are the **Munro School** for boys, the **Hampton School** for girls, and the Moravians' **Bethlehem Training College for Women**.

Keep to the right at the **Southfield** junction (the road to the left heads for Alligator Pond and Mandeville). A turn to the south leads after a couple of miles to **Lover's Leap**, a 1,500-foot escarpment dropping directly into the blue waters of the Caribbean below. The slope is nearly perpendicular; sometimes you can look down at small airplanes making their way along the coast.

Treasure Beach is another 10 miles or so, at the end of the road through Pedro Cross. Swimming can be tricky, as waves crash the shore and there is a vicious undertow where the land is not protected by a reef. But the gray sand beach is secluded and comfortable, and many villas are available for rent— even if electrical outages are frequent.

The local residents of Treasure Beach are very friendly and helpful. Many are also unusual for their blue eyes, blondish hair, café-au-lait complexions, and slightly Scottish accents. A popular explanation is that their ancestors were Scottish seamen who were shipwrecked on this shore.

Storm
clouds over
Lover's
Leap.

THE RED HOT RHYTHMS OF REGGAE

What's that music playin' on the radio?
What's that music playin' everywhere I
go?
I don't think I've ever heard
A sweeter feelin' in the whole wide world
Than that music playin' in my heart . . .
— Gil Scott-Heron in *Storm Music*

So sings poet-songwriter Scott-Heron in homage to reggae, the hot, raw recipe of rhythm and syncopation that is as synonymous with Jamaica as is jazz with New Orleans, salsa with Puerto Rico, soul with Detroit, and blues with Chicago. In little more than a decade, the rugged sound of reggae has fought its way up from cheap amplifiers fronting shabby record stores in the slums of Kingston to the sophisticated sound systems of the First, Second and Third World elite. Reggae has left its mark on the compositions of Paul McCartney, the Rolling Stones, Paul Simon, Eric Clapton, Elton John and Stevie Wonder. And it carried a tough, streetwise kid named Bob Marley from the ghetto to international stardom.

Reggae music has crossed language barriers, broken down race and class lines, patched up political schisms and dissolved religious differences. It has displayed a remarkable ability to drain hostilities and peel away peoples' prejudices. Its narcotic beat rarely fails to stir the most narcoleptic of cardiovascular systems. Eyes blink open; thumb and index finger rub and snap, rub and snap. Blood pulses into pelvic areas, sparking seated buttocks to bounce from one cheek to the other. Those who stand are soon swaying, their knees reacting with a dip and lock, dip and lock; their forearms swinging as nimbly as the hinged limbs of a puppet.

Even the government, once so anxious about the power of reggae that the music was relegated to the deadly dawn hours of radio, has finally surrendered. It has recognized reggae for what it is — the heartbeat that kept a nation alive during its darkest decade.

The universal appeal and acceptance of Jamaica's unique reggae sound has turned the island into what one writer called "The Third World Nashville." Recording studios

Preceding pages: fans celebrate the early morning hours of Reggae Sunsplash 1982. At left, the late reggae king, Bob Marley.

and record shops abound. Two of the largest studios are Tuff Gong International, a legacy of the late Bob Marley which is now headed by his wife, Rita; and Dynamic Sounds, operated by Byron Lee when he is not performing with his legendary Dragonaires. These and dozens of other studios crank out hundreds of new titles each month in an attempt to satisfy the voracious appetite of Jamaica's listening public. New singers, bands and studios appear and disappear overnight. And international stars like Wonder and McCartney make regular trips to Jamaica's studios to learn the latest reggae riffs and lay down a few tracks.

Despite the diversification, reggae music is the elixir that keeps Jamaica's recording industry healthy, much as country-and-western music fuels the studios of the real Nashville. The story of the evolution of that music is a fascinating journey through Jamaica's colorful musical history.

'Down the Way Where the Nights Are . . .'

The story starts with a myth that still prevails in some circles — that an import from Trinidad called calypso is Jamaica's music. There are two possible reasons why.

The first was a talented Jamaican singer named Harry Belafonte. Belafonte recorded folksy commercial tunes like "The Banana Boat Song," "Jamaica Farewell" and "Island in the Sun." The albums on which these hits appeared also served up a healthy portion of songs with a calypso flavor. The American recording company that turned the handsome Belafonte into an international star apparently saw little difference between two tiny islands in the Caribbean, let alone differences in their music or even in their dark-skinned inhabitants.

In addition, calypso became so popular throughout the Caribbean that visitors believed each island had its own variation of the lively music. Jamaican entrepreneurs shamelessly perpetuated the myth during the tourist boom of the 1950s by filling their North Coast hotels and nightclubs with calypso bands.

In reality, Jamaica did have a brand of popular music of its own — mento. Mento descended from the music and dance that slaves from Africa used to enliven the drudgery of life on Jamaican plantations. Cruel masters often tried to beat the vestiges

Drawn after Nature & on Stone by I. M. Belisario.   Printed by A. Duperly.

BAND of the JAW—BONE JOHN—CANOE.

Kingston Jamaica — Aug. 1837.

234

of African culture out of the souls of their slaves, but some cultural traditions inevitably persisted. Their music survived even after the authorities discovered that rebellious slaves used drumming to communicate with other pockets of dissidents on the island. University of West Indies historian Edward Brathwaite noted in a study of Creole society in Jamaica: "It was this drumming, which the authorities and the missionaries tried unsuccessfully to eradicate by legislation and persuasion, respectively, which retained and transmitted important and distinctive elements of African/folk culture into the period after Emancipation."

The slaves also took a decidedly African approach to the fashionable Spanish, French and English salon and court dances of the

embraced amoral and malicious themes that grew out of the slanderous *mauvaise* language of Trinidad and the more genteel, but barbed, linguistic traditions of *picong*.

The Copacetic '40s and '50s

Mento leaned toward more playful, almost pornographic lyrics. The '40s and '50s produced such memorable hits as "Belly Lick," "Goosie Till a Morning," "Dr. Kinsey's Report," and "Night Talk"—most banned from radio airplay. Clyde Hoyte sang "Daphne Walking":

"Go a Poco meeting de other day
Sing de hymn but a could not pray
All me mind was on Daphne walking
Every night ah sleep a dreaming

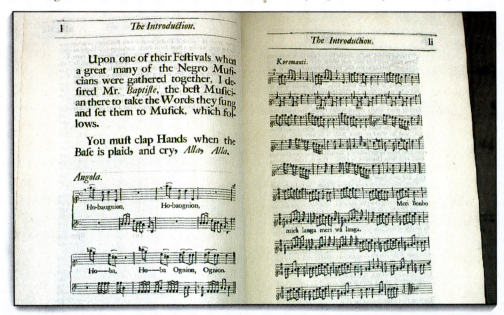

19th Century. Traces of the Parisian Quadrille can still be recognized in contemporary Jamaican folk dances. At first, mento was essentially music that accompanied a dance believed by some to have been sired by the quadrille. It called for a slow, undulating hip movement and close body contact below the waist that is commonly called "dubbing."

Thus, the assumption that mento is merely a Jamaican version of calypso is not accurate. Both forms acted as vehicles for social commentary, and even protest, but calypso

Isaac Mendes Belisario's light look at a Jamaican musical combo of the mid-19th Century (left). An old musical history shows the African influence on island music (above).

Her BEBOP waistline still de bother me . . ."

In the vernacular of the day, these were "sending" tunes and "rhygin rhythms," copacetic music to which every respectable *langalala* could spin, break away or spree. The purveyors of mento included the titled ones—Lord Lebby, Lord Power, Lord Fly, Lord Flea, Lord Messam of MoBay, Count Sticky—and bands like The Ticklers and the Pork Chops Rhumba Box Band of MoBay.

Mento gained its foothold in rural areas where large crowds flocked to lively *brams* dances in pre-transistor radio days. The country bands consisted of a rhumba box (an adaptation of the African thumb piano), bongos, guitar and shakers. Even aristocrats sought mento bands to add spice to their society dances.

But by the early '50s, mento began to fade under an assault of popular music transmitted from the United States. The lack of recording facilities in Jamaica at the time, which might otherwise have preserved and popularized mento, hastened its demise. Yet, it had already firmly established itself in the island's musical evolution. According to folk-music researcher Marjorie Whylie, "In the context of popular Jamaican music, mento could well be regarded as the matrix."

The Dukes Of
The 'Sound Systems'

Jamaica's first radio station, an amateur effort called ZQI, turned itself on in 1939. It broadcast live and taped programs of European classical music and American pop, and smaller servings of Jamaican folk and classical tunes. Radio Jamaica replaced ZQI in 1950, but continued to feed the island a diet heavy on mainstream American music. Yet many islanders had begun tuning in to powerful stations in the southern United States that pumped out the exciting, danceable beat of rhythm-and-blues. Louis Jordan, Fats Domino, Amos Milburn and Roscoe Gordon became the rage in Jamaica.

Rhythm-and-blues put stress on the second and fourth beat of the musical measure—the afterbeat—not unlike mento. R & B groups also pioneered the electrification of the guitar and organ, and later the bass. These instruments became fundamental in the development of popular Jamaican music.

In addition to its marked similarity to local rhythms, R & B also soared in popularity on the crest of a Jamaican phenomenon called the "sound system," a prototype of the disco. "Sound system men" trucked outsized speakers fed by powerful amplifiers to hired halls and beer gardens in every nook and canefield of Jamaica. People packed the dance halls when "the systems" thundered to the latest rhythm-and-blues '45s just in from New York and Miami.

Rivalries erupted between the systems men of the '50s. Two of the greatest were the glittering Duke Reid and Clement Dodd, who disc-jockeyed under the *nom de guerre* Sir Coxonne. Michael Thomas graphically described Reid's style in an article in *Rolling Stone* magazine:

Duke Reid used to arrive at his dances in flowing ermine, a mighty golden crown on his head, a .45 in a cowboy holster, a shotgun over his shoulder, and a cartridge belt across his chest. He was gorgeous, gold rings on every finger and thumb, the perfect gaudy image-melt of Hollywood gangster and high camp aristocrat. He'd have himself carried through the throng to his turntables, and then he'd let one go, the latest Lloyd Price, a rare old Joe Turner, and while the record played, Duke would get on a mike and start DJing, going "Wake-it-Up, Wake-it-Up" and "Good God" and "Jump shake-a leg."

The success of Reid and Coxonne spawned more competing systems—Nick's, Tom's, the Mighty Sebastian, each promising systems that challenged the sound barrier and "exclusive" singles. Reid and Coxonne regularly flew to New York to sniff out new music. When they found it, they would

scratch off the record labels to throw the competition off the scent for as long as possible. Spies and strong-arm men soon entered the picture.

Consequently, Jamaican artists began to take a cue from American rhythm-and-blues. Early vocalists like Laurel Aitken, Derrick Morgan and Owen Gray cut records strongly influenced by the New Orleans R & B sound. At first intended mainly for the systems market, their recordings found their way into the hands of the public. So Reid and Coxonne exchanged their sound systems for recording studios. By 1959, a record industry weaned on rhythm and blues and a modicum of calypso/mento began producing music that wasn't quite either, but which was very Jamaican.

The evolution of contemporary Jamaican music as depicted in album covers—from the legendary Don Drummond (above) to the Skatalites and "Toots" Hibbert (right).

Jamaica's early musicians often developed their skills in military bands. One group at Alpha Boys' School proved particularly fertile ground. Established in the 1890s by the Sisters of Mercy order of Roman Catholic nuns, Alpha catered to underprivileged youths and orphans. They included trombone players Rico Rodriquez and Don Drummond, tenor sax players Tommy McCook and Roland Alphanso, alto saxman Lester Sterling, trumpeter Johnny Moore, lead guitarists Jah Jerry and Ernest Ranglin, drummer Lloyd Knibbs and Drumbago, bass players Lloyd Brevette and Cluet Johnson and pianists Jackie Mittoo, Gladstone Anderson and Theophilus Beckford. These giants of Jamaican musical history graduated to jobs in dance bands or north coast hotels

behind the beat in the best jazz tradition. Vocalizing was kept to a minimum, allowing the musicians more room to play. The cumulative effect proved several degrees cooler than steamy R & B. Beckford had officiated at the birth of ska.

The onomatopoeic sound of the piano comp—ska-ska-ska-ska—gave this newborn musical form its name. The island's musicians suddenly found themselves with a music of their own to play, explore and cultivate.

The Rise and Fall of the Skatalites

Sir Coxonne succeeded in corraling Alpha's band of iconoclastic musicians; as a result, his Studio One amassed a catalog that

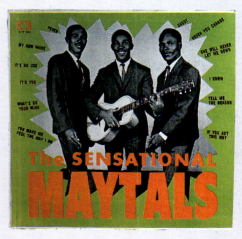

until Reid, Coxonne and another systems man-turned-producer named Prince Buster coaxed them into the recording studio.

While this pool of talent was experimenting in the studio, the government's Jamaica Broadcasting Corporation (JBC) took to the air waves in 1959. Its programmers demonstrated a sensitivity for indigenous music that had previously been missing on local radio. In fact, the JBC played a milestone tune into prominence.

Beckford's "Easy Snappin'" walked the line between rhythm-and-blues and boogie-woogie. In the process, it stumbled upon a new musical style. Beckford nimbly poked out a steady boogie-woogie riff on his piano in the first and second beat. So did Jah Jerry's guitar, prior to his solo. Cluet Johnson walked his bass on a straight four while Papa Son's brushwork accented the first and second beat. The horns of Alphanso, Rodriquez and Ossie Scott, meanwhile, laid back

is a veritable thesaurus of Jamaican music. From its ranks rose the Skatalites, comprised of McCook, Alphanso, Moore, Drummond, Mitto, Jerry, Brevette, Sterling and Knibbs. Although short-lived, the group left Jamaica a lively, largely instrumental musical form that fostered its own peculiar dance movement—a bobbing torso seemingly powered by a piston-like arm movement. Dancers grunted—uh, uh, uh,—virtually echoing the horns and guitar.

Trombonist Drummond dominated ska in much the same way that Bob Marley came to dominate reggae. Drummond developed a highly personal instrumental style that successors have yet to surpass. A significant number of his compositions reflected minor blues melodies, melancholy, and a kind of non-verbal protest, an expression of his own deteriorating mental state. It was this rebelliousness in Drummond's music, and his conversion to the Rastafarian faith, that ultimately had a tremendous impact on the aspiring young musicians of his day.

Ras Tafari, with its spiritual godhead in Ethiopian Emperor Haile Selassie and its other African cultural inspirations, redefined the folk rhythms of *kumina* and *burru* beginning with the 1959 Ffolkes Brothers hit, "Oh Carolina." That song introduced the legendary drumming of Count Ozzie, a musical guru and ardent follower of Ras Tafari who had considerable influence on the music of the Skatalites.

But ska peaked in popularity by 1966. Drummond, its most eloquent exponent, murdered his sweetheart and was committed to a mental asylum where he died in 1969. The Skatalites disbanded. Singers began to encroach upon the music that had been dominated by instrumentalists, articulating what the horn men had only hinted at. Musicians soon took a back seat to the vocalists. "Rock steady" had arrived.

'Renting a Tile'

Perhaps as a result of the pensive "What do we do now?" period that followed the euphoria of independence, the tempo of Jamaican music slowed down. More emphasis was put on syncopation. The drop of the drum, characteristic of mento's rhythmic structure, became more pronounced. The guitar strum of rock steady also harked back to mento. The style freed the bass from timekeeping and gave it an infinitely more melodic role, again a possible throwback to the manner in which mento bands used the rhumba box. As its name implies, dance strongly motivated rock steady. But it was slower and more languid than the high-energy exercises sparked by ska. Dancers swayed to Delroy Wilson's "Dancin' Mood" and Alton Ellis' "Rock Steady" as if glued to one spot, keeping all their frustrations in that little space—"renting a tile."

The lyrics of some of these new tunes mirrored the poets' attitudes toward their people's place in Jamaican society. They did not always like what they saw. Consider Bob Andy's "I've Got to Go Back Home":

I've got to go back home
This couldn't be my home
It must be somewhere else
Can't get no food to eat
Can't get a job to get bread
That's why I've got to go back home...

As the lyrics became even angrier, rock steady gave way to reggae. This new emphasis on what songs had to say opened the door for a flood of Jamaican vocalists. Ironically, the best had begun their careers during the heyday of instrument-oriented ska. One of the most successful was Jimmy Cliff, a skinny teenager with a soothing voice.

Born in Somerton, a small town on the outskirts of Montego Bay, Cliff left home for the lights and lures of Kingston. There he lived in its gaping pits of poverty singing and recording several rhythm-and-blues-type numbers for sound systems men who balked at playing them. But in 1962, the 14-year-old Cliff persuaded Beverly Records producer and owner Leslie Kong to give him a break. Kong did and never regretted it. Among Cliff's biggest hits for Kong's label was the 1964 story of a storm, "Hurricane Hattie." That same year Cliff migrated to Great Britain. England's swelling population of

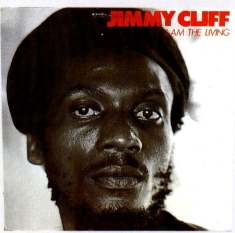

Jamaicans re-adapted ska and called it "blue-beat." Cliff signed with Island Records in London in 1965 and scored with hits including "Many Rivers to Cross," a brooding ballad about his own hard times and struggles to survive. After winning a Brazilian song contest in 1968, Cliff returned to Jamaica where he immediately cut his first international hit for Leslie Kong, "Wonderful World, Beautiful People."

Cliff's biggest break came when producer-director Perry Henzel cast him in the lead role of a movie, *The Harder They Come*. Cliff portrayed Ivan O. Martin, a singing, gun-slinging tragic hero, whose story (to a point) paralleled Jimmy's life. The film became a classic cult film and is credited with

Two faces of contemporary reggae: Jimmy Cliff, as he appeared on a record sleeve (above), and Winston Rodney, better known as Burning Spear (right).

238

launching reggae music into the world lime-light.

Cliff did not fare quite as well as his music, however. His subsequent conversion from a rebel singer into a clean-cut Muslim apparently lost him many of the fiery, young fans looking for anti-establishment heroes. Ironically, these fans turned to another Jamaican singer that Cliff had introduced to Kong, a man who wore his snaking locks like a crown and claimed the throne of the king of reggae. His name was Robert Nesta Marley.

Cliff has remained original and philo-sophical about his unfairly diminished role in the development and popularization of reg-gae. "My role has been as the shepherd who opens the gate. Now we're going into a

uses in an "open-throat" style in the best traditions of American gospel music. Toots' style has been inspired by Ray Charles and Otis Redding.

His trio, Toots and the Maytals, has sur-vived every twist in popular Jamaican music and still runs singles up the local charts. Clement Dodd produced the group's first hit, "Six and Seven Books," in 1962. For Prince Buster's label, they produced several topsellers including "Pain in my Belly." After serving time in prison on charges of dealing ganja, Toots bounced out in 1966 with a song based on his experience called "5446 Was My Number." He followed it up with the timeless reggae anthem, "Pressure Drop."

In Stephen Davis' definitive book, *Reggae*

different pasture," he said. With Marley gone, Cliff may get another much-deserved crack at the title. His international stature has continued to grow steadily, if not drama-tically, and he commands massive followings in Africa, Brazil and the Soviet Union.

Toots and the Maytals: 'Comin' From the People'

Whatever happens to Cliff, he has still fared better than the man who apparently gave Jamaica the word reggae, if not the music itself. Frederick "Toots" Hibbert re-corded his first single the year before Cliff burst into prominence. Fame has eluded Toots despite a powerful voice that he

Bloodlines, Toots boasted: "I invented reg-gae. Wrote a song called 'Do the Reggay' in 196- I don't remember when, but I wrote it anyway. It's true. Reggae just mean comin' from the people. Everday t'ing, like from the ghetto. So all of our music, our Jamaican rhythm, comin' from the majority. Everyday t'ing that people use like food; we just put music to it and mek a dance out of it, y'know. I would say that reggae come from the roots of the reggae that is the ghetto. When you say reggae you mean regular, majority. And when you say reggae it mean poverty, suffering, Ras Tafari, everything. Ghetto. It's music from the rebels, people who don't have what they want."

Regardless of its literary origins, reggae,

as the music came to be called about 1968, took the mild protests of the rock-steady poets into the realm of all-out social protest as restlessness increased among Jamaica's poor majority and rivalries intensified between the two political parties that promised salvation. Many groups even added militant touches to their songs. This marked the era of the "Rude Bwoys," as the word "boys" comes out sounding when spoken in emphatic patois.

Birth of the Wailers

In the midst of this rapidly changing music and social scene of the mid-'60s, behind walls of corrugated tin and plywood in West Kingston's tough Trench Town, four youths named Junior Brathwaite, Peter (Tosh) MacIntosh, Bunny Livingston and Bob Marley began rehearsing. When Clement Dodd opened his Jamaica Recording and Publishing studios in 1964, the group was just one of many that came knocking on his door.

"When they first came in, they were like most other groups just starting out—young, inexperienced and willing to learn," Dodd recalled. "I coached them, worked on their songwriting. I had an album from the States by all the top soul artists. Bob Marley liked the Impressions, the Tams and the Moonglows the most. You can hear the influence on some of his early songs." That influence is most apparent in some of the group's slow, romantic songs like "It Hurts to Be Alone." Faster ska hits like "Simmer Down" featured superlative backing by the Skatalites.

As the gangs of tough, unemployed "Rude Bwoys" began roaming the streets of Jamaica, they protested their poverty by looting, shooting and defying the police. The music of Bob Marley's group echoed the times. They took the name Wailing Rude Bwoys before shortening it to the Wailers. Marley expressed the feelings of defiant youth in the composition called "Rudie":

Jailhouse keeps empty
Rudie gets plenty
Baton sticks get shorter
Rudie gets taller...

Derrick Morgan, the Clarendonians and Desmond Dekker of "Poor Me, Israelites" fame, also took up the tenor of the times. But it was the Wailers who prevailed. With a major assist from producer Lee Perry, they transformed reggae into its best-known form. Others claim to have created the style. Clement Dodd said he patented the sound when experimenting with an echo unit when his guitar began strumming the now-familiar

chaka-chaka-chaka rhythm. But as one writer put it: "Reggae is not just a music, it is more a philosophy, with the advice handed out to a danceable beat."

In an interview with *Rockers* magazine, Bunny Livingston Wailer offered another definition and description of reggae in perfect patois:

Well mek me tell you little history about Africa and reggae. Africa a one nickname; Ethiopia is the real name fe the whole a dat place. Reggae means the *Kings* music from the latin *Regis* e.g. like Regal. Now Ethiopia (Africa) is a place with plenty King so they have to be entertained with the King's music. So from you a play reggae with the heavy emphasis pon bass and drums, you a mingle with the spirit of Africa. The rhythm is connected to the heartbeat...

Bob Marley understood that. His metaphysical imagery, his embrace of Rastafari and its inseparable association with the music, made reggae a musical style to be reckoned with.

Stir It Up, Rub It In

Embittered by the token pay that producers offered Jamaican artists of the times, the Wailers disbanded in 1967. Marley went to live with his mother in Wilmington, Delaware. But after a few months he returned to Jamaica, where he reorganized the Wailers.

This time, the group formed its own label called Wailin' Soul. Despite a string of hits including "Bend Down Low," "Stir It Up" and "Nice Time," they still failed to turn a profit. To add to the misfortunes, Bunny Livingston was jailed for nearly a year on ganja charges.

The restive Marley left Kingston again, this time for the parish of St. Ann, where he had been born in the village of Rhoden Hall in 1945. He tried planting corn instead of singing. But a black American singer named Johnny Nash came to Jamaica in search of talent. Story has it that when Nash saw Marley performing on television, he immediately set out for the country to find him.

The Wailers agreed to record an album for Nash's production company. Nash's own version of Marley's "Stir It Up" climbed into the Top Ten in many countries. Marley also collaborated on a film score with Nash in Sweden and penned the popular "Guava Jelly" with its immortal refrain: "You've got to rub it on my belly like guava jelly."

Meanwhile, Lee Perry had put together one of the great reggae studio bands, the Upsetters, for his new record label of the same name. Led by brothers Aston and

Carlton Barrett, the Upsetters released several instrumental hits named for Italian spaghetti westerns, "The Return of Django" and "The Liquidator."

Before these records could fill the void left by Marley's departure, however, he returned from overseas. The Wailers teamed up with Perry to produce some of their finest work: two classic reggae albums, *Soul Revolution Part Two* and *Soul Rebel*. One featured a song called "Duppy Conqueror" that firmly established Marley as a powerful songwriter with its description of his release from a prison stint.

Yes me friend
Dem set me free again
Yes me friend
Me dey pon street again.

Marley's melodies also broke new ground. The timing and the manner in which the importance of the instruments was apportioned just sounded different. It embraced all the popular musical forms that preceded it, but Marley's brand of rhythm struck original notes that have come to symbolize reggae.

The money finally began trickling in. The Wailers used it to form their own company, Tuff Gong, in 1970. Late the next year, they exploded their biggest hit to that date, "Trench Town Rock."

Above, a young fan of reggae and the Rastafarian religion that inspires much of the music takes a turn on stage at Reggae Sunsplash.

In 1971, the art of the DJ also resurfaced in the form of a raving toastmaster named U Roy. Rooted in the Jamaican folk tradition of rhythm games and later in the performances of the sound systems men, U Roy and his fellow practitioners strung together nonsense lyrics, rhymes and commentary to the background of reggae instrumentals in an innovative manner. His one-of-a-kind classic was "Wear You to the Ball."

In 1972, Marley's group joined forces with the Upsetters. Bob did lead vocals and played rhythm guitar, Tosh sang and also strummed guitar, Bunny sang and handled percussion, Eral Wire Lindo controlled the keyboards, Aston "Family Man" Barrett played bass, and Carlton Barrett pounded drums. The new incarnation of the Wailers rocketed to international fame under the tutelage of a part-Jamaican producing genius named Chris Blackwell.

Blackwell and Marley Catch Fire

The London-born Blackwell had come to Jamaica as a youth with his Irish father and Jamaican mother. He led a privileged childhood between a palatial Kingston home that has since been turned into the Terra Nova Hotel and a country estate in St. Mary. The versatile Blackwell worked as an aide-de-camp to two British governors of Jamaica, Sir Hugh Foote and Sir Kenneth Blackburne. He also was a real-estate salesman, a scooter hirer and a water-ski instructor in Montego Bay before a cousin persuaded him to try his hand at recording.

Blackwell first hit the top of the charts with his production of Laurel Aitken's "Little Sheila." Pioneer singers Owen Gray and Jackie Edwards also joined his stable of talent.

In 1959, Blackwell joined with Leslie Kong and two other partners to establish Island Records, the label that helped make Jimmy Cliff an international star. It established headquarters in a looming house on Hope Road that now houses Tuff Gong's offices. Rapidly growing sales of Island's records in Britain prompted Blackwell to migrate there. In 1962, his cover version of Millie Small's "My Boy Lollipop" became the international hit that cinched his reputation as a successful producer of early British rock as well as Jamaican music.

The Blackwell-Marley association spawned the Wailers' first internationally acclaimed album, *Catch A Fire*. Critics in the United States and Great Britain praised it as the advent of a new wave in rock music. Similar applause greeted the release of the follow-up, *Burnin'*.

But the sweetness of success soon soured. Bob Marley's overwhelming stage presence and voice singled him out as the soul of the group. Tosh and Bunny left in 1975 to launch solo careers of their own. Tosh has since developed his own international following with albums like *Legalize It* and *Bush Doctor*. Bunny (Livingston) Wailer has turned elusively inward and unpredictable after several stunning efforts, led by *Blackheart Man*.

Acclaim for a Musical Messiah

Bob Marley became a solo act in essence, too, but beefed up his act with an expanded

musical messiah. His own government in Jamaica awarded him the nation's third highest civil honor, the Order of Merit. That made him the Honorable Robert Nesta Marley, O.M. Marley became fabulously wealthy. Still, he never forgot his roots as he sang in one of his most poignant songs. "No Woman, No Cry":

Said I remember when we used to sit
In the government yard in Trench Town
Observing all the hypocrites
Mingle with the good people we meet . . .
And then Georgie would make the fire light,
I seh, log would burnin' thru the nights
Then we would cook cornmeal porridge,
Of which I'd share with you . . .

By 1981, most of the world had acclaimed

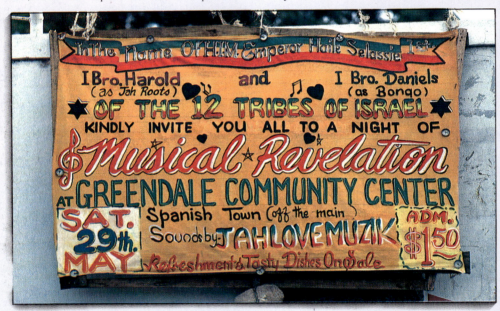

version of the Wailers and a set of soulful back-up singers called the I-Threes. They consisted of his wife, Rita, Marcia Griffiths and Judy Mowatt. With their backing, Marley danced, stomped, sang and shook his shaggy mane to greater success beginning with the release of *Natty Dread* in 1975. Albums like *Rastaman Vibration, Exodus* and *Survival* followed. They included such enduring singles as "Natural Mystic," "Jammin" and "Positive Vibration."

The Third World gave Marley his warmest receptions. He hailed the transformation of Rhodesia into Zimbabwe with a song and a triumphant concert at the Independence Day celebrations in Salisbury on April 17, 1980. The Zimbabweans hailed him as a

Marley as an international superstar and a major influence on contemporary music. Only the stubborn, stagnating studios in the United States resisted this Third World upstart. But at the same time, they made hits of Marley compositions recorded by others—like Eric Clapton's version of Marley's "I Shot the Sheriff."

Ironically, it was during a tour that Marley hoped would finally make his mark on America that his meteoric rise to fame suddenly ended. At the age of 36, at the height

A poster on a Kingston wall invites all to one of the city's frequent reggae extravaganzas (above). The Mighty Diamonds welcome dawn with a song at Sunsplash '82 (right).

of his popularity, Marley died of brain cancer in Miami's Cedars of Lebanon Hospital on May 11, 1981.

Jamaica showered its fallen hero with a funeral the likes of which only Jamaicans could stage. Marley lay in state at the National Arena in Kingston from 8 a.m. to 7:30 p.m. on May 20. His body was dressed in a blue denim suit, a Bible propped in his right hand, his guitar in his left. A tam in the red, green and gold colors of the Ethiopian flag covered his head, and his locks were neatly arranged on his shoulders. An estimated 24,000 people filed passed his casket that day, among them the prime minister and most other government officials.

The following day, Marley was eulogized at a funeral ceremony conducted by mem-

evolving, or is beginning to stagnate without the guidance of its master practitioner.

Marley's wife, Rita, has taken over Tuff Gong Records and is becoming a star in her own right. "One Draw," a lengthy single banned from Jamaican radio because of its celebration of ganja smoking, still became a monster hit on the island and sold more than 50,000 copies in the United States. But American fans and promoters bristled when she canceled a major tour of five U.S. cities—something Bob would never have done.

Four of Bob's 10 children, meanwhile, have pulled their own sound together in a group called the Melody Makers. Led by the teenaged Ziggy, the group also consists of Sharon, Cedella and Steve. They broke into

bers of the Ethiopian Orthodox Church. His wife, five of his children and his mother eulogized him with some of his own songs. Then his body was driven to a gravesite far from Kingston, in the hills of the parish of St. Ann near his birthplace. The funeral procession stretched for 55 miles.

Reggae Without Marley

Ironically, now that Marley is gone, Americans have finally begun showing signs of discovering his music. And despite Marley's absence, the record studios of Jamaica are cranking out more reggae music than ever. Still, many wonder whether Jamaica's unique brand of contemporary music is still

the Jamaican Top 40 with a number called "What a Plot" in which Ziggy wailed in a manner reminiscent of his father.

Outside, the Marley clan, numerous challengers to Bob's preeminence have emerged and reemerged. Jimmy Cliff has been climbing the charts with metronomic regularity. The venerable Dennis Brown and Gregory Issacs have begun moving reggae toward the musical mainstream. That has earned Brown a contract with A & M Records and Issacs a spot on the Island Records label.

The Mighty Diamonds, Toots and the Maytals, Burning Spear, Roy Shirley, Lloyd Parkes and We the People Band, Byron Lee and the Dragonaires, Leroy Sibles (an original Heptone), and John Holt continue to ride new reggae rhythms to the top of the local charts. Holt wrote "The Tide is High," which became an international hit for the reggae-influenced new-wave group Blondie.

Newer groups making an international impact include Third World and Black Uhuru. Stevie Wonder helped engineer Third World's *You've Got the Power* album onto the American rhythm-and-blues charts even before it hit Jamaica. Black Uhuru is a one-woman, two-man trio whose albums have had phenomenal success in the United States and Europe. And there are signs that a popular group called Chalice could also hit overseas.

Foreign Reggae Phenoms

Another phenomenon has been the rise of foreign reggae groups. Most notable are Great Britain's Steel Pulse, who regularly appear at Jamaica's ultimate celebration of music, Reggae Sunsplash. The 1982 Sunsplash saw the emergence of an even odder phenomenon—a group of Caucasians from Kentucky and Chicago called Blue Riddim Band, who earned ovations from the tough, tired Jamaican audiences.

New Wave groups like the B-52s and the Police owe an obvious debt to reggae. One Jamaican journalist commented: "The irony is that a group like Third World actually opens shows for the group Police, which is in essence a copy of Jamaican groups from the early '60s, shiners suits with 'high-water' pants and all!"

The local scene, meanwhile, has undergone a revival in the "dub" and DJ forms of reggae. Dub essentially strips the music down to its basic elements, as *Showman* magazine noted:

Dub records often start out sounding like conventional reggae—a singer intones an opening phrase, keyboards and guitars begin clickclacking against each other in percussive counterpoint, bass and drum back into step, a horn section contributes an anticipatory fanfare. But almost immediately the music begins to unravel. The singer and horns vanish, leaving only a ghostly shimmering electronic echo. Bass and drums crunch dutifully around as snatches of guitars, keyboards and other instruments appear out of nowhere, repeat themselves for a measure or two, and then evaporate. Sometimes the instruments fall in together for part of a verse and the music's textures thickens. Sometimes almost everything disappears

and one hears a single drumbeat, a bass note, then nothing, nothing at all."

The scant dub background has been used by poets like Mutabaruka who recite their words over the sound. Hence, the emergence of a new group of "dub poets."

Yellowman and 'Mr Chin'

DJ harks back to the days of the sound systems and fast-talking ad-libbers like I-Roy, U-Roy and Big Youth. The latest rage is a slim, pale-skinned albino, Winston Foster, better known as Yellowman. Not since Edgar and Johnny Winter broke into pop music as albinos have the likes of Yellowman been seen.

His negroid features, sparse beaded hair, yellow clothes and glasses add to his bizarre appearance. But Jamaicans love him. He proved the sensation of the 1982 Reggae Sunsplash in Montego Bay as thousands of loyal fans waited until 6:30 a.m. to watch him take the stage, where he bobbed back and forth reciting the lyrics to hits like "Mr. Chin," "I'm Getting Married in the Morning," and "Mad Over Me." His insistence on spouting "slackness," the Jamaican term for raunchy lyrics, has caused many of his songs to be banned from radio airplay. Yet he still had six singles in the Top 40 and two in the Top Ten simultaneously.

Yellowman, in the manner of many reggae stars, overcame a rugged life as an orphan abandoned to Kingston's Maxfield Park Home and Alpha Boys' School. In addition, he had to overcome the stigma of being an albino, and Jamaicans often shouted the name "*dundus*" at him as he walked the streets. His success has brought him his own home in Kingston's Franklin Town and a yellow BMW.

Jamaica's own annual orgy of music, sun and sin—Reggae Sunsplash—has also become a sellout event. Attendance now tops 150,000 each year. Increasing legions of foreign fans make the summer pilgrimage to Montego Bay, where they hear the latest sounds Jamaica has to offer.

For four days, bands and soloists parade across the stage, from late night to well past dawn. Rastafarian hawkers peddle vegetarian I-tal food and sinsemilla. At times, black, brown, white and yellow join hands in the middle of the night. They sing, smile and sway in unison. Reggae music has brought them together.

This vintage juke box still spins sounds at The Country Club in Kensington (right). Following pages: Byron Lee's Dragonaires.

Drawn from Life, and Lithog. by I.M. Belisario.

"KOO, KOO, OR ACTOR=BOY."

Kingston. Jamaica.

Printed by A.Duperly.

DANCE AND DRAMA: EVERYBODY IS A STAR

Jamaicans pride themselves on their sense of rhythm, their love of laughter, their loose-limbed style. It's not peculiarly Jamaican, of course. It's Caribbean. It's African. It's a reflection of the many cultures blended into one unique style, a marriage between the Old World and the New.

Jamaicans boast that they make drama of everything. A man on the sidewalk peeling pineapples will wave his knife like an artist to "mad" the crowd of admirers he is convinced have gathered to watch him. A man who lops off the top of a green "water coconut" to share the cool, sweet liquid inside will flash the broad-bladed machete known as a *wamparah* in sweeping arcs, using far more energy than the simple task requires.

The epitome of Jamaican street drama unfolds when a man tries to back up his truck. Inevitably, a crowd gathers for no apparent reason. One man casts himself in the role of traffic director. He gives instructions to the driver to "back-back" or reverse back. (Jamaicans often repeat words for emphasis.) The trusting driver back-backs as far as he is directed, then crashes into a wall. The annoyed traffic director walks off muttering, "Me never tell you fe back-back so far." The bystanders laugh. It's pure theater.

Thus it comes as no surprise to find, in such a society, that those who entertain on stage must sweep and soar and rise on every occasion to satisfy the demanding audiences. Jamaican audiences can be cruel in their detachment, sitting on their hands until those onstage have earned their approval. But when the performers do gain that respect, the Jamaican audience embraces them.

There is a side of Jamaica which many visitors, too timid or ill-informed to venture beyond the walls of their vacation villas, often go home without experiencing. The collective love of the Jamaican people has spawned an internationally acclaimed dance company, a national theater group with a distinctively Jamaican style of presentation, and numerous performing groups and ensembles that distinguish themselves in their own dynamic ways.

Preceding pages: students perform folk dances at Kingston Parish Church. At left, a 19th Century John Canoe troupe member.

Regrettably, Jamaica's cultural image has long been linked with contortionist limbo dancers, kerosene-guzzling fire eaters, and calypso dancers who gyrate to endless reprisals of "The Banana Boat Song" and "Island in the Sun." Island tour companies would do well to exploit the sophistication of many modern travelers by mounting bus tours to Kingston to showcase what Jamaica really has to offer in the realm of dance and theater.

A Dance to Prominence

Even novice travelers would enjoy a performance of the National Dance Theatre Company of Jamaica, popularly called the NDTC. It vividly embodies the rich tapestry of expression that draws its inspiration from the island's diverse ethnic influences. The company is based in Kingston. Its annual season runs from mid-July to mid-August, but there is also a mini-season in November and December. Special performances include a sampler of religious works from the Company's extensive repertoire, held at the Little Theatre at dawn on Easter Sunday every year. It's definitely worth rising with the sun to see.

The NDTC is an ensemble of dancers, musicians and singers dedicated to exploring the seemingly innate sense of stylized movement in the Jamaican soul. It started out in 1962 as an offshoot of that year's independence celebrations. A grand dance show called "Roots and Rhythms" was staged at a gala attended by Britain's Princess Margaret and U.S. Vice-President Lyndon Johnson —and the NDTC was born. Two young men, Rex Nettleford and Eddy Thomas, were the catalysts.

"For 20 years the Company has grown alongside the independent state of Jamaica, for 20 years it has weathered the winds of political and social change as the emerging nation struggled to make independence more than just a change of flag; and if there is one way in which this company can set a standard for the nation, it is in the discipline that maintains grace under pressure," wrote Nettleford on the occasion of the Company's 20th anniversary in 1982.

The multi-talented Nettleford now juggles his time between his professor's duties at the University of the West Indies, lecturing on the international circuit, directing the Trade

Union Education Institute and the University's Extramural Department, and writing books on the nation's culture and development. Somehow, he has also managed to continue as director of the NDTC, as the choreographer of many of its presentations and as one of its most beloved and best known dancers.

Whetting the World's Appetites

"To the exoticist who merely wants his appetite whetted with writhing bodies, the Jamaican dance company may well prove a disappointment. . . . like all serious artists, the Jamaican dancers have given priority to works of intrinsic artistic merit rather than indulged the folksy exoticism which they know wide-eyed foreigners and folksy chauvinistic patriots all too frequently demand," Nettleford said.

Still, audiences around the world have discovered that the NDTC fulfills their need for more than "writhing primitive bodies." The Jamaican Company has been acclaimed in concerts from Mexico City to Moscow, from Adelaide to Atlanta, and points in between. Elected heads of government and blood royalty have thrilled to performances of the NDTC. And the dancers have triumphed in spite of the thin air of Mexico City and bouts of jet lag incurred by jaunts from Jamaica to Australia. They have been cheered by homesick Jamaican immigrants and expatriates in Brooklyn and Toronto, Cardiff and London. Young Muscovites have tried to barter company members right out of their blue jeans, and Canadian parliamentarians in black tie surprised the Jamaicans by turning up unannounced at an early overseas performance in a small Canadian town.

One of the NDTC's most unusual experiences occurred at the first Caribbean Festival of the Arts in Guyana in 1972. Local officials had arranged for an entire performance of the Company to be broadcast live— over radio. Journalist-playwright Barbara Gloudon was tapped for the unenviable task of sitting on a ledge in a Georgetown theater, from which she could see only half the stage, and describing the performance to Amerindians in the Guyanese forests, while Kumina drums similar to Guyana's *kweh-kweh* drums pounded out rhythms in the background.

Ballets of the Spirit

The repertoire of Jamaica's dance company incorporates eclectic dance forms rang-

ing from the indigenous to classical to modern, reflecting the island's decades of exposure to external influences. Locally produced titles include "Street People" and "Backlash" with their vignettes about life in the ghetto. The Rastafarian sub-culture inspired "Two Drums for Babylon," and "Court of Jah" is performed totally to the reggae music of Bob Marley.

"The folklore of Jamaica abounds not so much in movement as in songs and stories. Jamaican dance creators have therefore plunged adventurously into the creative and the abstract, making dances out of universal ideas and composing ballets of the spirit rather than the letter of Jamaican folklore," Nettleford explained. "This has led to exploration rather than to the boldly authentic

commercialized transference from the field on to the stage."

Other works choreographed by Nettleford, Thomas and other members of the company incorporate ancient rituals with African roots like Kumina, Etu and Pocomania, while the modern techniques of the Martha Graham School in New York lend contemporary themes to the NDTC repertoire. Company members have a standing invitation to train at the Graham School in New York. Even Prime Minister Edward

National Dance Theatre Company director Rex Nettleford dances the part of the Obeahman in a number called "Myal" (above). Louise Bennett in the Pantomime "Queenie's Daughter."

Seaga, a patron of the NDTC, has contributed his vast knowledge of Jamaican folk culture. During his days as Finance Minister, he served as a consultant in the creation of works like "Myal" and "Pocomania."

The Jamaican government has traditionally thrown its support behind the island's artistic movements, a fact that has undoubtedly contributed to Jamaica's preeminence in Caribbean artistic and cultural circles. Yet, neither the NDTC or any other performing group has ever received financial support from the government. They flourish strictly on the willingness of company members to excel and attract throngs of paying customers.

NDTC members, for example, receive no pay for their professional efforts. Many work

full-time as secretaries, teachers, doctors and attorneys—then spend long, grueling hours in training for each year's performances. Their only reward is the warm applause of their fellow Jamaicans, the occasional cheers of an international audience, and the praise of critics like the reviewer for the prestigious *Dance and Dancers* magazine who wrote: "Jamaica is the only Caribbean island to have built a company of this kind. . . . It is amazing what has been achieved."

Festival!

Dance is only a small part of the cultural fruits that bloom throughout the island in mid-summer each year. The weeks leading up to the annual Independence Day celebrations on August 6 have simply been designated "Festival!"—with an exclamation point. Painters, public speakers, singers, woodcarvers, sculptors, musicians, photographers, even chefs roll out their best work and most polished performances in competition for prizes and plaudits.

Festival! emerged from old Jamaican community traditions of Christmas morning concerts, "tea meetings" of songs and dances and recitations, and church fund-raising rallies. It also provides an outlet for the Jamaican flair for "showing off." In the 1950s, the Jamaican government began organizing this hodgepodge of events into a single, massive outpouring of talent. Now, a formal Festival Movement meanders through the countryside each year encouraging competition in various artistic endeavors. Finals are held during Independence Week in Kingston. Many are nationally televised.

Obviously, Trinidad's internationally famous Carnival celebrations provided a spark for Jamaica's Festival! Gate receipts and business sponsorships have added a touch of commercialization to the festivities. But the importance of Festival! surfaces in the deep involvement of schools throughout the island. They seize the opportunity to motivate their students to maintain and further develop island traditions. Parents pass on customs to the young who incorporate them in speech, drama, dance and music. Young people thus learn traditional dances like "Bruckin Party," a sly satire on goings-on in the days of the Great Houses when "*bakkra*"—the white master—held grand balls which servants and laborers watched through the windows.

The Jamaican penchant for coining words to fit any phrase has produced a verb that describes what happens during the annual Festival! Jamaicans "festibrate." Visitors to the island during July and August should make it a point to join in the festibrations.

Pantomime in Patois

An old Jamaican phrase advises that "we tek bad sinting mek laugh." Roughly translated, this means the speaker tempers potential tragedy with humor. Nowhere is this Jamaican characteristic more in evidence than in a 40-year-old tradition called the National Pantomime.

Although the word pantomime evokes visions of a performance without words, Jamaicans adapted the word to describe a fast-moving musical comedy with plenty of dialogue in the local patois—a blend of standard English and the Twi dialect of West Africa. Far from being a silent show, this delicious concoction produces a potent piece of theater alive with wisecracks, send-ups of peculiarly local situations, and lampoons of historic events. Pantomime "makes sport" of grave matters, and mimics the foibles, the heartbreaks and the joys of Jamaican life. The Pantomime audience in turn responds with continuous peals of laughter and even joins in repartee with the performers, becoming an integral part of the show itself.

People of all ages, from all walks of life and every part of the island, descend on downtown Kingston for the annual National Pantomime offering. Many even charter

British favorites.

But as Jamaicans always do, they soon transformed English tradition into their own thing. They added characters from Jamaican folklore like Anansi, the West African spider god, and his innumerable prodigy—Brer Tacoma, Brer Tiger and others. Soon playwrights brought in caricatures of public figures like politicians and police chiefs. English music-hall songs gave way to indigenous rhythms, including the drumming frenzies of Pocomania and the beat of Christmas time's John Canoe (Jonkanoo) dances. Contemporary rhythms like ska and reggae eventually found their way into pantomime scripts like that of "Johnny Reggae." "Carib Gold" in 1960 and "Banana Boy" in 1961 saw the introduction of sophisticated dance

buses to transport entire towns and villages to Ward Theater, the traditional venue for the Pantomime. The tradition dates back to the years when Jamaica's Little Theatre Movement, the Caribbean's oldest theatrical ensemble, staged traditional versions of the English Pantomimes that were based on fairy tales. Actors and actresses performed in standard formulas: a Dame, for example, always appeared in a comic, exaggerrated manner so that there was no confusion about the actual male identity of the performer. A Principal Boy and a Principal Girl routinely added romantic interest and a villain provided the conflict in the story line. "Beauty and the Beast," "Sleeping Beauty," and "Pandora's Box" were among these early

movements ushering in the establishment of the NDTC in 1962.

The Pirate Princess And the Politician

A distinctive innovation of the National Pantomime is its use of "topicalities." Topical vignettes comment on and usually satirize current Jamaican events that are the talk of the island. Jamaica's all-time queen of the theater, Louise Bennett, invented the art

The themes of selections in the repertoire of the Jamaican National Dance Theatre Company draw on the rich island heritage. Above and at right, company members in concert.

254

form in an impromptu moment on stage one year.

"It was in one year's Pantomime that things went wrong backstage," she recalled. "There was what you would call an uncomfortable pause in the action, so the director shoved me in front of the curtain and told me to do something. . . . anything!"

The irrepressible Miss Lou, as Jamaicans fondly call their Earth Mother of an actress, asked her audience for suggestions. They implored her to "mek joke." So she did, leading them in a folk song in which she ad-libbed jokes about current topical events.

Now when the public utilities break down, topicalities produce a National Pantomime figure who invokes the gods to "let there be light, let there be light . . . and water too."

dimension to the National Pantomime performances. Spectators relegated to the rough seating in the highest tier of Ward Theater have been particularly vocal. One year a young hero proclaiming his love for the reluctant heroine was interrupted by an impatient member of the gallery who shouted: "Tell him yes mek me go get the bus and go hom." Another song writer inadvertently loaded his show with songs about fools. In the midst of an endless string of songs in which one actor or another admitted to being a fool, the gallery indicated its irritation by taking up the chant, "If you a fool, me no fool, so done the foolishness." The fool songs were cut before the next performance.

No matter the story line, scenes from the

Or when a character falls ill, he will mimic utilities' officials by telling the audience to sympathize with him "because mi number six generator break down."

Public figures provide a popular target for topicalities. Minister of Public Utilities Pearnel Charles earned the nickname "Hurricane Charles" when he tackled inner-city problems like illegal street vending in a whirlwind campaign. Not unexpectedly, a sudden on-stage gale called Hurricane Charles livened up the plot of "The Pirate Princess" when it blew down vendors' stalls and plunged the town into confusion. The minister laughed as loudly as the rest of the audience.

Audience participation adds another

National Pantomime may parody a moon landing or the peccadilloes of a public figure. The framework of the story might as easily be about a prince or princess, a mythical Jamaican beast, or the local ghosts known to every spirit-fearing Jamaican as *"duppies."* In the end, magic inevitably helps good triumph over evil.

Pilgrimage to the Pantomime

The island's finest designers of costumes and stage settings, leading composers and musicians, playwrights and directors regard it an honor to be part of the Pantomime team each year. Major actors, actresses, dancers and singers donate their time and talent. Miss Lou and the late Ranny Williams led the headliners for years. And the pantomime has made household names of performers like Charles Hyatt, Oliver Samuels, Lois Kelly Miller and Leonie Forbes.

The Pantomime opens its season at 6 p.m. on Boxing Day each year. That's the day after Christmas in Jamaica, a traditional English holiday when the gentry used to share the boxed-and-bowed remnants of their Christmas feast with the poor.

Audiences continue to grow each year, as do the number of performances. Twenty performances were considered an accomplishment in the early days of the show. The 1981/82 production of "The Pirate Princess" broke all attendance records with 124 continuous performances that ran beyond Easter.

"The Pirate Princess" spoofed the fictional adventures of two real-life women pirates, Anne Bonney and Mary Read. They served in the crew of the infamous Captain John "Calico Jack" Rackham until their capture off the coast of Negril in 1726. The play was written by Barbara Gloudon, who has penned five of the National Pantomime productions—more than any other person. In addition to performing in more than 30 of the shows, Louise Bennett has also written or helped write many.

Increasingly elaborate stage sets and the lack of proper theater facilities outside the capital city have confined the annual production to the venerable Ward Theater in the heart of Kingston. But that has not kept Jamaicans from making their annual pilgrimage to the Pantomime—even if it means a hot and dusty bus journey.

Great Things
In Small Packages

A more recent phenomenon has been the increase of foreign visitors attending Pantomime performances. Most cannot keep pace with the rapid-fire dialect of the actors. Instead, they revel in the colorful sets, infectious music, and unbridled enthusiasm of the local audience which becomes involved from the first note of the overture to the last bar of the curtain call. According to one visitor, "Even if you don't understand a word of what's being said on stage, it is a treat just to watch the audience react. The music and the

The National Dance Theatre Company also reflects Jamaica's African roots. At right, an erotic moment from "African Scenario."

setting are worth a visit to the Pantomime. It's a side of Jamaica we wouldn't have missed for anything."

The National Pantomime, NDTC and Festival! are only the most visible manifestations of Jamaica's rich tapestry of performing arts. Tucked in unexpected corners of Kingston and even small villages in the countryside are small theaters where amateurs perform like professionals. Kingston alone boasts the Barn Theatre, the Way Inn Theatre at the New Kingston Hotel, and the Way Out Theatre next door at the Jamaica Pegasus Hotel. Major playwrights like Dennis Scott, Barry Reckord, Louis Marriott, Sam Hillary, Trevor Rhone and Gloria Lannamann regularly unveil new works at these intimate venues.

Such smaller productions have a built-in advantage. They can be taken on tour through the villages and towns of the island where they reach an even greater, more appreciative audience. It's not uncommon in Kingston to find as many as six new plays or revivals, and a dance performance or two, all running at one time.

The Youngest Performers

The performing bug infects Jamaica's youngest citizens during the annual Schools Drama Festival. For more than 25 years, high school students have staged plays from Shakespearean classics to contemporary Caribbean favorites in an island-wide competition. Many Schools Drama Festival performers continue their theatrical interests into adulthood.

Since 1976, the Little Theatre Movement has also operated a national School of Drama as part of the Institute of Jamaica's Cultural Training Centre. Some have bemoaned the introduction of "drama education" as unnecessary in an island so full of natural talent. Nevertheless, the school systematically trains students in all aspects of the theater from acting to developing light and sound systems.

There is also Jamaican music—beyond the steady beats served up by discos, sound systems and reggae parlors. The Jamaica Folk Singers, led by Olive Llewin, have earned an international following for performances that weave music and movement into an educational form of entertainment. In addition, the National Chorale offers folk and classics.

The full spectrum of Jamaica's performing arts—dance, drama and music—adds up to an island that is one vibrant, glowing stage, even after the curtain has fallen.

FROM GHETTO TO GALLERY: THE ARTISTS' WORLD

Tivoli Gardens grows from the rubble of West Kingston. The street pavement is cracked and potholed; the vacant lots are indiscriminately littered; insects travel in hordes through the stale, humid air. In the scalding sun of a Jamaican afternoon, poverty glares at the people of Tivoli Gardens. But it has not blinded or stripped them of their self-esteem.

In defiance of the destitution that surrounds them, these people have transformed blockhouse architecture into an artistic wonderland. Tivoli Gardens residents have

from the ghettos of West Kingston. A mother and daughter, arm in arm, look out at a lake while father romps with a dog. These images are bold statements that prove rampant poverty has not robbed the richness of the Jamaican spirit.

The walls of Tivoli constitute only one example of the island's colorful tradition of "yard art." Turn the corner of another crumbling area not far away and discover smiling figures beckoning passersby into something called the "Texas Arena." Or look for the suave fellow with the slick hair

painted the walls of their flats—not just in solid shocks of color, but with individualized works of art. There are red, green and gold tributes to former Ethiopian emperor Haile Selassie, who is revered by the country's Rastafarians. There are pastel, pop-style pastiches that have now been made famous by reggae record album covers. A flowery paean bids visitors: "Welcome to our New City." Mostly, there are pristine landscapes and florals that remind residents of the natural beauty that lies only a few minutes away

At left, "Homage to Beethoven," from the palette of National Gallery Director David Boxer. Above, one of the paintings that decorate the walls of Kingston's Tivoli Gardens.

painted on the front of the Bridgeview "Restaurant and Disco-Style Pub" at No. 15 Naggo Head Road between Spanish Town and the Hellshire Hills.

Surprising strokes from the painters' brush decorate the island—from cliffside villages in the Blue Mountains to makeshift cafes in Negril. Even the execution, symmetry and poetry of the reams of political graffiti scrawled on every inch of unadorned island space before general elections underline the Jamaican's drive to express themselves, to create.

Unfortunately, honest, unpretentious "yard art" has inevitably "inspired" rows of banal woodcarvings, baskets, beads and paintings that gather dust on the shelves of the souvenir stands in Ocho Rios, Fern Gully, Montego Bay and other tourist hubs. This commercialization of genuine artistic values, mass-produced with little care or pride, is aimed at earning an easy buck from the indifferent visitor bent on bringing home a sample of "native art" to wave under the nostrils of envious neighbors and to fill the gap on the mantel piece between the Niagara Falls souvenir plate and the bowling trophies.

More satisfying—and worthy of the praise, attention and higher prices it commands—has been the work of the self-taught, intuitive artists, sometimes called "primitives," who have emerged from the masses of yard artists. Many actually hailed from the Tivoli Gardens and the Trench

since they were so unusual, so non-European and so different. Today, his works are almost impossible to purchase and command the highest prices paid for Jamaican art.

Those who followed him captured untrained, untampered visions of Jamaican life at the grassroots with honesty and clarity. Gaston Tabois, Mallica Reynolds (who paints under the pseudonym "Kapo"), Everald and Sam Brown, Albert Artwell, Allan Zion and Sydney McLaren comprise the vanguard of the artists who are Jamaican originals. They draw their inspiration from the country's colorful and complex traditions, not from the dictates of outside influences. As Norman Rae wrote in an essay for *Ian Fleming Introduces Jamaica*, "The

Towns of Jamaica.

John Dunkley, for instance, was a humble Kingston barber. Born in 1881, Dunkley, had limited schooling. But he followed many other young Jamaican men of that time and went to Central America to seek his fortune. Dunkley returned in the 1930s and set up his barber shop in a poor neighborhood of downtown Kingston. Although he had no training in art, he covered his shop and even the barber's chair with colorful patterns, flowers and motifs. He also began painting on canvas dark, almost morbid images: stunted tree trunks, embryonic rabbit holes and mesmerizing shapes and symbols that sometimes seem subtly Freudian. He did not sell many of his paintings during his lifetime

'locals' choose between the lurid—impossible except in bar-room decor—and the drab which rejects the temptations of our Technicolor island in a desperate attempt to keep faith with the emotional content of the theme."

Compared to the older and more internationally known works of the self-taught artists of neighboring Haiti, the works of the Jamaican school are less homogeneous and stylized and, consequently, often more interesting. Working in isolation from each

The surrealistic flights of fancy of artist Colin Garland show through in his painting of "Mr. and Mrs. Goose" (above). Artist Edna Manley relaxes at her home in Kingston (right).

other and from foreign influences, each of these artists developed a technique totally unique in style, and theme. Kapo's paintings and woodcarvings include lush landscapes and "Garden of Eden" images. The Browns produce bright paintings that mesh with the colorful essence of their Rastafarian themes and motifs. McLaren brings the human side of Jamaican life to the canvas in detailed landscapes and cityscapes.

The Early Artists

Almost every weekend in Jamaica, an art exhibition opens. Art lovers and hangers-on, from a handful to a crowd, mill around holding glasses of pink rum punch, the traditional opening drink. Wrapped in flowing tropical lounging robes, embroidered shirts, head wraps, and the electric Ethiopian colors of Ras Tafari, the crowd is as attractive as the paintings. They look at the latest offerings of the well-known and the up-and-coming. They chat. Usually a Jamaican personality gives a speech which the artist's friends applaud politely. They laugh at the jokes. Then they resume their chatter. They buy the best of the works and spirit them away to private collections in their villas, apartments and more modest residences.

In this way, Jamaicans celebrate an artistic tradition that dates back even before the Europeans set foot in the Americas. The island's first inhabitants, the Arawaks, used cave walls instead of canvas. Arawak drawings have been compared to prehistoric African art and resemble ancient Hawaiian petroglyphs. Figures of birds and humans carrying spears and wearing headmasks have been discovered in Mountain River Cave in the parish of St. Catherine. The Arawaks, in turn, may have inspired the figures in architectural friezes in Jamaica's first capital at Sevilla Nueva created by equally anonymous Spanish artists who accompanied Christopher Columbus on his voyages. These pieces are on display at the Institute of Jamaica in Kingston.

The earliest published works of note were the so-called Spillsbury prints executed by an unknown English artist and printed by one "Mrs. Spillsbury of London." They depicted the harbors of late 18th Century Jamaica. William Beckford, a wealthy property owner, brought two artists to Jamaica in 1773: Philip Wickstead painted portraits of the island's plantocratic families and George Robertson painted landscapes.

More famous itinerant artists followed and succeeded in capturing for posterity the essence of 19th Century Jamaica. James Hakewill's watercolors were transformed into aquatints and bound in one volume. Isaac Mendes Belisario, an Italian Jew born in England, arrived in 1830 and set up a studio in downtown Kingston where he produced portraits. He is best known for 12 sketches of the slave custom of Jonkanoo or John Canoe, a lively musical parade in grotesque costumes still celebrated during Christmas and New Year's holidays. Joseph Bartholomew Kidd, a Scottish painter, produced a series of sensitive sketches of Jamaican estates and the city of Kingston. Another interesting artistic development was the commissioning and importation of some of history's finest works of religious neo-classic sculpture to trim the island's Anglican churches, tombs and monuments.

Two famous pieces that still stand are the Rodney Memorial Statue in Spanish Town sculpted by John Bacon Sr., and the monument to Simon Clarke in the 18th Century Anglican Church in Lucea executed by John Flaxman.

But these early Jamaican works reflected a colonial society and virtually ignored the heritages of the African slaves and smaller pockets of indentured laborers from other countries. All that changed in the 20th Century with the emergence of nationalism in Jamaica and other British colonies.

The 1930s spawned traumatic events which prompted the island's black majority to join labor unions and political parties in a political awakening aimed at improving their lot in spite of continuing British control. The nationalistic feelings also surged through the veins of Jamaica's artists. A group of middle-class artists began to probe the Jamaican psyche, utilizing indigenous subjects and themes. European styles continued to influence their approach to brush and chisel, but their changing directions formed the nucleus of Jamaica's modern-art movement.

In the colonial social structure, some of these artists actually lived at the top. They were the privileged bourgeoisie among native Jamaicans. Among their leaders, in fact, was Edna Manley, the wife of one of the founding fathers of independent Jamaica, Norman Manley, and mother of former prime minister and present opposition leader, Michael. Mrs Manley mothered the

lish aesthetics," said Mrs. Manley, now a stately woman in her eighties. "It came out in the poetry. You had the poets in those days writing about the daffodils, snow and bitter winds they had never experienced. I told them, 'Why don't you describe the drought, when the sun gets up in the morning and is king of the world all day, and everything is parched? You can smell the seymour grass, and the sun goes down in a blaze of glory only to come up again tomorrow. The drought is on.' That is a very Jamaican and artistic and poetic theme. And we had the most terrific arguments over this."

The Jamaican establishment at that time "thought we were bonkers," Mrs. Manley added. Differences in attitudes toward the

infant art movement, helping to organize art classes at the Institute of Jamaica and inspiring others to meet and exchange ideas and opinions.

The personalities in Mrs. Manley's circle included poet George Campbell, artist Albert Huie, interior decorator and furniture designer Burnett Webster, photographer Dennis Gick, sculptor Alvin Marriott and novelist Roger Mais. These dynamic talents held provocative meetings where they would show each other the work they had been doing, which generated critiques and arguments.

"The great thing was to be able to see ourselves as Jamaicans in Jamaica and try to free ourselves from the domination of Eng-

arts exploded in 1939 when a group of 40 liberals stormed the annual general meeting of the Institute of Jamaica. The Institute had been created "for the encouragement of arts, science and culture in Jamaica," but the board of directors was perpetuating a colonial interpretation of arts and culture.

"Our leader was a lawyer, Robert Braithwaite," said Mrs. Manley, her dark eyes alive with the memories. "He pointed to the portraits of the English governors on the wall and said, 'Gentlemen! We have come to tell you to tear down these pictures and let

Painter David Pottinger puts the finishing touches on another work of art of his studio in Jamaica (above).

the Jamaican paintings take their place.' There was pandemonium. But we knew they could not ignore us anymore."

The incident at the Institute meeting sparked prompt action. Mrs. Manley and some volunteers began to give art classes. That mushroomed into larger, more formal training courses, until, in 1950, the Jamaica School of Art was established. The school has since trained most of the country's established artists. During his directorship in the 1970s, Karl Craig expanded the school and opened its doors to a wider segment of Jamaican society. Its success, particularly in obtaining assistance from international agencies, led to the creation of a Cultural Training Centre in Kingston in 1976. The Centre houses the Schools of Art, Music, Dance and Drama.

The National Gallery

The Institute also transformed a small collection of local art into a major establishment, the National Gallery. The paintings, sculptures, sketches and woodworks of most of the island's leading artists were initially housed in charming Devon House, itself a fine example of Jamaican architectural art. Steibel Jackson built the home in 1881 along the lines of buildings he admired during a 15-year stay in Venezuela. The elegant white wooden structure stands back from a wrought-iron gate on Hope Road in New Kingston. The National Gallery has since moved to more secure premises in the Roy West building on Kingston's waterfront.

The Gallery's current curator, a noted artist in his own right, is David Boxer, an art historian educated at Cornell University and Johns Hopkins University. Boxer has nurtured the young collection of works and has helped it to blossom into a major collection.

Leading names in the collection include: Carl Abrahams, whose masses of wormy shapes grow into trees and whose preoccupation with the Last Supper comes shimmering through; Karl Parboosingh, whose evolution from stark, plain images of Jamaican life to his later experiments in abstract are always vivid; Ralph Campbell, whose dreamy, semi-abstract landscapes are colorfully punctuated with human forms, and David Pottinger, whose realistic look at people and places mirrors the island. The lyrical ceramics of Cecil Baugh are also in the National Gallery along with the carvings of Mrs. Manley. Her powerful woodcarvings capture the shape and form of native Jamaican physique and spirit. They have earned her an international following.

The Gallery, in cooperation with the Smithsonian Institute, sent a representative group of Jamaican works on a North American tour in 1983.

By the 1960s and 70s, many young Jamaicans had studied abroad. They returned home with new ideas and strong styles. They applied their nationalistic themes to their external experiences in cubism, modern abstract, nordic expressionism, surrealism and other contemporary techniques. Their work added another dimension to the island art in the Institute.

Barrington Watson brought with him a romantic yet realistic view of the Jamaican people. The late Eugene Hyde produced Jamaica's first modern abstracts. Osmond Watson has become known for his angular, stark depictions of the human face. David Boxer is influenced by surrealism and depicts highly subjective themes. Australian-born Colin Garland has made a name for himself with his super-realistic symbols of man and beast. Hope Brooks has produced a fine series of textured environmental abstracts in pale colors.

Another product of the movement was Christopher Gonzalez whose work as a sculptor earned him a commission from the Jamaican government to fashion a statue of the late reggae superstar Bob Marley. This impressive work now stands in the National Gallery in New Kingston.

Gonzalez trained at the Jamaica School of Art, where he later taught, and at the California College of Arts and Crafts in Oakland. He now divides his time between Atlanta and Kingston. Gonzalez and many of his colleagues continue to explore the themes laid down by Edna Manley and her group. He spoke enthusiastically of the future of fine arts in Jamaica.

"The younger artists have a lot of potential and promise that they can create something unique and unusual," he said. Noting that U.S. artists look at his work as old-fashioned and romantic compared to their experiments in superrealism and the abstract, he said:

"American art is less people-oriented than ours. In Jamaica, we still deal with people as human beings. Maybe they will say that Jamaica is a more primitive place, but the human element is much stronger. The artist reflects this in his work."

And for the visitor to the island who has thrilled at the colorful spectrum of people singing, dancing, working and loafing their way through life in Jamaica, the focus on humanity makes Jamaican art that much more rewarding.

WHERE CRICKET IS A WICKET GAME

To the uninformed, cricket comes across as an utterly preposterous game. It stirs fuzzy images of something played in slow motion by straight-faced men stuffed into starched white uniforms. Aficionados brandish pretentious words and phrases like "batting for a century," "googly," "popping crease" and "bowled for a duck." Matches drag on for days. Scores pile up into hundreds of runs. It is the ultimate British cliché, an overwrought version of taking tea with crumpets, a bland mix of pomp and puffery.

To the knowledgeable, cricket is nothing of the sort. Not here in Jamaica. Not anywhere in the West Indies, for that matter. In Kingston's Sabina Park, the staging of a test match that pits the cricket stars of England against those of the Caribbean ignites as much excitement as a World Cup football match or a world heavyweight boxing championship. In Jamaica, test cricket is a celebration on the scale of Christmas, Thankgiving and Independence Day.

Even more importantly, cricket has traditionally mirrored the essence of life in Jamaica, Trinidad, Barbados and other former bastions of British colonial power. "Cricket was a stage on which selected individuals played representative roles which were charged with social significance," wrote Trinidad's great essayist and cricket enthusiast, C.L.R. James, in his book *Beyond a Boundary*. James made a convincing case for the importance of cricket in assuring the British that their colonies in the Caribbean were prepared for self-rule in the first half of the 20th Century.

Bails, Stumps and Wickets: The Intricacies of Cricket

The game of cricket has vague similarities to American baseball. A pitcher (called a "bowler") tries to hurl a ball (slightly smaller and heavier than a baseball) past a batsman. The batsman in turn attempts to hit the bowler's offering into the field, out of reach of the opposing team's defensive players.

Cricket revolves around a pair of inauspicious contraptions called "wickets," facing each other at a distance of 20 meters at opposite ends of a "pitch," or inner field. A wicket consists of three wooden sticks or "stumps" resembling apparatuses that might be used in a game of backyard croquet. The stumps are driven into the ground a few inches apart (so that the ball cannot go through them) and topped with two round pieces of wood called "bails." The bails fall off when a bowled, batted or fielded ball hits or "breaks" the wicket.

It is the job of the batsman—armed with a

three-foot-long paddle, flat on one side and rounded on the other—to defend his wicket against the bowler. He stands four feet in front of the wicket at the "popping crease," and from there swings at the bowled ball as it spins and caroms off the pitch at speeds approaching 100 miles per hour. The batsman can hit the ball in any direction, behind as well as in front of him. A clean hit allows him to run to the second wicket opposite his own, while his batsman-teammate, who has been protecting that wicket, exchanges places. If both reach their opposite wicket before it can be broken by a throw from the fielders, a run is scored.

The batsman and his teammate can continue to run back and forth between the

Legendary cricket star George Headley shows the form that made bowlers tremble in the 1930s (left), while youths dreaming to fill Headley's shoes play in the country (above).

wickets until a fielder returns the ball to the pitch and a wicket is threatened. If a batsman gets a good piece of a bowled ball and wallops it "beyond the boundary" of the playing field, it automatically scores six runs for his side.

A batsman can be dismissed in several ways. He can be bowled out (i.e., his wicket is broken by the bowler); run out (by a throw from a fielder); caught out (if a fielder catches a fly ball off the bat before it hits the ground); or stumped (if the opposition's wicketkeeper, akin to a baseball catcher, retrieves a ball and breaks the wicket with the batsman outside the popping crease). Various interference violations also result in the batsman's dismissal.

Until a batsman suffers one of these indig-

two innings, until both sides have batted twice. In international test matches, which pit any two of the world's leading cricket nations (England, West Indies, Australia, New Zealand, India, Pakistan, Sri Lanka and formerly South Africa), this can require 30 hours of competition spaced over five or six days, with breaks for lunch, tea, and restroom visits. Time limitations or other restrictions are usually called upon to keep most games shorter. School matches are often kept to a pre-stated number of "overs"—series of six or eight balls thrown by a bowler.

Given the time span of typical cricket matches, it is not surprising to find scores ranging from 200 to 500 runs per team. On rare occasions, first-class cricket teams have

nities, however, he is allowed to continue batting and scoring runs. The ultimate achievement of a batsman in cricket is to achieve a "century"—100 runs or more in a single innings. The antithesis is being "bowled for a duck"—going out without scoring.

11 Men Per Side, 10 Outs Per Innings

There are 11 men on a cricket side, and every one of them must bat before a side is retired and an innings has ended. Because there are two batsmen (at opposite wickets) in the game at one time, 10 outs constitute an innings. A match normally continues for

tallied more than 1,000 runs in two innings.

Of course, this oversimplified description of the game overlooks innumerable strategies, subtleties and idiosyncrasies. For instance, bowlers employ an entire range of tactics aimed at foiling the batter. They include the "googly," a ball spun in a counterclockwise motion so that it will spin away from a batsman after it bounces; and the "off-cutter," which bounces toward the batsman. There are fast-pace bowlers, who can deliver balls moving at more than 90 miles

The team portrait of the Jamaican cricketers that faced their arch-rivals, Barbados, in 1925 (above). Reserve players in protective gear watch the action from the sidelines (right).

per hour; medium-pace bowlers, who use more finesse to fool batsmen; and bowlers who deliver the ball with top spin or with slow, curving trajectories. The wicketkeeper and other fielders adjust their positions (on the instructions of the captain) according to the style of each bowler and batsman—much as an American baseball team might shift its infield and outfield to defend against batters known to pull their pitches.

It all adds up to a constantly changing, intriguing sport.

Michael Holding And
The Screams of Sabina

The cricket fanaticism that envelops Jamaica is most obvious during test match northeast coast. When Jamaica's own Michael Holding, the reigning No. 1 fast bowler in the world and possibly the fastest in history, begins his opening over, the tumult continues for much of the match. Holding may respond with a bumper or bouncer, a ball he can bowl at more than 90 miles per hour and make rise sharply off the pitch into the batsman's face. The poor batsman is forced to duck or swing his bat in defense. He is clearly unnerved.

Holding has parlayed his Jamaican fame into international cricket stardom. Already considered one of the sport's legends, he is a main reason why the West Indies have dominated test cricket since the mid 1970s.

Yet in the eyes of the public, the name of one Jamaican still spells cricket—George

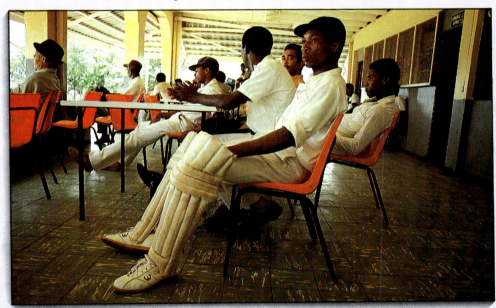

time at the island's main cricket venue, Sabina Park, just down the road from the Gun Court in West Kingston. Seats that can accommodate 12,000 are jam-packed beyond capacity. Males predominate, but there are numerous women and children. Some groups spread out major meals with courses from appetizers to dessert with coffee and tea. Liquor is in more than ample supply—especially the award-winning "national" beer, Red Stripe, but also rums, vodkas and whiskies.

All this alcohol helps fuel the noise. At Sabina, the din is said to surpass even that at Australia's notorious "Hill," the Sydney ground. The roar comes in layers, like storm-blown breakers crashing against the

Alphonso Headley. In cricket, Headley is on a par with his American baseball contemporary, Babe Ruth. But like another American contemporary, boxer Joe Louis, Headley was a black sporting hero with a constituency that stretched far beyond the field of play. He was born in the Canal Zone in Panama to a Barbadian father. His mother was a Jamaican who brought her son "home" at an early age to raise him.

A Headley Above the Rest

In the formative years of West Indies test cricket between 1928 and 1939, matches were real struggles. The teams won only one of 14 test matches played outside the West

Indies during that period. But they had a star. Even the fans of Australia and, more significantly, England, flocked to watch George Headley bat. Among many other achievements, he remains the only man ever to score two centuries in one test match at Lord's in London, the sport's world headquarters. If a comparison must be made, an American baseball player would have to hit a grand slam home run in every game of a World Series played at Yankee Stadium to equal the feat.

While undoubtedly the greatest batsman ever produced in the West Indies, some experts regard Headley as possibly second only to Sir Donald Bradman of Australia in the entire history of cricket. Bradman averaged a phenomenal 99.96 runs per innings,

dean of England's elegant cricket-writing fraternity, R.C. Robertson-Glasgow, described Headley in his collection called *Cricket Prints*:

> Great batting often has the beauty of the blast or the grandeur of the gale. In Headley's art, there is no noise. But it answers the test of greatness. As he walks down the pavilion steps, you expect in hope or fear. Only three or four can do this for you always.

The Roots of Caribbean Cricket

Cricket dates back to 16th Century England and has always been associated with that country and its larger associates, particularly India and Australia. By comparison,

or a century almost every time he came to bat. Headley ranks third on the all-time list at 60.83 runs per inning, slightly behind the 60.97 average of South Africa's Graeme Pollock. But Headley scored a test century once every four innings, the only player even close to Bradman's astonishing mark of one century per 2.7 innings. Cricket experts also point to the lack of support Headley received from his West Indian teammates. During the 10 years preceding World War II, Headley scored 10 test centuries, five times as many as his nearest teammate, Trinidadian Clifford Roach.

Headley's quiet personality and modesty bolstered his popularity. In one of the finest brief tributes ever paid to a sporting figure, a

the small, indigenous populations of the British Commonwealth islands in the Caribbean have only begun making great strides in the sport during the past 50 years or so. Yet the list of Jamaican cricket greats continues to grow. And that of tiny Barbados, population about 280,000 is even longer.

One reason for the rapid rise of cricket in the West Indies was that the British raj brandished the game as a byproduct of its colonial policy, often encouraging visiting teams to display the Union Jack and teach

Jamaican cricket fans, protected from the blazing sun by umbrellas, jam Sabina Park to watch the nation's favorite sport (above). A wicketkeeper's-eye view of the action (right).

the locals some English "culture." West Indians from all levels of society learned quickly and players of European descent are still found on teams fielded by the West Indies. By the turn of the 20th Century, most of the region's oldest clubs had come into existence and had begun inter-colony competitions (since succeeded by the annual Shell Shield matches). With limited other opportunities for education or advancement in society, young black men discovered that cricket could bring them both recognition and comparatively good incomes.

The success stories of George Headley and Trinidad's great 1930s all-rounder, (equally skilled in batting and bowling), Learie Constantine, encouraged them. Cricket propelled Constantine through law

account for the unlikely fact that the West Indies won six of the eight series they played against England in England between 1950 and 1980, but only two of six played against England on their West Indian home pitches during virtually the same years.

Six Decades of Cricket Milestones

But many great milestones have been recorded at Kingston's Sabina Park. In 1930, England's late Andy Sandham scored 325 runs, the first triple century in test history and the highest test score ever—until it was beaten by Bradman a few months later. During the same match in which Sandham made history, Headley scored the first of two

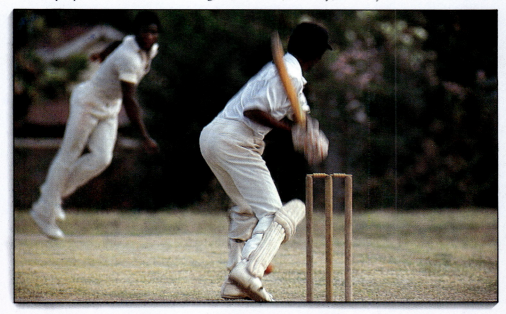

school and the Trinidad government cabinet, into the post of High Commissioner to Great Britain, and finally into the history books at the first fully black member of the House of Lords. Hundreds of young black islanders followed the examples set by Headley and Constantine and began to swing cricket bats, break wickets, and bowl the googly.

Success breeds success, of course. As more young West Indians took up cricket, the teams got better. They began earning the support of their fellow citizens, and West Indian teams traveling to play in Great Britain even got a spiritual boost from the cheers of their countrymen who had immigated to England. Perhaps that helps

test double centuries he was to make at Sabina. The next one occurred in 1935. Twenty-four years later, in 1959, Garfield Sobers of Barbados put up the existing world record score of 365 runs for a test innings here. Sobers, whose statistics and abilities rank him as the sport's all-time leading all-rounder was later knighted and presently lives in Australia.

Jamaica has produced other fine players. They include batting stylists like Lawrence Rowe, the last man to score more than 300 runs in a test match innings in 1974; J.K. Holt Sr., the most famous Jamaican cricketer before Headley and father of the great J.K. Holt Jr.; and O.G. "Collie" Smith, who rose from the ghetto to become one of the nation's finest all-rounders before his tragic death in an automobile accident in the early prime of his career. Alfred Valentine, one of the game's best slow left-arm spin bowlers, made a major contribution to the West Indies' first overseas victory against England in 1950—a feat which made him and his right-handed Trinidadian colleague, Sonny Ramadhin, heroes of a famous calypso tune. Maurice Foster combined his cricketing prowess with a championship for the West Indies in table-tennis doubles. Finally, in the oft-forgotten position of wicketkeeper, Jamaica has produced virtuosos Jackie Hendricks and Franz Alexander. That Jamaican sportsment often excel on several playing fields is evident in the outstanding contributions also made to football (soccer) by Alexander and Holt Jr.

Like Father, Like Son

Another Jamaican success story epitomizes the phenomenal rise of West Indies cricket during the 20th Century. In the summer of 1923, Jamaica's Ernest Rae, playing for the West Indies touring team of Jamaica, Trinidad and Tobago, Barbados and British Guiana, went to bat against an English county team in Great Britain. He stroked the ball and received a smattering of polite applause from the British crowd. But he scored an out shortly afterward and a proper English gentleman snidely asked him: "Were the cheers for your thousand (runs) for the season, Mr. Rae?" Rae parried with a simple retort: "No, my fifty!"

Today, Rae's son Allan, formerly a successful test cricketer himself, is president of the West Indies and Jamaican Cricket Board of Control, which makes him the leading administrator in the region that reigns as the undisputed, albeit unofficial, champion of test cricket.

While that title is as intangible as a claim to the championship of American collegiate football, the record is clear. The West Indies have lost only one series since 1976, that of a highly dubious defeat in a questionably-umpired game against New Zealand. The West Indies also were ranked No. 1 in test cricket from 1962 to 1967. In the history of test cricket, only Australia has maintained a better overall win-loss record than the West Indies. But Australia and England played their first test match in 1877 after centuries of dabbling in the sport. The West Indies played their first test match in 1928. In addition, the West Indies won World Cups of one-day cricket held in England in 1975 and 1979, but lost to India in 1983.

Curried Goat Amidst the Wickets

Jamaica College on Old Hope Road in Upper St. Andrew, above Kingston, is a high school modeled on the great private institutions of England. It sits well back from the road behind acres of grassy playing fields. Its brooding north gate opens on a semicircular drive that skirts an ivy-covered chapel and three solid old buildings which sport the kind of shingle roofs usually reserved for castles in the British countryside. Every Saturday afternoon from February through April, players in prim white uniforms and two umpires in dark pants and white coats scramble about the lawn fronting Jamaica College, lending further credence to its colonial airs. Perhaps 50 onlookers quietly watch the match.

It is just a few steps from the rarified atmosphere of Jamaica College and the supercharged grandstands of Sabina Park to the ghettos of Kingston. Here, the future Holdings and Headleys practice their bowling and batting strokes. Sometimes they make do with a misshapen piece of wood and a few stones. On special occasions, when neighborhoods come together for a big local match, there may be a well-worn but authentic bat and a ball that has seen many better days. A dusty, uneven field must make do for a pitch.

Jamaicans at all levels of society love their cricket. In Great Britain, it is a summer game that readily gives way to football (soccer) in the winter. In Jamaica, serious competitive cricket matches may be played from January to August, and an International Festival of Cricket is held in September every year.

When there is no cricket at home, an important test match half a world away in Australia may infect the entire island. Ears are glued to transistor radios. "Listening" house parties begin early and continue until dawn in deference to the time difference.

And there are few things that compare with a "curry goat" match on a weekend or public holiday. A meeting between a city team and a country team provides the perfect excuse for legions of cricketers, family and friends to head for a country pitch loaded down with curried mutton, chicken, rice and bottles of spirits. The equipment may be primitive. The rules may not be strictly enforced. But the cricket is always good in Jamaica, and all are welcome.

A batsman demonstrates the versatility of his bat during a match between the Jamaica Defence Forces and Kingston's policemen.

FROM CHO-CHO TO KULU KULU

Spicy and pungent, aromatic and enticing, greasy and filling, mouth-watering and hot, a blend of African, Chinese, Indian and European cuisines, yet individualistic in its appeal. This is Jamaican food, sure to tempt and please every visitor.

But despite its unsung charms, cuisine generally takes second place to drink in a discussion of Caribbean cookery. This is especially true in Jamaica, where its famed rum is sometimes thought of as the "Bordeaux of the Caribbean."

No matter where you go on the island of

villager to the city sophisticate, has his favorite local drinking spot. Drink fare runs the gamut from imported whiskies, wines and champagnes to white rum accompanied by the continuous "bang" of dominoes in a back room. Almost every restaurant serves beer; as the grade of service and quality improves, a wide choice of other drinks are also available. Not surprisingly, even many of the fast-food restaurants in Jamaica serve beer.

Jamaica has an award-winning local beer, Red Stripe. (It is also known as "The Police-

Jamaica, you are almost certain to find a bar within touching distance of any church. In other words, even though the license to run a bar is based on the British system of "bar, inn and tavern," they are everywhere. What's more, almost every corner grocery sells and serves beer and stout.

Drinking is as important to Jamaican culture as politics, perhaps moreso. Indeed, the fastest way for a visitor to penetrate the local lifestyle is to drop into the neighborhood bar.

Nearly every Jamaican, from the rural

man." because the uniforms of law enforcement officers are distinguished by a red stripe on the pants.) Red Stripe's brewers, Desnoes & Geddes, also produce Dragon Stout, which competes with the island's own Guinness Stout factory.

There are a number of liqueurs native to Jamaica, both home and commercially blended. Best known is Tia Maria, seen in better bars throughout the world. Other fine coffee and fruit liqueurs are produced by the small Sangster's Old Jamaica company high in the Blue Mountains. Fruit liqueurs in orange, ginger and ortanique (orange-tangerine) flavors have been blended from selected aged Jamaican rums and have won international gold medals in recent years.

Old Jamaica liqueur at "World's End" in the Blue Mountains, left. Above, rum punch on Negril Beach.

But as the world knows, it is rum that is synonymous with fine drinking in Jamaica.

Traditional Jamaican rums are dark and full-flavored, with a rich aroma. Commonly called Wedderburn or Plummer, these were the rums suplied to the British Navy for some 200 years. Rum was the drink of the slaves on every West Indies sugar plantation. It was introduced to England in 1655 when Jamaica was captured from the Spanish. It was previously known to continental Europeans, however, after Christopher Columbus carried sugar-cane cuttings to the Canary Islands.

Rum is a spirit distilled directly from cane and aged in oaken casks. Because sugar is already present in the cane, there is no need for preliminary malting to convert starch to

death in *kumina* ceremonies, an even better rum is "kulu kulu." This is the rawest of white rums, passed around a table in a common bottle or cup, as celebrants sing loudly from a hymnal while intermittently clearing their throats with pinches of brown sugar.

Appleton rum is Jamaica's best-known brand. It is made by the company of J. Wray & Nephew, who also market Coruba rum overseas. Appleton rum is exported to 64 countries. Sales on the United States market have increased in recent years, thanks to the effects of the Caribbean Basin Initiative.

There are two principal blends of Appleton rum. Appleton White is light, smooth and mellow, a blend which maintains a subtle taste and delicate aroma. Appleton

sugar. In this sense, rum is considered superior to vodka, whisky or gin. It is one of the purest of alcoholic beverages, retaining much more of its natural flavor than other drinks.

Today, Jamaica produces a full range of rums, from light to dark, fermented in the two processes of continuous and slow stills.

To the common man, however, the only real rum is white rum. He drinks it in its unadulterated stage of fermentation, 100 percent over proof, and chases it with water or milk. On rainy days, he even splashes it on his head and face to prevent him from catching cold or chills!

To the traditional Jamaican "Nine Nighter" who celebrates the transition of life to

Special, available in more than 800 cities worldwide, is a blend of old Jamaican dark rums with a taste and smoothness of its own.

If your spirituous licentiousness extends to the world of drugs, a word in the right ear will introduce you to ganja steeped in white rum or local Red Label wine. This is highly recommended for its medicinal propensities. It can reportedly heal anything from the common cold to asthma to influenza.

If health is your kick, perhaps you should try dandelion tea, guaranteed to prevent bed-wetting. Soursop punch calms the

Jerk Pork stand at Boston Bay, above. Right, a street chef serves up crab claws (left) and fish and bammy (right).

274

nerves and reduces the pressures of city life. If you come to Jamaica during the "cold" weather of December, the locals will be picking sorrel for Christmas cheer: this herb is used as an appetizer mixed with ginger and rum and is said to be the elixir of life.

For those not inclined to strong drinks, there is a variety of soft drinks and fruit juices available. They include "Ting," a grapefruit-based drink; tamarind juice; a blended fruit punch of melons and bananas; Roots wine; and Irish Moss. Jamaican fruit juices have won several worldwide contests.

Discovering Nyam

Nyam is a Jamaican-African word which means, "to eat." After you discover the

second are the wayside food stops, many of which are located on visitor-driven routes, characterized by quaint shelters and equally quaint names.

Authentic Jamaican home cuisine is best sampled on weekends. Probably the most-talked-about delicacy is ackee, the national dish. This red-skinned yellow fruit, with a taste all its own, can only be eaten after the pod opens up, revealing three large black seeds set in yellow lobes. Unripe and un-opened, ackee is poisonous. These lobes are boiled, then blended deliciously with onion, peppers and salted cod imported from Canada. This Sunday morning special of "ackee and sal' fish" is often served with boiled green bananas, fried plantain, johnny cakes (fried flour dumplings) and bammies (cassa-

wonders of Jamaican cuisine, you will find yourself *nyam*-ing around the island.

From jerk pork to ackee and sal' fish, from rundown to callaloo, from curried goat to pig's trotters, Jamaican cooking is a once-receding art form now emerging with a new-found pride. From stamp-and-go to solomon gundy and matrimony, it is a Caribbean gourmet's dream.

Unfortunately, the tourist who sticks to resort hotel restaurants will never be exposed to the great majority of Jamaican foods. True, some hotels have become more adventurous in recent years, adding ackee quiche and staple soups like pepperpot and red pea to their menus; still, the true delights can only be found in home cooking. A close

va cakes).

The main course for Sunday lunch may be roast beef or chicken. It comes with mounds of rice and peas (usually gungo peas), white or yellow yams, the squash-like cho-cho, sweet potatoes and pumpkins.

Saturday's main meal, the lead-in to the Sunday feasting, may have consisted of stew peas and rice, red beans cooked down with pig's tail, salted beef and dumplings spiced and peppered and caressed to a steaming mouth-watering brew. Or perhaps lunch was a pot of beef soup simmered with yams, dumplings, sweet potatoes and cho-cho, topped with a large slice of avocado pear and hard-dough bread.

Picture yourself as part of a typical

Jamaican family sitting down for a big meal cooked out of (at best) two common pots or kerosene tins. The serving dishes include nature's own locally produced utensils, such as a banana leaf for the meat; and rejected sophisticates of the Western world, such as plastic dishes to contain the rice and yams. For starters, place a helping of mackerel and boiled green bananas in your enamel plate. Take intermittent mouthfuls of blended portions of avocado and boiled shrimp served from an empty dry coconut shell, wash them down with rum and coconut water, top it off with freshly picked guavas or naseberries or plums or the abstractly tasting otaheite apples, and complement your meal with a cup of the finest blend of homemade coffee. Then help yourself to slices of fresh pineap-

ple as the conversation moves from the national political scene to neighborhood gossip.

Fruits of Land and Sea

Jamaica abounds in arable land where the widest range of fruits and vegetables can be produced. There is no time of year when one fruit or another is not in season, be it mangoes or pomegranates. As the fortunate visitor meanders the island's byways, he or she can stop and sample naseberries or papayas or star apples.

Seafood is exquisite. Peppered shrimps are a delicacy of the Black River area. Elsewhere, fish is roasted or peppered or stuffed and roasted on a sheet of zinc.

You can also choose your own "jerkers" stand and savor freshly jerked pork or chicken or fish, again spiced with pepper and cooked slowly under zinc, Boston-style, on a bed of pimento wood. (The hardy pimento tree, which produces the renowned superior-quality pimento spice, is found in Jamaica.)

At times of celebration, there is the inescapable goat's or ram's head soup. This is followed by curried goat and rice, a meal which always opens the commencement and closes the completion of a work program.

There are even treats for the gourmet searching out aphrodisiacs. Turtle eggs in red wine are a delicacy of Clarendon. Fresh oysters with a blend of vinegar and pepper are another favorite. Rare booby eggs from Goat Island (Port Esquivel) are favored when they can be found. But beware of the Jamaican woman who puts pumpkin buds in your soup. This is as sure a way as saltpeter to cut a man's nature and keep him faithful forever!

A listing of unusual or indigenous Jamaican food might include the following:
- Breadfruit, a large, green, starchy fruit that is served boiled, roasted or fried. It is a dietary staple.
- Callaloo, a leafy vegetable like spinach.
- Cassava, a root vegetable ground into flour for making cakes. It should not be eaten raw, as it contains cyanide; neither should it be taken in combination with ginger, because the action of the acid on cyanide creates poisonous prussic (hydrocyanic) acid in the stomach.
- Cho-cho, a pear-shaped prickly-skinned vine vegetable similar to squash.
- Matrimony, a dessert which blends orange segments with star apple pulp in cream.
- Naseberry, sometimes called sapodilla, a small brown fruit with a jelly-like flesh.
- Ortanique, a citrus fruit crossbred from oranges and tangerines.
- Otaheite apple, a maroon fruit with a tasty white interior, native to the South Pacific.
- Rundown, mackerel or salted cod boiled in coconut milk and eaten in a mush with onions and peppers.
- Solomon gundy, spiced pickled herring.
- Stamp-and-go, batter-fried sal' fish fritters, usually eaten as a snack.
- Star apple, a round purple fruit, whose seeds are seen set in a star-like fashion when it is cut crosswise.

Rural children sell sticks of ackee near Flat Bridge, left. Right, the traditional way to carry a fruit basket.

Ganja, the 'Sacred Herb'

In the 1950s, island jukeboxes jumped to the beat of calypso and lyrics that implored listeners to "take her to Jamaica where the rum comes from." Today, discos rock to the beat of reggae and songs that say, "Hey, Rastaman, hear what I say, give me some of that Sensi."

"Sensi" is short for *sinsemilla*, a Spanish word describing a potent form of seedless ganja—or marijuana, also known as grass, herb, weed and pot. Increasing international acceptance of marijuana use by people of all ages and all socioeconomic groups has made Jamaican ganja as popular an intoxicant as the country's rums.

Ganja is smoked in religious rituals by thousands of Rastafarians who consider it the "weed of wisdom" and by members of the Ethiopian Zion Coptic Church who call it "a sacred herb." Thousands more drink ganja as a cure-all. They take it in tea or steep it in white rum or wine, with or without pimento seeds, as a tonic. Others steam ganja and eat it as a vegetable; pastry lovers bake it into their cakes.

Few mass political meetings or packed football matches have occurred during the past few years without clouds of ganja hanging over the proceedings. In Kingston cinemas, it's often impossible to determine whether the audience's exuberant outbursts come in response to the film or as a result of breathing the pungent air

The Biggest Open Secret

Jamaica's ganja industry, in fact, is the nation's biggest open secret. In spite of nonchalant attitudes toward its use and availability, it is officially illegal. But that doesn't keep it from being one of the island's largest private businesses.

In 1981, *Time* magazine estimated that ganja illegally flown and shipped out of Jamaica was earning the traffickers $1 billion U.S. dollars annually. *Newsweek* magazine put the figure at $1.1 billion for ganja smuggled from Jamaica into the United States. Only Colombia provided more; Mexico had fallen to No. 3. Recent U.S. government figures estimate that 10 percent of the marijuana sold in the United States is of

A farmer checks out his plot of sinsemilla ganja (left). His illegal plantation was hidden among legal crops deep in the mountains.

Jamaican origin; its street value has been determined to be in the area of US $2.4 billion.

Some 8,000 large-scale growers supply the bulk of Jamaica's market. Leaders of the industry include key figures in other walks of life, among them lawyers, doctors, diplomatic corps members, policemen and soldiers. But few of these "respectable" dealers in ganja risk direct contact with their dubious enterprise. They merely provide financing for ganja seeds, food supplies, insecticides and fertilizers, pay others well to tend the fields, then wait for the big return on their investment.

The Greening of Jamaica

In spite of its contemporary synonymity with Jamaica, *cannabis sativa*—the botanical term for ganja—is not native to Jamaica or anywhere else in the Caribbean or the Americas. Ganja came to Jamaica, Trinidad and Guyana in the satchels of indentured laborers imported from India in the middle of the 19th Century. Like the Rastas and Coptics of modern-day Jamaican, Hindus of those times revered this so-called Indian hemp as a "holy plant."

Sugar-estate plantation owners soon determined that the use of ganja diminished the productivity of their laborers. Thus, the first legislation introduced in Jamaica to outlaw the use of marijuana stemmed from capitalistic concern about productivity and profits, not from any moralistic regard for the health and well-being of fellow humans.

Still, the use of ganja grew slowly as the numbers of East Indians increased. The birth of the Rastafarian movement in the 1930s provided another boost in its use in Jamaica. But ganja did not become a major influence until the "Greening of America" in the 1960s brought the "reefer" out of the ghettos of Harlem and into the mainstream of life in the United States.

Mexico served as the first primary source of supply for the surging American market. But stringent border inspections instituted by U.S. law enforcement agencies forced American dealers to turn to alternative sources for ganja. Jamaica, only two hours' flying time or an easy sail from the Florida peninsula, topped their shopping lists. By 1974, about 70 percent of the ganja grown in Jamaica wound up in the United States.

Experts put the current percentage at close to 96 percent.

Only the most unobservant or uninformed traveler in Jamaica could fail to stumble upon a stalk or two of the familiar herb sprouting from weed patches on construction sites, or growing near the garden of Bob Marley's grave at Nine Miles. Yet these are only minor manifestations.

Down on the Farm

St. Ann, the "Garden Parish" on the North Coast, has in recent years earned the nickname, "The Ganja Parish." Vast plantations also checkerboard rural St. Andrew, St. Thomas, Portland, St. Mary, Manchester and many of Jamaica's other parishes.

Although ganja literally seems to grow like a weed in Jamaica's lush tropical climate and terrain, proper cultivation for export is expensive and time-consuming. Farmers say it flourishes in a variety of soils. "But the red land really agrees with it. It brings out the crop quickly," said one Clarendon grower, who prefers the bauxite-rich soil of his parish.

Methods of cultivation vary, but like any plant, the seed must first be sown in a nursery in a manner no different from sowing tomato seeds. The seeds of quality plants fetch prices of 50 to 60 Jamaican dollars per quart.

Ganja seedlings sprout to about a foot high in a month, then are transplanted two feet apart to the field. Ganja for export or the commercial market gets its own plot of land. For domestic or personal use, growers plant it among other cash crops like corn, cassava or peas. Gungo peas are often planted on the periphery of a ganja field to disguise its main crop. For the most part, though, other money-making crops are cultivated separately in the event of a raid where police destroy the innocent plants right along with the ganja.

Bat Droppings and 'Goat's Shit'

Water supplies, which can be undependable during severe drought conditions like those that existed in the spring of 1982, are also critical. Experienced farmers water their plants once every four days and use only organic fertilizers such as poultry manure or bat droppings. One popular type of ganja is known as "Goat's Shit," its name taken from the droppings used to fertilize it. As one farmer put it, ganja grown with inorganic fertilizers "can't take the market. It makes the trees too big. They make the ganja mad."

Growers frequently weed their ganja fields to prevent grass from choking the prized plants, and spray with insecticides. In short, the crop is cared for as carefully as a mother might nurture a child. Farmers or their hired hands usually live in huts at the edge of the fields, which for obvious reasons lie far from the comfort of towns and villages.

When the plants' seeds start to ripen or "collie," the farmer must guard against attacks from the sky. Birds—including bald pates, ground doves, parrots and parakeets—enjoy dining on ganja seeds. Slingshots and scarecrows fashioned from tin pans and bits of cloth are standard equipment at this stage. One very Jamaican scarecrow employs magnetic tapes from cassette or reel-to-reel recorders which when strung through ganja fields "sing" in the wind and drive away skittish birds.

Barring droughts, insect or bird invasions or police raids, the ganja crop reaches maturity about five months after transplanting. Some stalks attain heights of nine feet in the rich Jamaican soils. Then it is time for the harvest. First, leaves are cut off; seeds are saved and stems removed for making hash oil. Some farmers "cure" their product by putting the leaves on a tarpaulin in the sun and turning them regularly for maximum exposure. They are left out through the night and morning dew to prevent the leaves from becoming too crisp and crumbly, and thus less desirable to smokers.

Lamb's Bread, Collie, Bush Cotton and Mad

Various types of ganja are harvested. Sinsemilla is the generic term for the strongest variety. Burr, Cotton and Lamb's Bread all fall within this category, although Cotton is extremely rare; according to one ganja farmer, it is not unusual to get only one Cotton plant from a 10-acre field of ganja. McConey is milder but very popular, Goat's Horn less so. Bush, Collie and Mad are the ordinary varieties of the plant. Collie has its legion of smokers, but Bush and Mad, particularly the latter, are of low potency and not highly regarded.

Most farmers harvest their own crop to maximize profits and eliminate Jamaican middlemen. "Them too cheap, sah. We prefer the plane man them, the white man them. The Jamaican buyers want to give you only $60 Jamaican for a pound weight, but the white men buy good. The men to get in touch with are the planemen," said one

Clarendon farmer, who admitted dealing with the same ganja pilots for eight years. He said at least seven planes make pick-ups at the neighborhood illegal airstrip each week, except (inexplicably) Wednesdays. "I supply them all the while."

In January 1970, security officials estimated that 40 private airstrips existed in Jamaica. Now the number of private, official and illegal airstrips is believed to be near 120. Illegal strips rarely resemble the real thing and are camouflaged by moving shacks onto them when they are not in use. Some ganja flights, arranged by dealers with good connections, even leave official aerodromes under the cover of night. The *Daily Gleaner* occasionally runs aerial photographs of rugged-looking runways thought to be used in

"In this business you can spend a year and set your family right. You can build a house, buy a car. You can live a comfortable life. I have seen guys who couldn't change their pants and since this ganja business, they can change dozens of pants now. It has helped a lot of people in Jamaica," explained one prospering grower.

In a country haunted by high unemployment, low wages and a lack of job alternatives for undereducated citizens, the temptation to get rich off ganja has proved strong, in spite of the laws against it. Parliament continues to resist calls to legalize or ease penalties against ganja. But therein lies its value. Legalization in Jamaica, in concert with similar moves in the United States, would make ganja just another crop, like

the ganja trade, to assist authorities trying to close them down. Some airstrips even sport navigational beacons. Loading is swift, with pilots rarely shutting down their engines as up to forty 100-pound bags are hoisted aboard in 15 minutes. Payment is cash on board. The next stop is Florida and the markets of the U.S.A.

Legalize It?

Many Jamaicans call ganja "the poor man's friend."

The distinctive bud of a ganja plant (above) is attractive and occasionally used decoratively in Jamaica to the dismay of lawmakers.

tobacco for cigarettes or sugar cane for rum. Its price would plummet and the huge profits would evaporate. One wonders whether the influential growers and buyers in both the United States and Jamaica have mounted surreptitious campaigns against pro-legalization legislation.

It is virtually impossible to envision a unilateral move by the Jamaican government to lessen or abolish its ganja laws without the blessing of the United States. Despite liberalized legislation against its use in some states, the Reagan Administration has escalated its drug enforcement efforts in Florida and other parts of the country. Florida officials have even sprayed homegrown fields with paraquat, a poisonous herbicide, to discourage the growth, the sale, and use of marijuana.

Sacrament and Medicine: The Jamaican Dilemma

Meanwhile, Jamaica's Parliament has been less strict in its actions. The legal ramifications are many when dealing with a drug that a significant number of the population considers a sacrament or at least a medicinal godsend, while an equally significant number rely on its cultivation for economic livelihood.

The government introduced mandatory imprisonment for growing ganja in 1964 only to abolish that penalty in 1972. In 1969, Parliament outlawed cultivation of the female, male or any crossbreed of the ganja plant. Previously, it had been illegal only to grow the pistillate, or female, form.

Jamaica's joint Parliamentary Committee on Ganja recommended in 1977 that personal use of the drug be decriminalized and up to two ounces of ganja be permitted to be found on premises without punishment. There has been no action on that recommendation or any apparent follow-up study since. Jamaica's security officials have maintained a semblance of actively pursuing and punishing growers and smokers. In 1980, for instance, security forces seized 88 light aircraft, five ocean-going vessels, and ganja valued at about US $400 million. They also arrested 200 people involved in the drug traffic. But analysts believe that for every plane seized that year, 10 accomplished their missions. More vigorous action has been hampered by the well-known fact that police and soldiers in high and low places have a stake in the trade.

Ganja and the No-Funds System

Recommendations for a large-scale effort to spray Jamaica's plantations with paraquat have been ruled out because so many farmers still plant the herb among food crops. Crop substitution? "Even if you plant 1,000 banks of yam, you can't get from it the money you would get from one acre of ganja," one farmer noted.

At the economic end of the debate, Jamaica's "no-funds" licensing system grants an import permit to anyone who guarantees that no foreign exchange is required in payment for imported goods. The law has made illicit drugs one of the country's biggest foreign-exchange earners: ganja dealers provide the U.S. currency for licensees, who in turn repay them the equivalent in Jamaican dollars. The parallel black market, necessitated by the no-funds system in a country starved for U.S. dollars, is believed to have been fed by a ganja-bred US $100 million in 1980. Some economists fear legalization of ganja and destruction of the free trade that exists without government bureaucracy would lead to a sudden devaluation of the Jamaican dollar and could bankrupt the shaky economy.

The arguments for and against legalization of ganja rage on in Jamaica, as they have in the United States and other countries for years. The difference here is that for many the issue is moot.

Certainly, visitors to Jamaica find the plant in ample supply. Indeed, many young visitors from the United States, Canada and Europe come to Jamaica solely to sit in the sun and get high on the grass. It's usually available at resort areas from young men who stand for hours outside hotel gates and even from hotel employees trying to make some money on the side. Even deep in the rugged interior, wanderers may be flagged down by youths toting a flour sack full of ganja.

It's also inexpensive. Ganja cigarettes ready-rolled in Rizla papers and called "spliffs" sell for as little as two and no more than 10 Jamaican dollars, depending upon their size and the buyer's bargaining abilities. Prices for larger quantities are negotiable. A healthy helping wrapped in old newspapers may sell for as little as 20 Jamaican dollars.

But ganja users must always bear in mind the official penalties. The Dangerous Drugs Act states that for the possession of ganja, first offense carries as a sentence "a fine not exceeding $1,000 (US $560) or imprisonment for a term not exceeding three years or both such fine and imprisonment." For subsequent convictions the fine is increased to $2,000, imprisonment to not more than five years. Sentences for cultivating, selling, or otherwise dealing in ganja can bring up to 10 years' imprisonment. Offenders under the act are every person who manufactures, sells or otherwise deals in prepared ganja. It's an offense to have ganja in one's possession, or to occupy premises used for preparing, smoking or selling ganja. It is likewise an offense to have any smoking paraphernalia in one's possession.

At right, "dreadlock" celebrates Ras Tafari by smoking ganja in the sacramental manner—with a handmade "chalice."

PARDON MY PATOIS!

English-speaking visitors to Jamaica often wonder what language is spoken on the island, especially after they encounter their first Rastaman espousing the glories of "Jah" or a good-natured beachboy who inquires: "Everyt'ing kool, mon? Everyt'ing *irie*?" The newcomers soon think their tour guide lied in telling them everyone here speaks English. That is an understandable reaction—except to Jamaicans, who are under the impression that Jamaicans speak English and Americans, British and Canadians speak in unintelligible dialects.

later uses the word "physic" to connote the act of purging. Jamaican country children all know that when their parents threaten to "physic" them, it means castor oil next morning. "Salt physic" is the Jamaican terms for Epsom salts, a most unpleasantt laxative administered in a most unpleasant manner.

African slaves, brought to Jamaica centuries ago, adopted the speech mannerisms of their British masters. In their new Caribbean home, a rampant use of biblical phraseology crept into the distinctive patois. The Bible is

Indeed, Jamaicans do speak English, but some of it is so ancient that even the British have abandoned it. William Shakespeare and his contemporaries might understand, though.

For instance, Jamaicans use the word "up" as an intensive. A car that is "smash up" is in much worse shape than one that has merely been in a smash. You "slip up" when you trip, you "soak up" when you make a mess of a job and, as even Americans know, you get "beat up" when you suffer a serious mugging.

Compare this to the character Jacques in Shakespeare's *As You Like It*. He tells of hunters who haunt the Forest of Arden and "shoot the deer and kill them up." Jacques

a fixture in the homes of Christians and Rastafarians alike. So when parting, a mere goodbye seems inadequate when one can say: "Peradventure I wi' see you tomorrow." And most visitors to the island will agree that a Jamaican mosquito "biteth like a serpent." Jamaicans even refer to themselves as "righteous judges" rather than mere people.

Some of the most colorful of Jamaican expressions can be traced back to the languages of West African countries like Gha-

"Cuss-cuss never bore hole in skin" is the way Jamaicans on the telephone (above) or chatting on the road (right) would tell each other that "hard words break no bones."

na. Early arrivals from these lands found it difficult to pronounce barbaric language constructions like *th*. Thus, "the" became "de," "then" became "dem," and "that" became "dat"—a speech pattern that conformed with those of Africa and which persists here today. *Th* at the end of a word proved particularly tricky. If a Jamaican man says his girlfriend has beautiful "teet," rest assured he is complimenting her dental work, not her bustline.

To further simplify the Africans' transition to life in colonial Jamaica and its strange tongue, the peculiarities of English grammar were often simplified or totally abandoned. Both case and gender were ignored in favor of simply "him"—for men, for women, for you or I alike. A young girl or woman became "gal." But the plural became "de gal dem." In fact, the plural "dem" applies to almost everything—cars, people, dogs, even children.

Vowel Games, Syllable Shifts

Jamaicans play speech games with vowels, especially the letter *a*. A garden can become either a "gyarden" or a "gorden," depending on the gentility of the speaker.

The influence of Africa is also found in the way Jamaicans shift syllables and rearrange the stress to suit their purposes. A mattress becomes a "mat-rass." A tomato becomes either "tomatis" or "salad," depending on its size. The ubiquitous surname Smith becomes unrecognizable to the Jamaican visitor as "Simmit."

Words with African roots that linger in contemporary patois include *putta-putta* for mud, *duckanoo* for a particular kind of pudding, and "*Anansi* story" for fairy tale. (In the Akan language of Ghana, *Anansesem* means "words about the spider.")

More recent years have found yet another form of African influence creeping into patois—the language of the Rastafarians. Central to their speech is the emphasis on the singular "I" or the plural "I and I" to underline the importance of the individual. Thus, divine becomes "I-vine," Ethiopian is "I-thiopian" and wonderful or fabulous has simply become *I-rie*.

Jamaicans regard time and distance as subservient to the individual. Thus the often misunderstood phase "soon come" should be interpreted to mean that the speaker will turn up sooner . . . or later.

Another source of confusion for the unwary is the use of measurements unkown elsewhere. Who besides a Jamaican knows that a *gill* is a quarter of a pint? Or that a "big *gill*" is just a little bit more? This is a crucial piece of knowledge when one is buying a drink of white rum.

In measuring land, the old English unit of chains is still employed. The original measuring chains used by surveyors were comprised of heavy wire links, each link exactly 7.9 inches long, so that the chain could be folded and carried in a bag. One hundred links equalled a chain of precisely 22 yards, the length of a cricket pitch. If a Jamaican tells you that your destination is "a few chains from here," it is not far away. If it is "a stone's throw," on the other hand, it may be anywhere from a few yards to a half-mile or more.

In fact, scientific quantities of time or measurement are not important. It is the

quality of the time or the amount of rum that really counts.

The ultimate key to Jamaican speech is the word *rass*. Originally, it meant backside, bum, derriere. It still retains that meaning in Jamaica, but as Tweedledee told Alice, it also "means what I intend it to mean." Thus, a man who is a "tiefin *rass*" is a dishonest thief. On the other hand, "Come here, you ole *rass*, mek I buy you a drink!" may be used when men greet their friends. Jamaicans may even say to each other with envy: "Dat is a *rass* house." Or a man who spots an attractive woman walking past may lean over to his friend and smile, "Dat gal pretty to *rass*"—about which no further comment is necessary.

GUIDE IN BRIEF

Traveling to Jamaica

By Air

If you've ever seen the television commercials or travel posters gently urging you to "come to Jamaica," rest assured that getting here is usually a cinch. Annually more than 12,000 airline flights arrive on the island. Most visitors pass through Donald Sangster International Airport in the northern coastal city of Montego Bay—which reigns as the nation's tourism hub. Flights headed for the capital of Kingston to the southeast land at Norman Manley International Airport.

At either airport, it's common to see Jamaicans loaded down with bulging handbags. Why? Because they're bringing in goods from other countries priced considerably cheaper than their Jamaican counterparts. Visitors, however, should keep their carry-on luggage to a minimum in preparation for the lengthy hike between the plane and the immigration and customs checkpoints. And if your plane lands during one of the many passenger waves that often descend on the airports, expect a prolonged check-in wait. In the Montego Bay airport, you can fill up the time spent waiting for your luggage by stopping by the Visitor Services booth or sipping on the Jamaican rum offered at the Appleton Rum booth. The Kingston traveler should concentrate on nabbing one of the elusive baggage carts.

There are 12 airlines that provide service to Jamaica. The national carrier is Air Jamaica, which makes frequent flights to Montego Bay and Kingston from Miami, New York, Philadelphia, Los Angeles, Atlanta, Baltimore, Toronto and will be starting flights to Newark and Tampa shortly. American Airlines heads for the island's two major cities out of New York. Eastern arrives in Montego Bay from Atlanta and Miami. Air Canada offers nonstop service from Montreal and Toronto to MoBay. Challenge Airlines flies in from Miami.

British West Indies Airlines (BWIA), Antillean Airlines (ALM) and Cayman Airlines link Jamaica with neighboring Caribbean islands. VIASA flies from Venezuela to Kingston, and Cubana Airlines has a route between Havana and Kingston. British Airways' London flights stop in Bermuda, the Bahamas and Miami before heading on to Jamaica. The Soviet Union's Aeroflot also provides service to the island, but reservations must be made in the USSR with confirmation possible through Air Jamaica. To contact the airlines in Jamaica, call:

Aeroflot, 922–4661 (Kingston).
Air Canada, 928–6211 (Kingston), 952–5160 (Montego Bay).
Air Jamaica, 922–4661 (Kingston), 952–4300 (Montego Bay).
American Airlines, 928–7305 (Kingston), 952–5950 (MoBay).
Antillean Airlines, 926–1763 (Kingston).
British Airways, 922–5245 (Kingston), 952–3771 (Montego Bay).
British West Indies Airlines (BWIA), 928–7376 (Kingston).
Cayman Airlines, 926–1762 (Kingston).
Challenge Airlines, 924-8501/2
Cubana Airlines, 922–3460 (Kingston).
Eastern Airlines, 928–6271 (MoBay).
VIASA, 952–5530 (Montego Bay).

By Sea

The seaworthy traveler who prefers a leisurely ride coupled with a short stay can select from 17 cruise ships that include Jamaica on their stop-and-go itineraries. Ocho Rios on the country's northwest side is the most popular port of entry, followed by Montego Bay to the northwest and Port Antonio in the east.

The main drawback to taking the sea route is the hassle involved in extending your stay beyond the ships' one-to-two-day docking time. Most cruise tickets are sold for round-trip voyages and you'll probably want to avoid the logistical maneuvering involved in a change. But to insure your ship stops in Jamaica, cruise lines that include the island on their schedule are:

Carnival Cruises (*Mardi Gras*), 1–800–327–9501.
Chandris Line (*Victoria*), no number available.
Commodore Cruises, (*Boheme*) no number available.
Costa Cruises (*Daphne*), 212–682–3505.
Hadag (*Astor*), no number available.
Hapag Lloyd Cruises (*Europa*), 312–332–0090.
Holland America (*Veendam*, *Volendam*), 1–800–223–6655.
Home Lines (*Atlantic*), 1–800–221–4041.
K-Lines/Hellenic (*Constellation*), 1–800–223–7880.
Norwegian Caribbean (*Southward*), 1–800–327–7030.
Paguet Line (*Rhapsody*), 1–800–221–2160/2490.
Royal Caribbean Line (*Nordic Prince*, *Song of Norway*, Sun Viking), 1–800–327–6700.
Royal Cruise Lines (*Royal Odyssey*), 415–788–0610.
Royal Viking Line (*Royal Viking Sea*, *Royal Viking Sky*), 1–800–227–4246.
Sitmar Cruises (*Fairwind*), no number available.
Sun Line (*Stella Solaris*), 1–800–223–5760.

Travel Advisories

Immigration

Anyone arriving from a Western country usually can bypass the health clearance in the airports. But all passengers must stop at the immigration checkpoint to submit proof of citizenship and flash a return ticket. A passport is the ideal international calling card, although U.S. and Canadian citizens can get by with a birth certificate or voter's registration card. All other visitors must show a passport and in some cases a visa, with the same rules applying to children. Check with authorities in your own country for specifics.

Airport officials also stamp the immigration card you fill out on the plane and ask for your Jamaican address. Save the card. It's required for your departure trip, which must be taken within the next six months.

Cruise-ship passengers skip this process under blanket ship clearance.

Customs

Jamaican officials pride themselves on extending a cordial welcome to visitors. One way they show off is by speeding up the customs process with a brief but thorough luggage inspection. Regulations prohibit anyone from bringing flowers, plants and fruits or any uncanned meats and vegetables into the country. Jamaican law also bans the transport of firearms or ammunition into or out of the country. Simply put, what you can bring in are personal belongings, 25 cigars, 200 cigarettes, one pint of liquor (excluding rum), a half pound of tobacco and one quart of wine.

It's what you can take out, though, that can become rather complicated. The first thing to remember is, most questions can be answered by calling Manley International Airport in Kingston at 928–6062 or Sangster International Airport in Montego Bay at 952–5160.

General guidelines for U.S. citizens allow $300 worth of duty-free goods after a 48-hour stay. If you're worried about overstepping the limit, you can mail an unlimited number of gifts worth up to $10 each back to the States—provided one person doesn't get more than $10 worth in a day. Such gifts cannot include perfume, cigars, cigarettes or liquor.

The only pets allowed to come in the country must hail from the United Kingdom or, in the case of dogs and cats, be born and bred in the United Kingdom.

Currency

Feel free to bring as much of your own money as you please. To make island purchases easier, exchange your own currency for Jamaican dollars at one of the banks, hotels or international airports. The official rate as of mid-1985 was 5.50 Jamaican dollars to the U.S. dollar. Jamaican law strictly forbids foreign currency exchanges with anyone other than an authorized dealer, but the black-market trade for U.S. dollars flourishes. If you're approached on a street corner, watch out for counterfeit money.

If you choose the underhanded method, expect problems trying to exchange any leftover Jamaican dollar for your own currency at the end of the trip. For legal transactions, save your receipts to speed up the conversion process. And remember to stash away enough U.S. money to pay for the hotel bill, car-rental fee and duty-free purchases.

Traveler's checks can be used throughout the island, as can most major credit cards particularly American Express.

Up to J$200 can be reconverted to foreign currency upon leaving Jamaica, if exchange receipts are provided.

Tax Reminder

Jamaica levies a little-known but all-important $20 departure tax that must be paid before you can board the plane. You can dispense with the worry by including the tax in your ticket payment and by having your receipt ready when your baggage is being checked for you to leave. The tax can be paid in Jamaican money or its equivalent in foreign exchange.

Travelers also pay a little-noticed room tax that's added into the hotel bill. During the summer season, it's US$4-$8 and in winter it's US$8-$12, depending on the hotel category.

Getting Acquainted

Climate

So many North Americans and Europeans winter in Jamaica because there *is* no winter. The average temperatures along the coast and plains range between 80 and 90 degrees Fahrenheit (27°C to 32°C) year-round. In the hills, it's a bit cooler, dropping to the 70s and even the high 60s (about 20°C to 25°C), while at the top of Blue Mountain Peak, the island's highest point, temperatures have been known to drop below 50°F (10°C) on rare occasions. The coolest months are November through April.

The rainiest times are May-June and September-October. Rain averages 77 inches annually, although some parts of the island, notably the north coast of Surrey, can get three times that amount in certain years. Hurricanes can strike anytime between June and October, but are most common in August-September. See detailed information later in Guide in Brief.

There is more variance between daytime and night-time temperatures. Day breezes blow off the sea to cool the land; night breezes come in from the mountains, making conditions a bit chillier.

Clothing

Lightweight tropical clothing is best throughout the year. A light sweater is suggested for evenings, especially in the winter or for excursions into the hills. If you're climbing into the Blue Mountains, carry a warmer jacket and wear good walking shoes. On the beaches, you can keep cool and comfortable in swimwear, but don't wear the same minimal cover in the business districts of the cities—particularly not in Kingston.

Tanning

First and last rule for tanning: Don't overdo it. Yes, the sun is shining; yes, the beach is inviting; yes, the water is sparkling; and yes, the breeze is refreshing. But in your eagerness to purchase that healthy, glowing look, you might emerge looking more like a boiled lobster than a bronzed deity. No matter what the skin color, first apply a sunscreen and then gradually follow up with tanning oil.

Pests

There are two kinds of pests in Jamaica: the human kind and the insect kind. The human kind quickly sum up your tourist status and barrage you with straw goods, wood carvings, cocaine and ganja for sale. The insect kind organize into mosquito squads bent on attacking your blood system. Deal with the mortal nuisances with a polite "thank you, but no." Mount a counteroffensive on the thirsty bloodsuckers with a strong dose of insect repellent spray and a burning mosquito coil.

Common Sense

Don't leave home without it. Just because you're on vacation doesn't mean you should shed all normal precautions. Place your jewelry and other valuables in the hotel safe until they're needed. When walking in crowds, women should clutch their handbags close to their bodies and men should transfer their wallets to front pockets. Carefully scrutinize the goods of all sellers proffering "fantastic" deals, and never forget that ganja and cocaine are illegal even though freely offered.

Etiquette

There are only a few ironclad rules of etiquette the traveler should be concerned with in Jamaica. No. 1: don't refer to Jamaicans as "natives," ignoring their cherished nationality. No. 2: don't expect continued quality service without occasionally saying the words "thank you" or "please." And No. 3: don't shove a camera in people's faces and begin snapping away without asking their permission.

Soon Come

The bustling activity evident in most of Jamaica's larger cities often belies a laidback, unruffled attitude many Jamaicans adopt. It's an attitude that almost functions as a defense mechanism for the inevitable breakdowns and delays in electricity, mail, water, telephone service, train schedules, etc., that often occur. Since howls of protest and insistent demands for service generally yield few results, it's best to adopt the Jamaican approach and with a shrug of the shoulders patiently utter, "Soon come."

Tipping

Tipping is definitely allowed and encouraged in Jamaica, a land that depends heavily on the largesse of visitors. The standard 10 to 15 percent gratuity is the norm in most areas, but make sure the tip hasn't already been added to the hotel or restaurant bill.

Time Zones

The country operates on Eastern Standard Time throughout the year. If you arrive between April and October, you will have to put your watch forward one hour. Remember to change it back when you leave.

Business and Banking Hours

The majority of business offices operate from 8:30 a.m. until 4:30 p.m. Monday through Friday, with few open on Saturday. Banks are open Monday through Thursday from 9 a.m. to 2 p.m., and Friday from 9 a.m. to noon and 2:30 p.m. to 5 p.m. The main offices of some major banks include:

Bank of Commerce, 121 Harbour St. (Kingston), 59 St. James St. (Montego Bay).

Citibank, 63–67 Knutsford Blvd. (Kingston)

National Commercial Bank, 77 King St. (Kingston), 41 St. James St. (Montego Bay)

Royal Bank Jamaica Ltd., 37 Duke St. (Kingston), Sam Sharpe Square (Montego Bay)

Scotiabank Jamaica, Duke & Port Royal Streets (Kingston), Sam Sharpe Square (Montego Bay).

Electricity

Most of the country runs on 110 volts and 50 cycles of electrical currents, although some of the larger hotels use 220 volts. If you need a transformer, most hotels can supply them.

Photography

While you'll want to capture the character-rich visages found in Jamaica, it's easier to find a receptive subject if you offer the right incentive. A few people will accept money, while others will accept a picture of their own which makes a Polaroid a handy item to carry along with your 35-millimeter camera. Shoot most of your pictures during the early morning or late afternoon hours, because the midday sun tends to bleach out color shots.

Holidays

Out of all the holidays celebrated in Jamaica, Christmas holidays and Jamaican Independence Day (first Monday in August) rank as the most festive occasions. Independence Day celebrations are marked by colorful parades, street dances, music, festivals and a rip-roarin' good time.

Other holidays when businesses are closed include New Year's Day (Jan. 1), Ash Wednesday, Good Friday, Easter Monday, Labor Day (May 23), National Heroes Day (third Monday in October), Christmas Day (Dec. 25) and Boxing Day (Dec. 26).

Wedding Bells

Always popular as a honeymoon site, Jamaica also beckons as an idyllic spot for the wedding itself. Couples can apply for a license after a 24-hour stay on the island and should bring along birth certificates and, where appropriate, divorce papers.

In Kingston, licenses are dispensed at the Registrar's Office from 8:30 a.m. to 4:30 p.m. Monday through Friday and 8:30 a.m. to 12:30 p.m. Saturday. The Montego Bay office is open from 8:30 a.m. to 4:30 p.m. weekdays and from 8:30 a.m. to 4:30 p.m. weekdays and from 8:30 a.m. to 12 noon Saturday. Any priest, marriage officer or registrar can perform the ceremony.

Tourist Information

Tourist Board and Embassies

An estimated 552,000 people don't just descend on one country during the course of a year. Some organization must mold a method to the madness of such a mass influx. And in Jamaica, that organization is the Jamaican Tourist Board.

The board answers your questions before and after you arrive, issues maps and brochures on the places you want to see, and can even help you find a Jamaican who shares your interests. It is that last function that has garnered much of the attention since the late '60s with the success of the "Meet the People" program, linking island visitors with Jamaicans. For more information, you can contact the board's local and/or overseas offices, the addresses of which are included in the Appendix. Besides the board, embassies/high commissions of 24 countries have found a home in the town of Kingston. Refer to the Appendix for the addresses.

Transportation

Island Flying

For short jaunts across the island, Trans Jamaican Airlines flies to the major cities and provides connections for flights at the two international airports. The local planes land at domestic airports in Kingston, Mandeville, Montego Bay, Negril, Ocho Rios and Port Antonio, all for a reasonable price. But be forewarned that while the homegrown airline boasts a creditable safety record, schedules are apt to change without much notice.

To get the most up-to-date timetable, call 923-8680 in Kingston, 962-3228 in Mandeville, 952-3254 in Ocho Rios and 993-2791 in Port Antonio.

Wings Jamaica Ltd. offers charter flights. Prices vary according to destination. Contact them in Kingston at 923-6573.

Buses

The rural areas are served by mini-buses that criss-cross the back and main roads, making impromptu stops as well as scheduled ones. Since no central agency handles the bus schedules, the only way to find out where the buses are going is to ask the driver. Fares are low, but there is not much elbow room and the music is loud. Because of the haphazard routes and crowded conditions, few tourists are bold enough to tackle the country system.

In the major population centers like Kingston and Montego Bay, the bus system isn't much better for the uninitiated. Here, too, mini-buses have taken over, traveling on the regular routes once used by the now vanished Jamaica Omnibus Service. Frequency is erratic, and the best way to travel is with someone who knows the system. Fares range between J80¢ and J$1.60, but increases are expected.

Trains

A rambling train ride from Montego Bay to Kingston, or vice-versa, gives you an inexpensive, breathtaking tour of the island countryside. For an economical J$25.00 first class and J$12.50 second class, the train makes at least one stop in each parish along a route that takes you from the beach, through the mountains, and back to the coast again.

The train departs Kingston 6.50 a.m. and 3.00 p.m. daily. From Montego Bay, departure times are 6.45 a.m. and 2.45 p.m. The trip takes approximately six hours.

It's rather easy to get a seat on the weather-beaten but sturdy railway cars, but a little harder to pin down the operating schedule. Check to see how much of the Montego Bay-Port Antonio route is back in operation as repairs continue following a hurricane brush a few years ago. You can contact the Kingston station by calling 992-6620 and Montego Bay by calling 952-0297.

Rental Cars

You'll probably find the Jamaican driving experience somewhat akin to a demolition derby as you steer to avoid potholes, goats, cows, pedestrians and seemingly crazed oncoming drivers. But not to worry, the most important driving rule you need to remember while tooling around the country is to stay on the left side of the road.

"U-Drive" or rental-car operations in Jamaica include such big-name agencies as Avis, Budget Rent-A-Car, Hertz, Martins Jamaica and National Car Rental. Try to reserve a car before you arrive on the island to avoid the frequent surges in demand. Once you arrive, look for agency representatives at the two international airports, tourist centers and special desks in the hotels.

To rent a car, you must be at least 21 years old with a valid driver's licence from any country. Anyone between 21 and 25 will be required to post a bond to meet insurance regulations and all payments must be made in either foreign currency or with a major credit card.

You can also rent motorcycles, mopeds and bicycles. Inquire at your hotel desk.

Taxis

Few taxis in Jamaica carry meters, so you should first ask the cost of the trip and whether payment is in U.S. or Jamaica dollars. Fares in the resort areas are easier to gauge because most taxis—or "contract carriages"—clearly display their rates on the outside of the car doors. If in doubt, feel free to strike up a few rounds of bargaining with the driver.

You can expect the cost of a brisk ride from the airport in Montego Bay to the hotel area to range from US $5 to $10. In Kingston, a run from the airport to downtown should be about US $15. Taxis are summoned either by a telephone call or the more common method of flagging them down in the street. The licensed ones display a red Public Passenger Vehicle (PPV) plate somewhere on the car.

Accommodation

To accommodate the hundreds of thousands of tourists and visitors to Jamaica, dozens of hotels, inns and guest houses have sprung up. They dot the island, with more along the coast in resort areas and fewer as one moves inland. But there is always somewhere to rest your head.

Quality and price vary greatly, from ultramodern package resorts for those who want to live in the lap of luxury, to tiny guesthouses and villas for those who are happy with the comforts of home—and less.

The appendix of this section includes a listing of hotels, selected at random. Their facilities and charges are, of course, subject to change.

Villas

You're basking in nature's generous gifts. An unending supply of clean fresh air fills your lungs with each breath you take, the sun is strong enough to bronze your back as you lounge under it, and the sea stretches for miles to the horizon and beyond. Nearby, stands the villa to which you've come to be "far from the madding crowd."

There are over 350 such villas and cottages available for year-round rental in Jamaica. These are not cluttered together; far from being an international holiday ground, they are sprinkled all over the island. You will find villas in Negril, Tryall, Rosehall, Reading, Ironshore, just outside Montego Bay, Mammee Bay, Ocho Rios, Oracabessa, Port Antonio, and even more out-of-the-way places. Some rise dramatically out of a long stretch of beach; others are set away in secluded hills; still others are built on the sea with balconied, second-story windows overlooking cliffs or sandy coves.

A constant attraction common to all these homes is the opportunity to live entirely at your own pace, doing what you want to do when you want; of having the privacy and convenience of a home together with the promise of romance, luxury and solace conjured up by such names as *East of Eden*, *Idle Hours* and *Come What May*.

The homes are all fully equipped with linen, towels, cutlery and dishes. Most have private swimming pools and a bathroom adjoining each bedroom. Qualified full-time household staff take over the drudgery of housekeeping; they will tidy up the place and (if requested) prepare exotic meals and make sure larders are replenished with food. (Usually villas are stocked with enough food and liquor to last two days for each new group of visitors.) Guests may alternatively opt for the experience of shopping in the fresh food markets for *calalloo* (Jamaican spinach), ackees, red peas, sugar cane, ortaniques, sweetsops and otaheiti apples.

During holiday season (Dec. 16 to Apr. 15), the average price for villa residents is US$470 per week per bedroom. The rate is US$350 during "off-peak" season (April 16 to Dec. 15.). Reservations can be made through most travel agents or the Jamaican Tourist Board or the Jamaican Association of Villas and Apartments, known as JAVA. They can be contacted in New York at 200 Park Avenue, Suite 229, New York, N.Y. 10166, tel. 212-986-4317/9, and in Jamaica at Pineapple Place, P.O. Box 298, Ocho Rios, tel. 974-2508.

Communications

Postal services

Every town in Jamaica has a post office, and every hotel can handle mail for you. Overseas airmail rates are:

To the United States and Canada, 55 cents per half-ounce; 35 cents for post cards.

To the British Isles and Europe, 70 cents per half-ounce.

To Asia, Africa, Australia and the Middle East, 95 cents per half-ounce.

Telecommunications

Although labor strikes cause frequent interruptions in service, the telephone system theoretically operates 24 hours a day. Direct connections are possible to North America and Europe. The area code for Jamaica is "809."

Inquiries for telegrams, cables and telexes can be made at post offices and hotel front desks. Inland telegrams cost approximately US$1 for 30 words.

The head office of Jamaica International Telecommunications Ltd. is at 15 North St., Kingston (tel. 922–6031). There are branch offices at Spanish Court in New Kingston (tel. 926–5602) and in Montego Bay at 36 Fort St. (tel. 952–4400).

News Media

Press

Two newspapers are published daily in Kingston and distributed throughout the island. The *Daily Gleaner* appears in the morning. It celebrated 150 years of publication in 1984. *The Star*, owned by the *Gleaner*, is an afternoon tabloid. The active Press Association of Jamaica is based in Kingston.

In Montego Bay, *The Western Beacon* is published twice weekly. For visitors to the island, publications include the *Tourist Guide*, published by the *Gleaner*; *The Visitor*; and the *Vacation Guide*.

Foreign newspapers, including *The New York Times*, *Miami Herald*, *The Times* of London, *Le Monde* and *Die Welt*, are available at hotels and bookstores in airmail editions.

Radio and Television

Jamaica is served by one television station (JBC-TV) and two AM-FM radio stations (JBC and RJR). All have their head offices and studios in Kingston.

Books and Magazines

Jamaica's biggest bookstore is **Sangster's**, with four branches in Kingston and one in Montego Bay. Here you can find a variety of books on all aspects of Jamaican life (see our suggested reading list), as well as foreign magazines and locally written and foreign novels. (Kingston shops are at 97 Harbour St., 33 King St., 144 Old Hope Rd., and in the Mall at the Constant Spring Shopping Centre. In Montego Bay, look for Sangster's in the West Gate Shopping Centre.)

Health and Emergencies

Tropical diseases like smallpox and yellow fever have been stamped out in Jamaica, where all tap water is chlorinated and filtered by modern methods. But even the strongest constitution might not be ready for the spicy island food, so take along your most effective antacid.

For minor illnesses and cuts and bruises, some hotels employ nurses to treat their guests. Major illnesses can be handled by specialists, most of whom practice in Kingston. Your travel agent can give you an up-to-date rundown of the island's health picture and tell you if any booster shots are needed.

All major towns have medical facilities. Large specialist hospitals are located in Kingston and Montego Bay:

Andrews Memorial Hospital, 27 Hope Rd., Kingston, tel. 926–7401.

Kingston Public Hospital, North Street, Kingston, tel. 922–0210.

Medical Associates Hospital, 18 Tangerine Place, Kingston, tel. 926–1400.

Nuttall Memorial Hospital, 6 Caledonia Ave., Kingston, tel. 926–2139.

St. Joseph's Hospital, Deanery Road, Kingston, tel. 928–4955.

University Hospital of the West Indies, Mona, Kingston, tel. 927–6621 or 927–4014.

Cornwall Regional Hospital, Mount Salem, Montego Bay, tel. 952–5100.

In addition, all parish capitals have infirmaries.

Antibiotics, tranquilizers and certain other drugs can be bought only on a doctor's prescription. Many other medications can be purchased at pharmacies located in all major towns.

Emergency Phone Numbers

Air-sea rescue	119
Ambulance	110
Fire	110
Police	119

Telephone Services

Directory assistance	114
Telephone repair service	115
Time of Day	117
Toll operator and assistance on local and intra-island calls	112
Overseas calls operator	113

Useful Telephone Numbers

American Express Travel Service		926–1260
Customs Airport General		
	(Montego Bay)	952–2776
	(Kingston)	922–8770
Donald Sangster Int'l Airport (flight info), Montego Bay		952–5530
General Post Office		922–5420
Immigration Dept.		922–1110
Jamaica Broadcasting Corp		926–5620
Jamaica Chamber of Commerce		922–0150/1
Jamaica Commercial Info Bureau		927–6495
Jamaica Hotel & Tourist Assn.		926–3635

Jamaica Library Service	926–3310/5
Jamaica Omnibus Services	926–2173
Jamaica Railway Corp.	922–6620
Norman Manley Int'l Airport (flight info.), Kingston	928–6077
Post & Telegraph Dept.	922–9430
Weather forecast & enquiries	
(Kingston)	926–4192
(Norman Manley Airport)	928–6055

Dining Out

There are tastes to please every palate in Jamaica's restaurants. Sophisticated hotel restaurants serve international cuisine, while cozy inns and roadside stands offer home-cooked local dishes. In the major towns, you can find everything from Kentucky Fried Chicken to excellent Chinese food, the latter a legacy of the island's large immigrant population.

The list of eating houses in the Appendix, while by no means exhaustive, offers a sampling of the various types of food available to the connoisseur.

Shopping

All over the island, there is a multitude of shopping possibilities. Many shops, offering a large variety of merchandise, at "in-bond" or duty-free prices, spell a paradise for shoppers. The vogue is shopping plazas and complexes which make it possible to do all your buying under one roof.

To trigger off reminiscences of your visit to the island, look for Jamaica's renowned hand-crafted items. These include Annabella boxes made of wood to serve as cigarette boxes and tiny trinket boxes; pimento-filled Spanish jars; beautiful hand-embroidered linens with motifs of birds and flora; silk and cotton batiked in daring colors. There are good crafts shops at the pier in Port Antonio on 'Cruise Ship' day; at City Centre and Bamboo Village in Montego Bay; and at Victoria Crafts Market on Port Royal Street in Kingston. Look for straw goods, woodcarvings and bead work at local markets and roadside craft stalls throughout the islands.

Another home product, a must for visitors either to bring home or to savor across the counters, is Jamaica's famous rums and liqueurs. Take your pick from internationally known names like Appleton, Coruba, Gold Label, Rumona, Tia Maria; and from names peculiar to the island, like Sangster's Old Jamaican.

Those who have an eye for intricately delicate jewelry, and a bulging wallet to pay for it, can find a first-class selection at major shopping areas in north coast resorts and in Kingston. Those with less money in their pockets should study the workmanship and ingenuity in the semi-precious stones set by Blue Mountain Gems, and Jamaican black coral jewelry. The highly fashionable shell jewelry created by former Miss World, Cindy Breakspeare, and colleague Donna Coore can be brought at the Italcraft, their Kingston boutique.

Jamaica is a treasure trove of fineries like bone china, crystal and figurines. These are some of the better buys as they are priced at far less than they would be in the United States. You can make your selection at shops like L.A. Henriques (in Montego Bay, Ocho Rios and Kingston), Americana (in Ocho Rios) and San-Hing's in (Port Antonio).

The fashion conscious can browse through the boutiques strung along the Gloucester Avenue hotel strip in Montego Bay, and in shopping malls like Beachview Arcade and Casa Montego Arcade.

Cultural Activities

A country as rich in history as Jamaica requires several museums to house the exhibits which relate to her arts and crafts, archaeology, antiques and so on.

In Kingston alone, there is the Institute of Jamaica which has a **Science Museum** and library; the **Coin & Note Museum** further downtown at the Bank of Jamaica; an **Archaeological Museum** and a **Maritime Museum**, among others. Three museums located in Spanish Town are the **Jamaica People's Museum of Craft and Technology**, the **Archaeological Museum**, and the **White Marl Arawak Museum**. Nearer to the east coast in Port Antonio, enlightening exhibits are found in **The Afro-Jamaican Museum** and the **Spice Garden**.

Jamaican artists' works are on display in a large number of galleries. The **National Gallery** is the repository of the finest works of art produced on the island. Other exhibitions can be seen at the **Bolivar Gallery**, the **Olympia International Art Centre**, the **Barrington Watson Gallery**, **Gallery Makonde**, the **Upstairs Downstairs Gallery** and the **Mutual Life Gallery**, all in Kingston. Further north in Montego Bay, galleries well worth visiting include **The Georgian Gallery**, the **Gallery of West Indian Art** and the **Budhai Gallery**.

Theaters, Dance and Music

Jamaica's lively tradition of performing arts— theater, dance and music—is surveyed in the feature section of this book. In Kingston, the cultural center, be sure to see the **National Pantomine** at the Ward Theatre between December and March or April. The **National Dance Theatre Company** and the **Jamaica Folk Singers** stage important mini-seasons at Kingston's Little Theatre; the dancers in December and the singers in March-April. Many smaller theaters also have regular seasons for stage plays; consult the daily newspaper for full details.

For classical and popular music, keep an ear out for performances by the **School of Music** (Institute of Jamaica), the **Jamaica Philharmonic Symphony Orchestra**, and the **National Chorale** during the early summer and early winter months. And consult the University of the West Indies for sporadic shows by and for students.

Jamaicans are movie fans, too. American-made films are most popular. The small but thriving local movie industry has tremendous support. Consult local newspaper or your hotel desk for offering in your area.

Nightlife

Many young visitors come to Jamaica with reggae music on their minds. They've brought along their dancing shoes. Night clubs, bars, discotheques, open-air theaters and concert halls throughout the island offer a regular fare of this rhythmic music. And a variety of other musical genres will please everyone's ear.

In Kingston, the most popular night spots include **Epiphany**, **Illusion**, **Scruples**, **Rumours**, the **Ritz**, **Turntable**, **Mario's**, and the **Red Carpet Club**. The **Jonkanoo Lounge** is at the Wyndham Hotel, New Kingston.

Montego Bay is the night-life center of Jamaica. The **Witch's Hideaway** at the Holiday Inn has been established longer than any other club. Also in the Rose Hall area, try **Disco Inferno** at Holiday Village or the **Hell Fire Club** at the Wyndham-Rose Hall Hotel. On MoBay's Strip, look for the **Fantasy** disco in the Casa Montego. In downtown MoBay, the **Banana Boat Club** is popular. At Montego Freeport, check out **The Cave** in the Seawind. For less flamboyant action, there's a nightly piano bar at the **Doctor's Cave Beach Hotel**.

The most popular clubs in Ocho Rios are The **Ruins** and **Decade** among the local crowds; **Silks** (at the Shaw Park Beach Hotel). You might also drop by **Footprints** in the Coconut Grove Shopping Centre. In Runaway Bay, look for **Jaws** at Club Caribbean and the **Plantation Room** at Runaway Bay Hotel.

Sports

A perfect tropical climate with bright skies and warm weather year-round have spawned a breed of sports enthusiasts. Visitors to the island will therefore find plenty of facilities provided at hotels, sports associations and health clubs.

Traditional sports for watching and participating range from very-British cricket to conventional badminton and universal horse racing at Caymanas Park. The list below serves as a brief guide to some of the more popular sports.

Golf

Caymanas Golf Club, Kingston
Constant Spring Golf Club, Kingston
Tryall Golf Course, Montego Bay
Ironshore, Montego Bay
Runaway Bay Golf Club, Runaway Bay
Upton Club, Ocho Rios
Manchester Club, Mandeville
Half Moon Golf Club, Montego Bay

Tennis

Liguanea Club, Kingston
Pegasus Hotel, Kingston
Jamaica Hill, Port Antonio
Dragon Bay, Port Antonio
Montego Bay Racquet Club, Montego Bay
Manchester Club, Mandeville
Negril Beach Club, Negril.

Horseback Riding

Chukka Cove Farm, Runaway Bay
Errol Flynn's Plantation, Port Antonio
Prospect Plantation, Ocho Rios
Dunn's River Stables, Ocho Rios
Hotel Astra, Mandeville
Seawind, Montego Freeport
Double A Ranch, Montego Bay
White Witch Stables, Montego Bay.

Water Skiing

Morgan's Harbour Club, Kingston
Royal Jamaica Yacht Club, Kingston
Blue Lagoon, Port Antonio
Club Caribbean, Ocho Rios
Americana Hotel, Ocho Rios
Ray's Parasailing, Negril
Coconut Cove Hotel, Negril
Montego Bay Yacht Club, Montego Freeport
Water Whirl, Montego Bay.

Sailing

Eden 2 Hotel, Ocho Rios
Negril Beach Club, Negril
Dragon Bay, Port Antonio
Half Moon Club, Montego Bay.

Yachting & Boating

Half Moon Club, Montego Bay
Eden 2 Club, Ocho Rios
Morgan's Harbour Club, Kingston
Royal Jamaica Yacht Club, Kingston

Scuba & Snorkeling

Sea Jamaica Aquatic Club, Ocho Rios
Island Dive Shop, Priory, St Ann, Ocho Rios
Dive Shop, Rick's Cafe, Negril
Sea Crab, Chatham Cottages, Montego Bay
Jamaica Reef Divers, Montego Bay.

Wind Surfing .

Jamaica, Jamaica! Hotel, Runaway Bay
Shaw Park Beach, Ocho Rios
Negril Beach Club, Negril
Dragon Bay, Port Antonio.

Jet Skiing

Sheraton Hotel, Ocho Rios
Montego Bay Yacht Club, Montego Freeport.

Parasailing

Ray's Parasailing, Sundowner, Negril
Negril Beach Club, Negril
Americana Hotel, Ocho Rios

Deep Sea Diving

Aqua Sports, Negril
Ruddy's Water Sports, Shaw Park Beach, Ocho
Rios
Sea Jamaica Aquatic Club, Ocho Rios

Foreign Investment

It's hardly surprising to know that Jamaica has been attracting overseas investments, especially ventures aimed at the export markets of the United States, Central and South America and the countries of the European Economic Community. One could perhaps attribute this to her strategic geographical location at the hub of the Caribbean.

There are no restrictions on ownership of foreign investments. The government encourages 100 percent foreign ownership, as well as joint ventures with local counterparts. Repatriation of invested capital is granted (at official prevailing rates of exchange) for all approved overseas investments. Repatriation of capital gains from real estate transactions is phased over an appropriate period.

Industrial and Export Incentives

According to Prime Minister Edward Seaga, "Investment is one of the most critical ingredients in the achievement of growth. We therefore encourage investment, by the tried principles of motivation, initiative and enterprise which experience has proved to be the only real basis of economic success."

In her move to encourage investment, the Jamaican government provides various incentives and motivations in the form of grants, tax relief and other exemptions. These include the Industrial Incentive Law and the Export Industry Encouragement Law by which enterprises are granted an income tax exemption. The former provides tax relief for up to nine years based on the quantum of local "value-added," computed to emphasize the employment content of the project. The latter grants a 10-year exemption to enterprises exporting to non-Caricom (Caribbean Commonwealth) countries. In addition, both laws give relief from import duties on machinery, equipment and raw materials during the concessionary period.

The Kingston Export Free Zone has been set up as an export center for manufacturing, warehousing and distribution activities. Production or operational space is available in modules of 6,500 square feet at an economical rental rate. If justified by size of operations, more than one module can be arranged. Investments in this zone must be financed solely with foreign exchange. Companies operating in the Free Zone enjoy minimal exchange control, freedom from quantitative restrictions, special security services, free management consultancy, a limited access to the Jamaican and Caricom markets, and exemption from customs duty, import licensing and income tax for profits earned from export sales.

Jamaica National Investment Promotion

Potential foreign investors are advised to obtain all information and assistance from the Jamaica National Investment Promotion Ltd. (JNIP), at the JDB Building, 15 Oxford Road, Kingston (tel. 929-4000, telex JANICO YA). This is the Jamaican government's central agency where all national projects are registered. It is part of the JNIP's function to expedite the processs of registration and to assist in clearing roadblocks. The agency's job is not complete until the investment is actually made, the company registered, and all criteria required by the Bank of Jamaica approved.

Interested prospective overseas investors may contact the agency's office in New York or the Jamaican trade commissioners based in London, Belgium, Germany, Canada and Trinidad.

Hurricanes

When they talk about hurricanes in Jamaica, they think of this jingle:
"June, too soon. July, stand by. August, prepare you must. September, remember. October, all over."

August is certainly the worst month for these tropical storms. But the official hurricane season begins on June 1 and continues into October. Throughout this period, you must be prepared for the possibility of a hurricane if you are visiting the island of Jamaica.

The most severe hurricane of the 20th Century struck Jamaica on Aug. 17, 1951. Hurricane Charlie ravaged the entire island, but saved its worst blows for Kingston and Port Royal. It claimed 150 lives.

Winds and rains from Flora in the 1960s and from Edith and David in the 1970s caused significant damage, although none of them caught the island with their full force.

On Aug. 6, 1980, however, Hurricane Allen— packing winds of 175 miles per hour—swung across the eastern end of Jamaica and devoured much of the north coast of the parish of Portland. Millions of dollars of damage was done to the agriculture and fishing industries, as well as to public works and tourism in the Port Antonio area.

The number of hurricanes that forms in a given year has ranged from as few as two to as many as 20, but most never swing into Jamaica. Still, the U.S. National Hurricane Center in Miami, Florida, tracks each of the massive storms carefully with sophisticated radar detection equipment, satellites and reconnaisance planes. It issues warnings throughout the Caribbean region in a spirit of international cooperation. In Jamaica, the office of Disaster Preparedness and Emergency Relief Coordination (ODIPERC) was established in 1980.

A hurricane forms when wind rushes toward a low-pressure area and takes on a distinctive swirling motion. It begins as a tropical disturbance, evolves into a tropical depression, and is classified a hurricane when winds reach 74 miles per hour. The size of storms can range from 60 miles in diameter to monsters more than 1,000 miles wide. Their patterns and routes remain difficult to predict. Hurricanes thought to be on the wane have reformed into bigger storms. Others move out to sea away from land areas only to double back and come ashore.

The average life of a hurricane is eight to 10 days. They begin to lose their punch and organization when they stray too far inland or over colder northern waters where tropical wind patterns are no longer able to feed them.

Jamaica residents are well versed on precautions that should be taken when a hurricane approaches. Newspapers and magazines publish special sections on the subject at the beginning of each season. Most coastal communities publish evacuation planes and routes.

Needless to say, tourists caught in Jamaica during an impending hurricane should drop plans to work on suntans or visit tourist attractions and follow ODIPERC advisories, television directives and common sense in riding the storm out.

Hurricane Developments

Tropical disturbance—This phase in a hurricane's development has no strong winds. But it may feature a weak counter-clockwise circulation of wind. Disturbances of this sort are common throughout the tropics in summer months.

Tropical depression—A small low-pressure system develops and the counter-clockwise rotation of air increases to speeds under 39 miles per hour.

Tropical storm—By now, the low-pressure system has developed winds ranging from 39 to 73 miles per hour and can be accompanied by heavy rains.

Hurricane—The low-pressure system has intensified to the point where strong winds of more than 74 miles per hour rotate in a counter-clockwise direction around an area of calm called the "eye." Storm tides may rise as much as 15 feet above normal and can surge as much as six feet in minutes.

Storm Advisories

Hurricane watch—This signal means that a hurricane may threaten your immediate area within 24 hours. It is time to begin taking final precautions against a direct hit. Stay tuned to radio or television for the latest storm information.

Watch precautions:
● Check car battery, water and oil and make sure your gas tank is full.
● Make sure you have new batteries for your radio and flashlight.
● Gather containers for storing clean drinking water. Fill drug prescriptions and make certain you have special medications like insulin on hand.
● Put together a survival kit consisting of non-perishable food (including a manual can opener), water (one-half gallon per person per day), eating and cooking utensils, personal toilet articles and sanitary needs (like diapers and toothpaste), bedding (or sleeping bags), changes of clothing, portable cooler and ice, and a first-aid kit.

Hurricane warning—This is issued when the storm has reached winds of at least 74 miles per hour and high water and storm surges are expected in a specific area within 24 hours. Warnings will identify specific coastal areas where these conditions may occur. Be prepared to evacuate your home or hotel, even if the weather does not appear threatening when the warning is issued.

Warning precautions:
● Clear your yard of loose objects, lawn furniture, garbage cans, bicycles, etc.
● Protect windows and take down awnings to secure your home. Also shut off gas valves, pull main electrical power switches, turn off main water pipes, open a window slightly, take all important papers with you and leave your swimming pool full and super-chlorinated.
● Complete the assembly of materials needed to take to a shelter or that you will need if you stay home.
● Prepare to evacuate if and when ordered. Consult ODIPERC or local emergency officials for more details.

If your area does not have an evacuation plan, check the elevation of your property above mean sea level, study the storm surge history of your area, and plan a safe evacuation route. Follow news bulletins closely and be prepared to take immediate shelter. If your home is above or away from areas threatened by high tides, stay put so you do not inhibit evacuation of people from those areas.

During the storm—Stay indoors and do not travel once the hurricane begins buffeting your area. When the eye passes over you, there will be a temporary lull in wind and rain that may last up to a half hour or more. Do not mistake this for an end to the storm, although you may take the opportunity to make emergency repairs. Prepare for resumption of the storm, possibly with even greater force, from the opposite direction. Wait for official word before leaving your home.

If ordered to evacuate—Follow instructions and designated routes as quickly as possible. Take blankets, a flashlight, extra clothing, medications, dietary food (if needed), infant necessities and lightweight folding chairs. Leave behind alcoholic beverages, pets, weapons or extra food.

The storm surge—Ninety percent of all hurricane-related deaths are directly a result of the storm surge. It occurs when a massive dome of water that can be up to 50 miles wide sweeps across the coastline near an area where the eye comes ashore. It is caused by an extreme drop in barometric pressure and the force of high winds pushing on open waters. The hammering effect of breaking waves and the surge act like a giant steamroller crushing everything in their path.

After the storm passes—Drive with caution when ordered to return home. Debris may fill some streets and cause hazardous conditions. Roads in coastal areas may collapse if soil has been washed from beneath them. Avoid sightseeing as you may be mistaken for a looter. Steer clear of downed or dangling utility wires.

Seek medical attention, if necessary, at designated disaster centers or hospitals. Stay tuned to radio stations for instructions about emergency medical, food, housing and other forms of assistance.

Re-enter your home with caution. Make temporary repairs necessary to correct safety hazards and to minimize further damage. Open windows and doors to air out and dry out the house and in case of gas leaks. Exercise caution when dealing with matches or fires. Report broken sewer or water mains to local utility departments.

Above all, do not take a hurricane lightly by inviting friends over for a "hurricane party." The deadly forces of wind, rain and tides that accompany a hurricane are no cause for celebration.

Further Reading

History and Politics

Barrett, Lloyd. *The Constitutional Law of Jamaica*. London: Oxford University Press, 1977.

Bell, Wendell. *Jamaican Leaders: Political Attitudes in a New Nation*. Berkley and Los Angeles: University of California, 1964.

Black, Clinton V. *History of Jamaica*. London: Collins, 1976. 4th Edition.

Black, Clinton V. *The Story of Jamaica*. London: Collins, 1965.

Black, Clinton V. *Tales of Old Jamaica*. Kingston: Sangster, 1979.

Bridges, George W. *The Annals of Jamaica*. 2 vols. London: Murray, 1828.

Carley, Mary Manning. *Jamaica: The Old and The New*. London: George Allen and Unwin, 1963.

Clerk, James Otway. *An Abridged History of Jamaica*. Falmouth, Jamaica, 1859.

Craton, Michael. *Searching for the Invisible Man*. Cambridge, Mass: Harvard University Press, 1978.

Cundall, Frank. *Chronological Outlines of Jamaica History 1492–1926*. Kingston: 1927.

Cundall, Frank, and Joseph L. Pietersz. *Jamaica Under the Spaniards*. Kingston: Institute of Jamaica, 1919.

Dallas, R.C. *The History of the Maroons*. 2 vols. London: 1803.

Dennis, Colin. *The Road not Taken*. Kingston: Kingston Publishers, 1985.

Dillion, J.T. *A Century of Progress: 1838–1933*. Kingston: 1933.

Earle, Stafford. *Basic Jamaica History*. Kingston: Earle Publishing, 1978.

Eaton, George E. *Alexander Bustamante and Modern Jamaica*. Kingston: Kingston Publishers, 1975.

Esquemeling, John. *Buccaneers of America*. London: 1684.

Foot, Hugh. *A Start in Freedom*. London: Hodder and Stoughton, 1964.

Gannon, John Charles. *The Origin and Development of Jamaica's Two-Party System 1930–1975*. St. Louis Graduate School of Art and Sciences of Washington University, 1976.

Gardner, William James. *A History of Jamaica From Its Discovery by Christopher Columbus to the Present Times*. London: E. Stock, 1873.

Graham, Tom. *Kingston 100: 1872–1972*. Kingston, Tom Graham, 1972.

Hall, Douglas. *Free Jamaica, 1838–1865: An Economic History*. New Haven: Yale University Press, 1951.

Hill, Richard. *Eight Chapters in the History of Jamaica*. Kingston: DeCordova, McDougall and Company, 1868.

Hill, Richard. *Light and Shadows of Jamaica History*. Kingston: Ford and Gall, 1859.

Hurwitz, Samuel J. *Jamaica: A Historical Portrait*. London: Pall Mall Press, 1971.

Ingram, Kenneth E. *Sources of Jamaican History, 1655–1838*. 2 vols. London: Inter Documentation Co., 1976. A bibliographical survey.

Lacey, Terry. *Violence and Politics in Jamaica 1960–70*. Manchester: Manchester University Press, 1977

Leslie, Charles. *A New History of Jamaica*. Printed for J. Hodges at the Looking-glass on London Bridge, 1740.

Long, Edward. *The History of Jamaica*. 3 vols. London: Frank Cass, 1774.

Manley, Michael Norman. *The Politics of Change: A Jamaican Testament*. London: Andre Deutsch, 1974.

Munroe, Trevor. *The Politics of Constitutional Decolonization: Jamaica 1944–1962*. Mona: U.W.I. Institute of Social and Economic Research, 1972.

Nugent, Maria Lady. *Lady Nugent's Journal: Jamaica 150 Years Ago*. London: 1939.

Olivier, Lord. *Jamaica the Blessed Island*. London: Faber & Faber, 1934.

Parry, J.H., and P.M. Sherlock. *A Short History of the West Indies*. London: Macmillan, 1956.

Phillippo, James M. *Jamaica: Its Past and Present*. London: Dawson, 1969.

Post, Ken. *Arise ye Starvelings*. The Hague: Martinus Nijhoff, 1978.

Robinson, Carey. *The Fighting Maroons of Jamaica*. London: Collins/Sangster, 1969.

Stone, Carl, and Aggrey Brown. *Essays on Power and Change in Jamaica*. Kingston: Jamaica Publishing House, 1977.

Taylor, S.A.C. *Pages from Our Past*. Kingston: Pioneer Press, 1954.

Van Sertima, Ivan. *They Came Before Columbus: The African Presence in Ancient America*. New York: Random House, 1976.

Wright, Richardson. *Revels in Jamaica, 1682–1838*. New York: Dodd, Mead, 1937.

People

Barrett, Leonard E. *The Rastafarians: The Dreadlocks of Jamaica*. London: Heinemann, 1977.

Bennett, Louise, *et al. Anancy Stories and Dialect Verse*. Kingston: Pioneer Press, 1950.

Brathwaite, Edward. *The Development of Creole Society in Jamaica 1770–1820*. Oxford: Clarendon Press, 1971.

Brown, Aggrey. *Colour, Class and Politics in Jamaica*. New Jersey: Transaction Books, 1979.

Cassidy, Frederic G. *Jamaica Talk*. London: Macmillan, 1971.

Clarke, Edith. *My Mother who Fathered Me*. London: Allen and Unwin, 1966 edition.

Cumper, George E. *The Social Structure of Jamaica*. Mona: University College of the West Indies, 1949.

Hart, Richard. *The Origin and Development of the People of Jamaica*. Montreal: International Caribbean Service Bureau, 1974.

Henriques, Fernando. *Family and Colour in Jamaica*. London: Eyre and Spottiswoode, 1953.

Heuman, Gad. *Between Black and White*. Westport, Conn., Greenwood Press, 1981.

Jekyl, Walter. *Jamaica Song and Story*. New York: Dover, 1966.

Kerr, Madeline. *Personality and Conflict in Jamaica*. Liverpool: University Press, 1952.

LePage, R.B., and David de Camp. *Jamaican Creole*. London: Macmillan, 1960.

Mbiti, John S. *African Religions and Philosphy*. London: Heinemann, 1969.

Owens, Joseph. *Dread: The Rastafarians of Jamaica*. Kingston: Sangsters, 1976.

Smith, M.G., Roy Angier and Rex Nettleford. *The Ras Tafari Movement in Kingston, Jamaica*. Mona: Institute of Social and Economic Research, 1960.

Wynter, Sylvia. *Jamaica National Heroes*. Kingston: Jamaica National Press Commission, 1971.

Arts and Culture

Baxter, Ivy. *The Arts of an Island*. Metuchen, N.J.: Scarecrow Press, 1970.

Bebey, Francis. *African Music: A People's Art*. London: Harrap, 1975.

Beckwith, Martha. *Jamaican Proverbs*. New York: Negro University Press, 1970.

Boot, Adrian, and Michael Thomas. *Jamaica: Babylon on a Thin Wire*. London: Thames and Hudson, 1976.

Clerk, Asley. *Music and Musical Instruments of Jamaica*. Kingston: 1916.

Cundall, Frank. *Sculpture in Jamaica*. London: William Clowes and Sons.

Dalrymple, Henderson. *Bob Marley: Music, Myth and the Rastas*. London: Carib-Arawak, 1976.

Davis, Stephen. *Reggae Bloodlines: In Search of the Music and Culture of Jamaica*. New York: Anchor Press/Double Day, 1977.

Ekwene, Laz E.N. *African Sources in New World Black Music*. Toronto: 1972.

Green, Jonathan. *Bob Marley and the Wailers*. London: Wise Publications, 1977.

Lewin, Olive. *Brown Gal in de Ring: 12 Folk Songs from Jamaica*. London: Oxford University Press, 1974.

Manley, Edna. *Focus: An Anthology of Contemporary Jamaican Writing*. Mona: University College of the West Indies, 1956.

McFarlane, J.E. Clare. *A Literature in the Making*. Kingston: Pioneer Press, 1956.

McFarlane, J.E. Clare. *A Treasury of Jamaican Poetry*. London: University of London Press, 1949.

Murray, Tom. *Folk Songs of Jamaica: 32 Songs With Words and Music*. London: University Press, 1952.

Nettleford, Rex. *Caribbean Cultural Identity: The Case of Jamaica*. Kingston: Institute of Jamaica, 1979.

Nettleford, Rex. *Roots and Rhythms: Jamaica's National Dance Theatre*. London: Andre Deutsch, 1970.

Nettleford, Rex. *Dance Jamaica*. London: Grove Press, 1985.

Tanna, Laura. *Jamaican Folk Tales and Oral Histories*. Kingston: Institute of Jamaica Publications, 1985.

Walton, Oritz M. *Music: Black, White and Blue*. New York: William Morrow, 1972.

Whitney, Malika Lee and Dermott Hussey. *Bob Marley: Reggae King of the World*. Kingston: Kingston Publishers, 1984.

Natural History

Adams, C. Dennis. *Flowering Plants of Jamaica*. Mona: University of the West Indies, 1972.

Avinoff, A. and Shoumatoff, N. *An Annotated*

List of Butterflies of Jamaica. Pittsburgh: Carnegie Museum, 1946.

Bond, James. Birds of the West Indies. London: Collins, 1960 edition.

Gosse, Philip Henry. Illustrations of the Birds of Jamaica. London: Van Voorst, 1849.

Gosse, Philip Henry and Hill, Richard. A Naturalist's Sojourn in Jamaica. London: 1851.

Kaye, W.J. Butterflies of Jamaica. Transactions of the Entomological Society of London, 1926.

Lack, David. Island Biology Illustrated by the Land of Birds of Jamaica. Berkeley & Los Angeles: University of California Press. 1976.

Sloane, Sir Hans. A Voyage to the Islands Madeira, Barbados, Nieves, St. Christophers and Jamaica, with the Natural History of the...last of those islands. 2 vols. London: 1707, 1725.

Stewart, D.B. (ed.) Gosse's Jamaica 1844-45. Kingston: Institute of Jamaica Publications, 1985.

Storer, Dorothy. Familiar Trees and Cultivated Plants of Jamaica. London: Macmillan for the Institute of Jamaica, 1958.

Swabey, Christopher. The Principal Timbers of Jamaica. Kingston: Department of Agriculture, 1941.

Photographic

Blake, Evon. Beautiful Jamaica, 4th Edition. Jamaica: Vista Publications, 1980.

Canetti, Nicolai. The People and Places of Jamaica. London: Peebles Press International, 1976.

Chen, Ray. Jamaica. Montreal: Ray Chen, 1985.

Duperly, Adolphe. Daguerian Excursions in Jamaica. Kingston: A. Duperly, 1844.

Egan, Anne. Jamaica in Pictures. New York: Sterling Publishing Co., 1967.

Rose Hall. Jamaica: Story of a People, A Legend and A Legacy. Kingston: Rose Hall Ltd., 1973.

Yeager, Bunny. Camera in Jamaica. Cranbury, N.J.: A.S. Barnes & Co., 1967.

Sports

Carnegie, James A. The Jamaican Tradition of Greatness in Sports. Kingston: Agency for Public Information, 1977

Dacosta, Eugene. Sixty Years of Horseracing in Jamaica. Jamaica, 1934.

Hannau, Michael P. Fishing in Jamaica. Hamilton: Buccaneer Publishing House. 1964.

Smith, Lloyd S. Public Life and Sport: Trinidad, Jamaica and Grenada. Spain, 1941.

Players: Monthly Sport Magazine. Kingston: Tony Becca, 1982.

Sports Annual 1980. Kingston: Publication and Productions Ltd., 1980.

Religion, Folklore and Witchcraft

Banbury, R. Thomas. Jamaican Superstitions. Jamaica: Mortimer C. DeSouza, 1849.

Beckwith, Martha. Jamaica Folklore. New York: American Folklore Society, 1928.

Buchner, J.H. The Moravians in Jamaica. London: Longman Brown & Co., 1854.

Coleman, Stanley J. Douglas, Isle of Man: The Folklore Academy, 1960.

Cumper, George E. The Potential of Rastafarianism as a Modern National Religion. New Delhi: Recorder Press, 1979.

Hogg, Donald W. Jamaica Religions: A Study in Variations. Michigan: Theses Yale University Phd., 1967.

Mullings, Bing. The 1860 Spiritual Awakening in Jamaica. Kingston: Jamaica Theological Seminary, 1972.

Seaga, Edward. Revival Cults in Jamaica. Kingston: Institute of Jamaica, 1982.

Fiction

Delisser, Herberts G. The White Witch of Rose Hall. London: Ernert Benn, 1929.

Duffus, Lee R. The Cuban Jamaican Connection. Kingston: Kingston Publishers, 1983.

Hearne, John. Voices under the Windows. London: Faber and Faber, 1956. Land of the Living. London: Faber and Faber, 1956. The Sure Salvation. London: Faber and Faber, 1983.

Hymann, Esther, Study in Bronze. London: Constable, 1928

Mais, Roger, Brother Man. London: Jonathan Cape, 1954.
The Hills Were Joyful Together. London: Jonathan Cape, 1953.

Marr, N.J. Nigger Brown. London: Museum Press, 1953.

Ogden, David. Jones, 38. Kingston: Kingston Publishers, 1985.

Patterson, H.O. Children of Sisyphus London: Hutchinson, 1964.

Ried, Mayne. The Maroon. London: Hurst and Blackett, 1862.

Ried, Victor Stafford. The Leopard. New York: Viking Press, 1958.

Salkey, Andrew. Escape to an Autumn Pavement. London: Hutchinson, 1960.

Wilson, Jeanne. No medicine for Murder. Kingston: Kingston Publishers, 1985.

Winkler, Anthony. The Painted Canoe. Kingston: Kingston Publishers, 1985.

General

Beckford, William. A Descriptive Account of the Island of Jamaica. 2 vols. London: 1796.

Black, Clinton V. Spanish Town: The Old Capital. Glasgow: Macclehose, 1960.

Cargill, Morris editor. Ian Fleming Introduces Jamaica. London: Andre Deutsch, 1965.

Cassidy, Frederic G. and R.B. LePage. Dictionary of Jamaican English. 2nd Edition. Cambridge: Cambridge University Press, 1980.

Henriques, Fernando. Jamaica: Land of Wood and Water. London: MacGibbon & Lee, 1957.

Henry, Mike. *Caribbean Cocktails and Mixed Drinks*. Kingston: Kingston Publishers, 1980.

Kupper, Adam. *Changing Jamaica*. London: Routledge & Kegan Paul, 1976.

Macmillan, Mona. *The Land of Look Behind: A Study of Jamaica*. London: Faber, 1957.

Miller, Elsa. *Caribbean Cooking and Menus*. Kingston: Kingston Publishers, 1983.

Sangster, Ian. *Jamaica: A Benn Holiday Guide*. London and Tonbridge: Ernest Benn Ltd., 1973.

Senior, Olive. *A to Z of the Jamaican Heritage*. Kingston: Heinemann, 1984.

Sibley, Inez. *Place Names of Jamaica*. Kingston: Institute of Jamaica, 1979.

Wright, Philip, and Paul F. White. *Exploring Jamaica: A Guide for Motorists*. London: Andre Deutsch, 1968.

Appendix

Accommodations

SURREY

KINGSTON AND ST. ANDREW

Luxury

JAMAICA PEGASUS, Box 333 (926-3690/9); 350 rms; AC, BP, BS(P), CA, GO, NC, RE, RM, RS, SP, SU, TD, TE, TEL, 12½%, *tb*

Expensive

WYNDAM-NEW KINGSTON, Knutsford Boulevard (926-5430); 200 rms; AC, BP, BS(P),CA, GO, NC, RE, RM, RS, SP, SU, TD, TE, TEL, 10% *tb*

HOTEL OCEANA KINGSTON, Box 986 (922-0920); 250 rms; AC, BP, B(P), BR, BS(P), CA, NC, RE, RM, SP, SU, TD, TE, TEL, 12%; *tb*

MORGAN'S HARBOUR, Port Royal, (924-8464/5); 24 rms; AC, B(P), BR, BS(P), CA, FI, RE, RM, SA, SK, 10%; *tb*

TERRA NOVA, 117 Waterloo Rd. (926-2211, 926-9334); 35 rms; AC, B(P), BR, BS(P), CA, NC, RE, RM, SP, TEL, 10%; *tc*

Moderate

THE COURTLEIGH, 31 Trafalgar Rd. (926-8174/8), 34 rms; AC, BS(P), CA, NC, RE, RM, SP, SU, TEL, 10%, *tc*

TROPICAL INN, 19 Clieveden Ave. (927-9917/8); 24 rms; AC, BS(P), CA, RE, RM, SP, SU, TEL, 10%; *tc*

Inexpensive

BEVERLY CLIFF GUEST HOUSE, 200 Mountain View Ave. (927-0951); 9 rms; BS(P), FI, PAC, SP; *tc*

CASA MONTE, Box 189 (942-2471/3); 18 rms; AC, BS(P), CA, CO, RE, RM, SP, SU, TEL, 10%; *tc*

HOTEL FOUR SEASONS, Box 190 (926-8805, 926-0682); 22 rms; AC, BS(P), CA, RE, 10%; *tc*

INDIES HOTEL, 5 Holborn Rd. (926-2952, 926-0989); 16 rms; AC, BS(P), RE, RM, 5%; *tc*

MAYFAIR, Box 163 (926-1610/2); 28 rms; BS(P), CA, PAC, RE, RM, SP, SU, 10%; *tc*

MEDALLION HALL, 53 Hope Rd. (927-5721, 927-5866); 10 rms; AC, BS(P), CA, RE, RM, 8%; *tc*

OLYMPIA RESIDENTIAL, Old Hope Rd. (927-9851); 20 rms; AC, BS(P), RE, RM, SU, TEL, 10%; *tc*

PINE GROVE GUEST HOUSE, Content Gap, St. Andrew, (922-3855); 20 rms; A, BS(P), CA, CO, PAC, RE, 10%; *tc*

RETREAT GUEST HOUSE, 19 Seaview Ave. (927-8853), 6 rms; *tc*

ROSENEATH, 8 Eureka Rd. (926-8090/1); 22 rms; AC, BS(P), CA, RE, RM, TEL, 10%; *tc*

SANDHURST GUEST HOUSE, 70 Sandhurst Crescent (927-7239) 40 rms; BP, BS(P), CA, PAC, RE, RM, SP; *tc*

SUTTON PLACE, 11 Ruthven Rd. (926-2297); 50 rms; AC, BS(P), CA, RE, RM, SP, SU, TEL; *tc*

WYNCLIFF, 222 Mountain View Ave, (927-5553); 9 rms; BS(P), CA, PAC, RM, SU; *tc*

PORT ANTONIO AND EAST COAST

Luxury

FRENCHMAN'S COVE HOTEL, Box 101, San San, (923-3224) 25 rms; AC, B(P), BR, BS(P), CA, CO, HO, RE, RM, SC, SK, TD, TEL, 10%, *tc*

MARBELLA CLUB, Dragon Bay, Box 176 (933-3281/3); 100 rms; AC, B(P), BR, BS(P), CA, CO, NC, RE, RS, SC, SK, SP, SU, TE, TEL, 15%; *ta*

TRIDENT VILLAS, Box 119 (993-2602, 993-2705); 26 rms; BP, B(P), BS(P), CA, CO, FI, HO, RE, RM, RS, SA, SK, SP, SU, TE, TEL, WS; *ta*

Expensive

JAMAICA HILL, Box 26 (993-3286); 44 rms; AC, B(P), BR, BS(P), CA, CO, HO, RE, RM, SP, SU, TE, TEL, 10%; *ta*

Moderate

BONNIE VIEW, Box 82 (993-2752), 30 rms; AC, BR, BS(P), CA, CO, RM, SP, TE, TEL, 10%; *tc*

DEMONTEVIN'S LODGE, 21 Fort George St., 15 rms; BS(P), CA, FI, RE, RM, 10%; *tc*

MIDDLESEX

OCHO RIOS AND NORTHSIDE

Luxury

JAMAICA INN, Box 1 (974-2514); 45 rms; AC, B(P), BS(P), FI, GO, HO, OC, RE, RM, SP, SU, TE, TEL, 10%, *ta*

PLANTATION INN, Box 2 (974-2501); 78 rms; AC, BP, B(P), BS(P), GO, OC, RE, RM, RS, SA, SK, SP, TE, TEL, WS, 10%, *ta*

SANS SOUCI, Box 103 (974-2353); 78 rms; AC, BP, B(P), BS(P), CA, GO, OC, RE, RM, SP, SU, TE, TEL, 10%; *ta*

Expensive

AMERICANA OCHO RIOS, Box 100 (974-2151/9); 325 rms; AC, BP, B(P), BS(P), CA, FI, GO, HO, JS, NC, OC, PA, RE, RM, SA, SC, SK, SP, SU, TD, TE, TEL, WS, 10% *ta*

COUPLES, Tower Isle P.O.; St. Mary (974-4271/5); 152 rms; AC, BP, B(P), BR, BS(P), HO, NC, RE, RS, SA, SC, SP, TE, TEL, WS; *tb*

EDEN 2, Mammee Bay, Box 51 (972-2382, 972-2300); 265 rms; AC, BP, B(P), BS(P), CA, FI, GO, HO, NC, RE, RM, RS, SA, SC, SK, SP, SU, TD, TE, TEL, WS, 10% *ta*

OCHO RIOS SHERATON, Box 245 (974-2201); 370 rms; AC, BP, B(P), BS(P), CA, FI, GO, HO, JS, OC, RE, RM, RS, SA, SC, SK, SP, SU, TD, TE, TEL, WS, 10%; *ta*

SHAW PARK BEACH HOTEL, Box 17 (974-2552/4); 118 rms; AC, BP, B(P), BS(P), CA, FI, NC, OC, RE, RM, RS, SA, SC, SP, SU, TD, TE, TEL, WS, 10%; *ta*

TURTLE BEACH APARTMENTS HOTEL, Box 73 (974-2801/5); 130 rms; AC, BS(P), CA, FI, JS, PA, RE, SA, SK, SP, SU, TD, TE, TEL, WS, 10%; *tb*

Moderate

GOLDEN SEAS RESORT, Oracabessa P.O. (974-3251); 50 rms; AC, B(P), BS(P), CA, CP, FI, NC, OC, RE, RM, RS, SA, SP, TD, TE, WS, 8%; *tc*

INN ON THE BEACH, Box 342 (974-2782/4); 46 rms; AC, BR, BS(P), CA, TD, TEL, 10%, *tb*

SILVER SEAS, Box 81 (974-2755, 974-5005); 83 rms; AC, B(P), BS(P), CA, FI, JS, NC, PA, RE, RM, SA, SK, SP, SQ, TD, TE, WS, 10%; *tc*

CASA MARIA, Box 10, Port Maria (994-2323/4); 30 rms; BP, B(P), BR, BS(P), CA, CO, PAC, RE, RM, RS, SP, TE, 10%; *tc*

HIBISCUS LODGE, Box 52 (974-2676); 20 rms; B(P), BS(P), CA, RE, 10%; *tc*

PINEAPPLE PENTHOUSE HOTEL, Pineapple Place, Box 263 (974-2727); 23 rms; AC, BS(P), RE, RM, SP, SU, 8%; *tc*

DISCOVERY BAY-RUNAWAY BAY

Expensive

EATON HALL GREAT HOUSE, Box 112 (973-3404); 36 rms; AC, BR, BS(P), CO, RE, RM, SP, SU, TD, TE, TEL, 10%; *ta*

JACK TAR VILLAGE, Box 112 (973-3404); 56 rms; AC, B(P), BS(P), RE, RM, SP, SU, TD, TE, TEL, 10%; *tb*

JAMAICA, JAMAICA! Box 58 (973-3435/7; 152 rms; AC, BP, B(P), BS(P), CA, FI, GO, HO, NC, OC, RE, RM, RS, SA, SC, SP, SU, TD, TE, TEL, WS, 10%; *ta*

Moderate

CLUB CARIBBEAN, Box 65 (973-3507/9); 116 rms; BP, B(P), BS(P), CA, CO, FI, GO, HO, JS, NC, OC, PAC, RE, RS, SA, SC, SK, SP, TD, TE, WS: *tb*

Inexpensive

BERKLEY BEACH, Box 20 (973-2066/7); 76 rms; AC, BP, B(P), BS(P), CA, FI, GO, NC, OC, RE, RS, RM, SA, SK, SP, TD, TE, TEL, 10%; *tc*

CARIBBEAN ISLE, Box 119 (973-2364); 14 rms; AC, BR, BS(P), CA, NC, RE, RM SP, 10%, *tc*

SILVER SPRAY, Box 16 (973-3413); 19 rms; AC, B(P), BS(P), CO, FI, GO, LA, RE, RM, SA, SP, TE, WS, 10%, *tc*

MANDEVILLE

Moderate

HOTEL ASTRA, Box 60 (962-3265, 962-3377); 22rms; BP, BS(P), CA, FI, GO, HO , RE, RM, SP, SU, TE, TEL, 10%, *tc*

Inexpensive

MANDEVILLE HOTEL, Box 78 (962-2460); 66 rms; AC, BS(P), CA, GO, HO, RE, RM, TE, TEL, SP, SU; *tc*

304

CORNWALL

MONTEGO BAY

Luxury

HALF MOON CLUB, Box 80 (953-2211); 191 rms; AC, BP, B(P), BS(P), CA, CO, FI, GO, HO, NC, OC, RE, RM, RS, SA, SP, SQ, SU, TD, TE, TEL, WS, 10%; *ta*

JACK TAR MONTEGO BEACH, Box 144 (952-4340); 127 rms; AC, BP, B(P), BR, BS(P), CA, GO, NC, OC, RE, RS, SA, SK, SP, SU, TD, TE, TEL, WS; *tb*

THE PALMS, Rose Hall, P.O. Box 186 (953-2160); 18 rms, AC, B(P), BS(P), CA, CO, SP, SU, TD, TE; *ta*

ROUND HILL, Box 64 (952-5150/5); 101 rms; BP, B(P), BR, BS(P), CA, CO, FI, GO, HO, OC, PAC, RM, RS, SA, SK, SP, SU, TD, TE, TEL, WS; *ta*

ROYAL CARIBBEAN, Box 167 (953-2231); 165 rms; AC, BP, B(P), BS(P), CA, FI, JS, OC, RM, RS, SA, SP, SU, TE, TEL, WS; *ta*

TRYALL GOLF AND BEACH , Sandy Bay, P.O., Hanover (952-5110); 44 rms; AC, B(P) BS(P), CA, CO, FI, GO, HO, RE, RM, RS, SA, SP, TD, TE, TEL, WS; *ta*

WYNDHAM-ROSE HALL BEACH HOTEL, Box 999 (953-2650); 508 rms; AC, BP, B(P), BR, BS(P), CA, FI, GO, HO, JS, NC, OC, RE, RS, RM, SA, SC, SK, SP, SU, TD, TE, TEL, WS, 10%; *ta*

Expensive

HOLIDAY INN, Box 480 (953-2485); 558 rms; AC, BP, B(P), BR, BS(P), CA, GO, HO, NC, OC, RE, RM, RS, SA, SC, SP, SU, TD, TE, TEL, 10%; *ta*

SANDALS, Box 100 (952-5510); 106 rms; AC, B(P), BS(P), CO, NC, OC, RE, RS, SA, SP, SU, TD, TE, TEL, WS; *ta*

TRELAWNY BEACH HOTEL, Box 54, Falmouth (954-2450); 350 rms; AC, B(P), BR, BS(P), CA, CO, FI, HO, JS, NC, OC, PA, PAC, RE, RM, SA, SC, SK, SP, TD, TE, TEL, 10%; *ta*

Moderate

BUCCANEER INN, Box 469 (952-2694); 18 rms; AC, BR, BS(P), CA, CO, OC, RE, RS, TD, TEL, 10%: *tc*

CARLYLE BEACH, Box 412 (952-4140); 52 rms; AC, BS(P), CA, RE, RM, SP, TD, TEL, 10%: *tb*

CASA MONTEGO, Box 161 (952-4150); 129 rms; AC, BP, B(P), BR, BS(P), CA, CO, NC, RE, RM, RS, SP, TD, TE, TEL, 10%; *tb*

CHATHAM BEACH, Box 300 (952-4780/1); 110 rms; AC, BP, B(P), BS(P), CA, NC, OC, RE. RM, RS, SA, SK, SP, TD, TE, WS, 10%; *tb*

CORAL CLIFF, Box 253 (952-4130/1); 32 rms; AC, BS(P), CA, RE, RM, SP, TD, TE, TEL, 10%; *tb*

DOCTOR'S CAVE BEACH, Box 94 (952-4355); 75 rms; AC, BP, B(P), BS(P), CA, FI, GO, HO, JS, NC, OC. PA, RE, RM, RS, SA, SC, SP, SQ, SU, TD, TE, TEL, WS, 10%; *tb*

HOTEL MONTEGO, Box 74 (952-3286/7); 35 rms; AC, BS(P), CA, RE, RM, SP, SU, TEL, 10% *tb*

MONTEGO BAY RACQUET CLUB, Box 245 (952-1895); 35 rms; AC, BR, BS(P), CA, CO, RE. SP, SU, TD, TE, TEL, 10%; *tb*

RICHMOND HILL INN, Box 362 (952-3859); 23 rms; AC, BP, BS(P). CA, FI, OC, RE, RM, SP, 10%; *tc*

SEAWIND BEACH RESORT, Box 69, Montego Freeport (952-4874, 952-4070/3); 452 rms; AC, B(P), BS(P), CA, CO, HO, JS, NC, RE, RS, SA, SC, SK, SP, SU, TD, TE, TEL, WS, 10%, *tb*

WEXFORD COURT, Box 239 (952-3679, 952-2854); 16 rms; AC, BS(P), CA, RE, RM, SP, TD, TEL; *tc*

Inexpensive

BEACH VIEW, Box 86 (952-4420/2); 54 rms; AC, BP, BS(P), CA, RE, RM, SP, TD, TEL, 10% *tc*

BLUE HARBOUR, Box 212 (952-5445); 22 rms; AC, BS(P), CA, RE, RM, SP, 10%; *tc*

CHALET CARIBE, Box 365 (952-1365); 28 rms; AC, B(P), BS(P), CA, JS, PA, RE, SA, SC, SK, SP, SU, TD, WS, 10%; *tc*

HARMONY HOUSE, Box 55 (952-5710); 21 rms; AC, BS(P), RE, RM, SP, TD, TEL; *tc*

KIRLEW GUEST HOUSE, Box 182 (952-1473); 6 rms; BS(P), CA; *tc*

LADY DIANE'S, Box 546 (952-4415); 16 rms; AC, BR, BS(P), CA, RE, RM, SP, TD, 10%; *tc*

MONTEGO GARDENS APARTMENTS, Box 220 (952-4838) 24 rms; BS(P), CA, PAC, RE, RM, SP, 10%; *tc*

MOUNTAINSIDE GUEST HOUSE, Box 1059 (952-4685); 5 rms; BS(P), SP, TD; *tc*

OCEAN VIEW, Box 210 (952-2662); 12 rms; AC, BS(P), CA, RE, RM, TD, 10% *tc*

ROYAL COURT, Box 195 (952-4531); 22 rms; AC, BS(P), CA, NC, RE, RM, SP, SU, TEL, 10%; *tc*

VERNEY HOUSE, Box 18 (952-4845, 952-2875); 26 rms; B(P), BS(P), CA, PAC, RE, RM, SP, TD, TEL, 10%; *tc*

NEGRIL & SOUTHWEST COAST

Luxury

COCONUT COVE, Box 12 (957-4216); 46 rms; AC, B(P), BS(P), CA, GO, HO, OR, RE, RM, RS, SA, SC, SP, SU, TE, WS, 10%; *ta*

Expensive

CHARELA INN, Box 33 (957-4277); 10 rms; AC, B(P), BS(P), RE, 10%; *tb*
HEDONISM II, Box 25 (957-4200); 280 rms; AC, B(P), BS(P), HO, NC, RS, SA, SC, SK, SP, TD, TE, WS; *tb*
SUNDOWNER, Box 5 (957-4225); 26 rms; AC B(P), BS(P), RE, RS, SU, 10%; *tb*

Moderate

NEGRIL BEACH CLUB, Box 7 (957-4220/1); 95 rms; AC, B(P), BS(P), CA, HO, NC, PA, RE, RS, SA, SC, SK, SP, SU, TE, TD, WS, 10%; *tb*
T-WATER COTTAGES, Box 11, (957-4270/1); 40 rms; AC, B(P), BS(P), RE, RS, SU, 10%; *tc*
WILTON HOUSE, Box 20, (955-2852); 4 rms; CA, B(P), BR, BS(P), FI, HO, RE, RM, SA, SK, WS; *tc*

Abbreviations for Hotel Facilities and Charges

AC	air conditioning in all rooms
BP	beauty parlor
B(P)	beach (private)
BR	beach rights
BS(P)	bath/shower (private)
CA	children accepted
CO	cottages
FI	fishing
GO	golf
HO	horseback riding
JS	jet skiing
NC	nightclub/discotheque
OC	orchestra
PA	parasailing
PAC	partial air conditioning
RE	restaurant
RM	room service
RS	resort shops
SA	sailing
SC	scuba
SK	skiing
SP	swimming pool
SQ	squash
SU	suites
TD	tour desk
TE	tennis
TEL	telephone in all rooms
WS	wind surfing
( )%	... added for gratuities

Accommodation Tax is now in effect, payable on a per-day-per-room basis for each occupancy (regardless of the number of people occupying that room):

ta: US $6; *tb*: US $5; *tc*: US $4.

Restaurants

SURREY

KINGSTON

Blue Mountain Inn, Gordon Town Road, tel. 927-7400; Continental and Jamaican cuisine.
The Chef's, 46 National Heroes Circle, tel. 922-4731; Jamaican and international cuisine.
The Coral, 89 Hope Rd., tel. 927-7556; Steak & Seafood.
Devon House, 26 Hope Rd., tel. 926-3580.
Dynasty, 20 Constant Spring Rd., tel. 926-4037; Chinese cuisine.
Emperor's Orchid, Wyndham-New Kingston Hotel, tel. 926-5430/9; Gourmet Chinese cuisine.
Fort Charles, Hotel Intercontinental Kingston, tel. 922-0920.
Golden Dragon, 9 Mona Plaza, tel. 927-08099; Chinese cuisine.
Hotel Four Seasons, 18 Ruthven Road, tel. 926-8805 or 926-0682.
Just Us, Holborn Road. Mexican cuisine.
Korea, 73 Knutsford Blvd., tel. 926-1428 or 929-4371; Korean cuisine.
Mayfair Hotel, tel. 926-1610; Jamaican and Continental cuisine.
The Orchid, 3 Waterloo Ave., tel. 926-8202.
The Plantation Terrace, The Courtleigh, 31 Trafalgar Rd., tel. 926-8174/8.
Restaurant Sutton Plaza, 11 Ruthven Rd., tel. 926-2297; Jamaican and Continental cuisine.
Ristorante d' Amore, Wyndham-New Kingston Hotel, tel. 926-5430/9; Italian cuisine.
Sammy's Kitchen, 17 Northside Drive, tel. 927-0939; Chinese cuisine.
Sea Witch, Knutsford Blvd., tel. 929-4386/7; Seafood.
Talk of the Town, Jamaican Pegasus Hotel, Knutsford Boulevard, tel. 926-3690.
Terra Nova, 17 Waterloo Rd., tel. 926-2211; continental cuisine.

PORT ANTONIO

Bonnie View Hotel, Bonnie View Street, tel. 993-2752.
Jamaican Hill Estate, San San, tel. 993-3286; Jamaican and continental cuisine.
Trident Hotel, Anchovy, tel. 993-2602; Russian and Viennese cuisine.

MIDDLESEX

OCHO RIOS

Almond Tree, The Hibiscus Lodge, Main Street, tel. 974-2183; Jamaican cuisine.
Anthony's, Pier 1, tel. 974-2716, 974-2755, 974-5005; seafood and Continental cuisine.

Carib Inn, Main Street, tel. 974-2445; seafood and Continental cuisine.

Casanova, Sans Souci Hotel, tel. 974-2353; international cuisine.

Chez Robert, Inn on the Beach; seafood and Continental cuisine.

Dick Turpin, Coconut Grove Shopping Centre, tel. 974-5007/8; English Pub and Restaurant.

The Garden of Eden, Eden 2 Hotel, Mammee Bay, tel. 972-2300; Continental cuisine.

Honeycomb Village, Main Street, tel. 974-2110; seafood and Continental cuisine.

The King's Arms, Harmony Hall, on main road to Couples, tel. 974-4222, 974-4233.

The Little Pub, Main Street, tel. 974-2324.

Moxon's of Boscobel, on main road to Couples, tel. 974-3234; Continental cuisine.

Nuccio's, DaCosta Drive, tel. 974-2333; Italian cuisine.

Seafare Restaurant, Main Street, tel. 974-2200; seafood, Jamaican and Continental cuisine.

The Victoria, Americana Hotel, tel. 974-2152/9. French cuisine.

RUNAWAY BAY

Runaway Bay Hotel, tel. 973–3435; Jamaican and continental cuisine.

Eaton Hall Great House, tel. 973–3404; Jamaican and continental cuisine.

CORNWALL

MONTEGO BAY

The Ambrosia, Wyndham-Rose Hall Hotel, tel. 953-2650; North Italian cuisine.

Brigadoon, Queen's Drive, tel. 952-1723; seafood.

Calabash, Queen's Drive, tel. 952-3891; Jamaican cuisine.

Carlyle Beach Pub & Bistro, Kent Avenue, tel. 952-4140.

Casa Blanca, Gloucester Avenue, tel. 952-0720; Italian cuisine.

Cat Cay Brasserie, Wyndham-Rose Hall Hotel, tel. 953-2650; Continental cuisine.

Club House Grill, Half Moon Golf Club, Rose Hall, tel. 953-228, 953-2314.

Diplomat, Queen's Drive, tel. 952-3353/4.

Fountain Terrace, Seawind Resort, Montego Freeport, tel. 952-4874.

Front Porch, Wexford Court, Gloucester Avenue, tel. 952-2854; Jamaican cuisine.

Georgian House, Union and Orange Streets, tel. 952-4914; Jamaican and Continental cuisine.

Harmony House, Gloucester Avenue, tel. 952-2503; Jamaican cuisine.

House of Chopsticks, Sewell Avenue, tel. 952-2560; Chinese cuisine.

House of Lords, Holiday Village, Rose Hall, tel. 953-2113/4; seafood.

King Arthur's, Ironshore, tel. 953-2250; Continental cuisine.

Le Papillon, Ironshore Golf Course, tel; 953-2800; French, Continental and Jamaican cuisine.

Marguerite's, Gloucester Avenue, tel. 952-4777; seafood.

On the Waterfront, tel. 952-2452; seafood.

Pelican Grill, Gloucester Avenue, tel. 952-3171.

Richmond Hill Inn, Union Street, tel. 952-3859.

Royal Caribbean Hotel, Mahoe Bay, tel. 953-2231.

Rum Barrel Inn, Market Street, tel. 952-2688.

Town House, Church Street, tel. 952-2660; seafood Jamaican style.

NEGRIL

Cafe au Lait, West End Road; French cuisine.

Charela Inn Hotel, tel. 957-4277; Jamaican and French cuisine.

Country Restaurant, Negril Beach; Jamaican vegetarian cuisine.

Negril Tree House Club, Negril Beach; Jamaican and Continental cuisine.

Rick's Cafe, West End Road; seafood.

Sundowner Hotel, tel. 957-4225; Jamaican cuisine.

Tourist Offices

JAMAICA

Kingston – 21 Dominica Drive, Box 360, Kingston 5.

Montego Bay – Cornwall Beach, tel. 952-4425. Gloucester Avenue, tel. 952-4426. Sangster Airport, tel. 952-3009.

Negril – tel. 957-4243.

Ocho Rios – Pineapple Place, tel. 974-2570. Special Projects, tel. 972-4243.

Port Antonio – Rafters Rest, tel. 993-2778. Dolphin Bay, tel. 993-2664.

BRITAIN

London, England – Jamaica House, St. James St., London SW1A 1JT, tel. 01-493-3467/8.

CANADA

Toronto, Canada – Suite 507, 221 Yonge St., Toronto, Ontario M4S 2B4. Tel. 416-482-7850.

MEXICO

Mexico City – Avenida Zola, No. 353, Col. Del Valle, Delegacion Benito Juarez, Mexico 03100, D.F. Tel. 687-92-22.

UNITED STATES

Chicago, Illinois — Suite 1210, 36 South Wabash Avenue, Chicago 60603, Tel. 312-346-1546.

Los Angeles, California — 3440 Wiltshire Boulevard, Suite 1207, Los Angeles, Ca. 90010. Tel. 213-384-1123.

Miami, Florida — 1320 South Dixie Highway, Suite 1100 Coral Gables, Fla. 33146. Tel. 305-665-0557.

New York, New York — 866 Second Avenue, New York 10017. Tel. 212-688-7650.

Embassies/High Comissions

Argentine Embassy — Dyoll Building, 40 Knutsford Boulevard, tel. 926-5588, 926-2496.

Australian High Commission — First Life Building, 64 Knutsford Boulevard, tel. 926-3551/2.

Belgian Embassy — Oxford House, 66 Oxford Road, tel. 926-6859, 926-67039.

Brazilian Embassy — First Life Building, 64 Knutsford Boulevard, tel, 929-8608.

British High Commission — 26 Trafalgar Road, tel. 926-9050.

Canadian High Commission — Royal Bank Building, 30 Knutsford Boulevard, tel. 926-61500.

Chinese Embassy — 8 Seaview Avenue, tel. 927-0850, 927-0459.

Colombian Embassy — British American Building, 53 Knutsford Boulevard, tel. 929-1701.

Costa Rican Embassy — 3b Haughton Avenue, tel. 929-6810.

Dutch Embassy —British American Building, 53 Knutsford Boulevard, tel. 926-2026, 926-1247.

French Embassy — 13 Hillcrest Avenue, tel. 927-9811/2.

German Embassy — 10 Waterloo Road, tel. 926-6728, 926-5665.

Indian High Commission — 4 Retreat Avenue, tel. 927-0486, 927-4270.

Israeli Embassy — Pan-Jamaican Building, 60 Knutsford Boulevard, tel. 926-8768.

Japanese Embassy — Hampshire House, 4 Reckadom Road, tel. 926-4736.

Mexican Embassy — British American Building, 53 Knutsford Boulevard, tel. 926-6891, 926-4242.

Nigerian High Commission — 5 Waterloo Road, tel. 926-6400, 926-6408.

Panamanian Embassy — First Life Building, 64 Knutsford Boulevard, tel. 929-5467.

South Korean Embassy — Pan-Jamaican Building, 60 Knutsford Boulevard, tel. 929-3035/7.

Spanish Embassy — British American Building, 53 Knutsford Boulevard, tel. 929-6710.

Trinidad and Tobago High Commission — Pan-Jamaican Building, 60 Knutsford Boulevard, tel. 926-5730, 926-5739.

United States Embassy — Jamaica Mutual Life Centre, 2 Oxford Road, tel. 926-4220, 926-4850.

Venezuelan Embassy — Royal Bank Building, 30 Knutsford Boulevard, tel. 926-5510, 924-5519.

Discography

BOB ANDY

RECORD LABEL	ALBUM TITLE
Sky Note	*Lots of Love*
Trojan	*Pied Piper* (with Marcia Griffiths)
Trojan	*Young, Gifted & Black* (with Marcia Griffiths)

ASWAD

Island	*Live and Direct*
Grove Music	*Hulet*
	New Chapter

BIG YOUTH

Negusa Nagast	*Hit The Road Jack!*
TR International	*Dread Locks Dread*
Trojan	*Natty Cultural Dread*
Trojan	*Screaming Target*

BLACK BEARD

Tempus	*Strictly Dub Wise*

BLACK UHURU

Island	*Solidarity*
Third World	*Chill Out*
	Love Crisis
	Red...Alert
	Sinsemilla

DENNIS BROWN

Music Works	*Just Not*
Laser	*Words of Wisdom*
Lightning	*Visions of...*
Third World	*West Bound Train*

BURNING SPEAR

Tuff Gong	HIM: *Haile his Imperial Majesty*
Island	*Garvey's Ghost* (dub)
Island	*Man In The Hills*

Island	*Dry And Heavy*
One Stop	*Social Living*
Studio One	*Burning Spear*
Studio One	*Rocking Time*

CHALICE

Pipe Music	*Stan' Up*
	Blasted

JIMMY CLIFF

Sun Power	*Power and the Glory*
A & M	*Wonderful World, Beautiful People*
EMI	*Unlimited*
Island	*Another Cycle*
Island	*Best of Jimmy Cliff*
Island	*Struggling Man*
Mango	*The Harder They Come*
Trojan	*Jimmy Cliff*
Veep	*Can't Get Enough Of It*
Warner Brothers	*Follow My Mind*
Warner Brothers	*Give Thanx*
Warner Brothers	*In Concert: The Best of Jimmy Cliff*
Warner Brothers	*Special*

DESMOND DEKKER

Trojan	*Double Dekker*
Trojan	*This Is Desmond Dekker*
Trojan	*You Can Get It If You Really Want*
Uni	*Israelites*

EEK-A-MOUSE

Tuff Gong	*Muskateer*
	Wha Do Dem

ERIC GALE

Micron	*Negril*

JOE GIBBS & THE PROFESSIONALS

JGM	*Someone Luv You Honey*
Fay	*King Tubby Meets the Upsetters*
Lightning	*African Dub, Chapter 2*
Lightning	*African Dub, Chapter 3*

OWEN GRAY

Total Sounds	*Forward on the Scene*

MARCIA GRIFFITHS

Tuff Gong	*Rock My Soul*
Sky Note	*Naturally*

THE HEPTONES

Greensleeves	*Good Life*
Island	*Book of Rules*
Island	*Night Food*
Studio One	*Freedom Line*
Studio One	*Heptones*
Studio One	*Heptones on Top*
Third World	*Better Days*
Trojan	*Heptones & Their Friends*

JOE HIGGS

Grounation	*Life of Contradiction*

JOHN HOLT

Volcano	*Police in Helicopter*
Creole	*Time is the Master*
Trojan	*Dusty Roads*
Trojan	*Holt*
Trojan	*One Thousand Volts of Holt*
Trojan	*Pledging My Love*
Trojan	*Still in Chains*
Trojan	*The Further You Look*

ISRAEL VIBRATION

Harvest	*The Same Song*

GREGORY ISAACS

African Museum	*Out Deh*
Conflict	*Extra Classic*
Deb	*Mr Isaacs*
Front Line	*Cool Ruler*

BYRON LEE & THE DRAGONAIRES

Trojan	*Rocky Steady Explosion*

BOB MARLEY & THE WAILERS

CBS	*The Birth of a Legend Parts 1 & 2*
Island	*A Taste of the Wailers*
Island	*Babylon by Bus*
Island	*Burnin'*
Island	*Catch a Fire*
Island	*Exodus*
Island	*Kaya*
Island	*Live!*

Island	*Natty Dread*
Island	*Rastaman Vibrations*
Island	*Survival*
Island	*Uprising*
Island	*Chances are*
Island	*Confrontation*
Maroon	*Present Soul*
	Revolution, Parts 2 & 3
Studio One	*The Best of Bob Marley & the Wailers*
Beverlys	*The Best of the Wailers*
Studio One	*The Wailing Wailers*
Trojan	*African Herbsman*
Trojan	*Rasta Revolution*
Trojan	*Soul Rebels*

RITA MARLEY

Tuff Gong	*Who Knows It*
Tuff Gong	*Haramba*

RAS MICHAEL & THE SONS OF NEGUS

Corporation Dynamic	*Freedom Sounds*
Grounation	*Rastafari*
Trojan	*Dadawah*
Trojan	*Tribute to the Emperor*

MICHIGAN & SMILEY

Tuff Gong	*Sugar Daddy*
Studio One	*Downpression*
Studio One	*Rub a Dub Style*

THE MIGHTY DIAMONDS

Channel One	*Stand Up To Your Judgement*
Front Line	*Deeper Roots — Back to the Channel*
	Fire on Ice
	Changes
	I Need a Roof
	Planet Earth

COUNT OSSIE & THE MYSTIC REVELATION OF RASTAFARI

Ashanti	*Grounation*
Dynamic	*Tales of Mozambique*

AUGUSTUS PABLO

Trojan	*Ital Dub*
Tropical	*This is Augustus Pablo*

PRINCE BUSTER

Melodisc	*Tutti Fruiti*

PRINCE FAR I

Front Line	*Message from the King*

PRINCE MOHAMMED

Burning Sounds	*African Roots*

MAX ROMEO

Island	*Reconstruction*

I ROY

Attack	*I Roy*
Micron	*Truth and Rights*
Trojan	*Hell & Sorrow*
Trojan	*Many Moods of I Roy*
Trojan	*Presentation I Roy*
Trojan	*Version Galore*
Virgin	*Crisis Time*

ERNIE SMITH

Federal	*Ernie*
Federal	*For the Good Times*
Federal	*Greatest Hits*
Trojan	*Life Is Just For Living*
Wildflower	*I'll Sing for Jesus*
Wildflower	*Pure Gold Rock Steady*

STEEL PULSE

Electra	*Earth Crisis*
Island	*Handsworth Revolution*
Island	*Tribute to the Martyrs*

TAPPER ZUKIE

Front Line	*MPLA*
Front Line	*Tapper Roots*

THIRD WORLD

Columbia	*Sense of Purpose*
	You've Got The Power
Island	*90° In the Shade*
Island	*Journey to Addis*
Island	*The Story's Been Told*
Island	*Third World*

NICKY THOMAS

Trojan	*Love of the Common People*
Trojan	*Tell It Like It Is*

TOOTS & THE MAYTALS

Coxsone	*Never Grow Old*
Dynamic	*Slatyam Stoot*
Dynamic	*The Sensational Maytals*
Island	*Funky Kingston*
Island	*In the Dark*
Island	*Reggae Got Soul*
Trojan	*From the Roots*
Trojan	*Monkey Man*

PETER TOSH

Intel-Diplo	*Mama Africa*
Rolling Stones	*Bush Doctor*
Virgin	*Equal Rights*
Virgin	*Legalize It*

THE TWINKLE BROTHERS

	Country Men
	Do Your Own Things
	Love
	Me No You
	Praise Jah
	Rasta Pon Top

U ROY

Virgin	*Dread in Babylon*
Virgin	*Rasta Ambassabdor*

UPSETTERS

Island	*Super Ape*
Trojan	*Eastwood Rides Again*
Trojan	*Double Seven*
Trojan	*Return of Django*
Trojan	*The Good, the Bad and the Upsetters*

BUNNY WAILER

Island	*Blackheart Man*
Island	*Protest*
	Bunny Wailer Sings the Wailers
	Rock and Groove
	Tribute (To Bob Marley)

DELROY WASHINGTON

Virgin	*I-SUS*
Virgin	*Rasta*

DELROY WILSON

Mr. Tipsy	*Dean of Reggae*
Eji	*Mr Cool Operator*
Jaguar	*Greatest Hits*
Trojan	*Bettah Must Come*

YABBY YOU VIBRATION

Grove	*Deliver Me From My Enemies*

YELLOWMAN

Power House	*Walking Jewelry Store*
	Live at Aces Disco
	Duppy or Gunman
	Mad Over Me

ART/PHOTO CREDITS

(Continue from page 9)

Jamaicans, Mount Ephraim, a biography of Norman Washington Manley, and numerous short stories. He has been honored as a Guggenheim Fellow and a Canada Council Fellow, and has received Musgrave silver and gold medals. In this volume, Reid contributed incisive word portraits of his countrymen in "The Jamaicans" and provided an inside look at Jamaica's "Vibrant, Spiritual Spectrum."

Clinton V. Black was well-prepared to write the in-depth history in this book, surveying Jamaica from Arawak times to the present day. Black has headed the Government Archives in Spanish Town since 1949. Born in Kingston in 1918, he has authored the standard island history text, The Story of Jamaica, and numerous other books, including history-guides to Spanish Town and Port Royal and a collection of Tales of Old Jamaica.

The lively travel section, giving readers a new look at popular old attractions as well as opening up new paths and places they may have overlooked before, was largely the work of three contributors: **Olive Senior, Dr. Ian Sangster** and the late **Ken Maxwell**.

Maxwell was one of Jamaica's leading figures in the field of communications. He maintained a public relations and advertising firm in Kingston, and he wrote and acted in the first television show every produced in Jamaica. He also authored documentaries and plays and did broadcast work for NBC in Chicago, CBC in Canada and BBC in Great Britain. For Insight Guide: Jamaica, Maxwell traveled through much of his homeland in a vintage Rover P4 gathering materials for chapters on South Middlesex, South Cornwall and the Cockpit Country, as well as the feature on the Jamaican language, "Pardon My Patois!" Tragically, he suffered a heart attack and died on Nov. 22, 1982, before seeing the fruits of his labors.

Senior took on the complex task of analyzing, dissecting and reassembling the sprawling capital city of Kingston and its surrounding region, including Port Royal, Port Antonio, and the Portland and St. Thomas parish countrysides. The author of books on Jamaican politics and culture, Senior took over as editor of the Jamaica Journal in 1982.

Sangster researched and produced the travel-section chapters about the north coasts of Middlesex and Cornwall counties, including the tourist centers of Ocho Rios and Montego Bay, as well as the Blue Mountains outside of Kingston. Indeed, Sangster's home is "High in the Blue Mountains," clinging to a cliff at World's End. Here, he spends most of his time producing the award-winning line of Old Jamaica liqueurs and rums. Sangster was born in Scotland, but emigrated to Jamaica in 1969 to become director of the Sugar Industry Research Institute, a position he still holds. He is the author of two books: Jamaica, A Holiday Guide and Sugar and Jamaica.

Dr. Heather Royes brought an extensive background in the field of communications to her work for Jamaica. The winner of several awards for her poetry, she holds a Ph.D. in mass communications from the University of Wisconsin. She has served as director of information for the office of the Prime Minister of Jamaica, cultural affairs officer for the Public Information Office, and third secretary for the Jamaican Embassy in Mexico City. For this book, she contributed the section entitled "From Ghetto to Gallery: The Artists' World" and provided information for Reid's piece on religion.

Dermott Hussey teamed with Zach to prepare the feature on "The Red Hot Rhythms of Reggae." His expertise comes from long years of bringing reggae music to the Jamaican public as a disc jockey for the Jamaican Broadcasting Company. He presently works for the JBC Television film unit. The co-author of Kingston Publishers' Bob Marley, Reggae King of the World, Hussey has produced numerous music documentaries for radio and television, and has written a large number of articles for newspapers and magazines.

Apa's resident expert on Jamaican politics was **Dr. Carl Stone**, the island nation's only public opinion pollster. A professor of political science at the University of the West Indies, Stone is the recipient of the national Commander of Distinction award for his contributions to scholarship. The Daily Gleaner newspaper has rated him Jamaica's outstanding columnist. Stone's numerous books include Democracy and Clientelism in Jamaica, Essays on Power and Change in Jamaica, and Jamaica at the Polls. For this volume, he surveyed "The Political Canvas: A Painting of Hope."

Barbara Gloudon, one of Jamaica's leading journalists, commentators and playwrights, prepared the chapter on "Dance and Drama: Everybody Is a Star." Formerly features editor for Gleaner Publications and chairperson of the Little Theatre Movement, she now leads her own communications agency in Kingston. Her most recent children's story, "Jack and the Gungoo Tree," won the 1982 National Award for Best Entertainment for Children.

Jimmy Carnegie was the source of this book's chapter, "Where Cricket Is a Wicket Game." Carnegie writes a sports column for the *Sunday Gleaner* and is the author of a biography of legendary cricket great George Headley.

Jamaican journalist **Lloyd Williams** researched and penned the mandatory piece on the island's infamous ganja trade. Williams has worked for the *Daily Gleaner* for more than 20 years, often reporting about the trafficking and abuse of drugs. He has been news editor since 1977. In 1982, Williams studied at Cambridge University in England as a recipient of a Nuffield Foundation Press Fellowship.

Much of the Guide in Brief material was compiled by **Patsy Pressley**, an American journalist with interests in the Caribbean, currently a staff writer for the *Evening Independent* in St. Petersburg.

Canadian author **Judy Allison** contributed valuable insights on Jamaica's Maroon people to several sections of the book.

Insight Guide: Jamaica owes its superb photography to the work of three principals: Zach, Hoefer and U.S. cameraman **David Stahl**. Hoefer, whose photographic work has appeared in major publications throughout the world and whose *Jalan-Jalan: Images of Malaysia* is considered a classic in the field of 8 × 10 photography, spent nearly a month poking his 35 mm Leicaflex cameras into various corners of the country.

Stahl, who is based in Sarasota, Florida, spent nearly a month in Jamaica on special assignment for Apa, after having met Zach in the offices of the *Floridian* magazine. Together, Stahl and Zach covered Reggae Sunsplash 1982 and the preliminaries of the Miss Jamaica (World) pageant. Stahl's work has appeared in such prestigious publications as *National Geographic* magazine.

Jamaican photographers who contributed to the creations of this book include **Maria LaYacona**, **Howard Moo Young**, **Dr. Owen Minott** and **Anthony DaCosta**.

LaYacona is an American by birth, a Jamaican by choice. She came to the Caribbean in 1955 on assignment for *Sports Illustrated* magazine, to cover an historic cricket encounter between the West Indies and Australia. Along the way, she fell in love with Jamaica, and has made it her home ever since. LaYacona had previously traveled the World as a photographer for *Life* magazine. She is now considered Jamaica's leading free-lance photographer.

Moo Young, a graduate of the New York School of Arts, was voted the champion photographer at Jamaica's 1982 Festival Photographic Competition. Born in Kingston, he is a partner in the advertising agency of Moo Young Butler Associates Ltd.

Minott, who makes his home in Montego Bay, is a rural physician by profession. But photography is his consuming passion. He saw his first contact print in the darkroom of Munro College, deep in the Jamaican countryside, and in his own words, "the magic of that first darkroom experience still lingers and colors my work as a physician."

DaCosta hails from Kingston, although he now makes his base in New York City. Schooled in the United States and Canada, he has won distinction in national photographic competitions, and has had one-man shows in New York, Toronto, Miami and Tampa.

The archives of the National Library at the Institute of Jamaica were a key factor in gaining a complete photographic picture of the island. National Library director Stephney Ferguson opened the drawers and doors of a collection reputed to be the finest in the world on the West Indies.

Thanks also go to the officials and employees of the Ministry of Information, the Ministry of Tourism, the Jamaica Tourist Board, the National Gallery, Hedonism II, Sandals Resort Hotel, Couples Resort Hotel, the Ocho Rios Sheraton, Sundowner Inn, Rose Hall Intercontinental, DeMontevin's Lodge, New Kingston Hotel, Blue Mountain Inn, Spartan Health Spa,, Martins Travel Service, and Synergy Productions Ltd.

Individuals who assisted with the making of the book in Jamaica included Andrew Henry, Corrine Chuck, Tino Geddes, Nikki Rich, Tony Aarons, Edna Manley and David Boxer and Carl Whitbourne.

The maps for *Insight Guide: Jamaica* were drawn in Singapore under the direction of cartographer Francis Tan. Vivien Loo contributed her energies to preparing final manuscripts and Guide in Brief material. The index was done by Linda Carlock.

Special thanks are in order for long deadline hours put in by Raymond Boey and his production team of Sam Chan, Molly Wee, Genie Lim, Karen Tang and Noiani Jantan. The efforts of Henry Lee, Alice Ng, Yvan Van Outrive, Diana Tan and Magdalene Teo also contributed to the final product.

To each and every one, *tenky* from *Jamaica*.

— Apa Productions

INDEX